THE END OF CONCERN

The End of Concern

Maoist China, Activism, and Asian Studies

FABIO LANZA

DUKE UNIVERSITY PRESS
DURHAM AND LONDON 2017

© 2017 Duke University Press
All rights reserved

Typeset in Whitman and Trade Gothic by
Graphic Composition, Inc., Bogart, Georgia

Library of Congress Cataloging-in-Publication Data
Names: Lanza, Fabio, [date] author.
Title: The end of concern : Maoist China, activism, and Asian
studies / Fabio Lanza.
Description: Durham : Duke University Press, 2017. | Includes
bibliographical references and index.
Identifiers: LCCN 2017019331 (print)
LCCN 2017021528 (ebook)
ISBN 9780822372431 (ebook)
ISBN 9780822369325 (hardcover : alk. paper)
ISBN 9780822369479 (pbk. : alk. paper)
Subjects: LCSH: Committee of Concerned Asian Scholars.
| China—Study and teaching (Higher)—United States—
History—20th century. | China—Relations—United States—
History—20th century. | United States—Relations—China—
History—20th century.
Classification: LCC DS734.97.U6 (ebook) | LCC DS734.97.U6 L35
2017 (print) | DDC 951.05071/173—dc23
LC record available at https://lccn.loc.gov/2017019331

Cover art: Design and illustration by Matthew Tauch.

TO SANDY, IN MEMORIAM

CONTENTS

ACKNOWLEDGMENTS ix

INTRODUCTION
Of Ends and Beginnings; or,
When China Existed 1

1. America's Asia: Discovering China,
Rethinking Knowledge 23

2. To Be, or Not to Be, a Scholar:
The Praxis of Radicalism in Academia 67

3. Seeing and Understanding:
China as the Place of Desire 101

4. Facing Thermidor:
Global Maoism at Its End 143

EPILOGUE
Area Redux: The Destinies of "China"
in the 1980s and 1990s 175

NOTES 195
BIBLIOGRAPHY 241
INDEX 257

ACKNOWLEDGMENTS

How did this all begin?

Memories are notoriously unreliable, and we often make up convenient origin stories. But I do like the one I crafted for this book, so I will stick with it; it might even be true. In my hazy recollection, the path leading to this volume started with a phone conversation. Alessandro Russo, friend and former mentor, had called to suggest that I submit a proposal to a conference on China and the Cold War to be held in Bologna, Italy. I was at the time frantically trying to write my first book on the May Fourth Movement, so I replied that the Cold War was way outside the scope of my current research—let alone my expertise. "Oh, come on!" he insisted, "Why don't you write something about the *Bulletin?*"

We must have had previous conversations on that topic because the suggestion did not apparently strike me as too outlandish. So I headed for the library, located the microforms of the entire run of the *Bulletin of Concerned Asian Scholars* (thankfully now fully available online), and wrote a first tentative paper on the topic. When the time of the conference came, I was already feeling way out of my depth among people who actually knew something about China during the Cold War. And that feeling got exponentially worse when I realized that Marilyn Young and Bruce Cumings, both former members of the Committee of Concerned Asian Scholars, were going to be there and would be listening to my presentation. Thankfully, they were incredibly gracious and encouraging. "Are you working on CCAS now?" they asked. "Maybe," I replied, noncommittally. But the more I thought about it, the more it sounded interesting: it combined a history of the field with a sideways view of the long sixties. *Plus,* I thought to myself, *this will be a quick project.* That was ten years ago.

Throughout these years, many people have offered intellectual and emotional support. Heartfelt thanks go first and foremost to the members of the Committee of Concerned Asian Scholars who were kind enough to find time to talk to me: Steve Andors, Marianne Bastid, Gail Bernstein, John Berninghausen, Molly Coye, Tom Engelhardt, Edward Friedman, Richard Kagan, Jon Livingston, Paul Pickowicz, Moss Roberts, Mark Selden, Susan Shirk, Saundra (Sandy) Sturdevant, Jonathan Unger, Ezra Vogel, and Marilyn Young. Sandy Sturdevant and Joe Moore were so generous to allow me access to their private archives, while Richard Kagan and Marilyn Young shared some precious documents.

Time for writing and doing research is the most valuable commodity for a scholar, and I benefited from two semesters of leave thanks to two research professorship grants from the College of Social and Behavioral Sciences at the University of Arizona. In the spring of 2014, the Eisenberg Institute for Historical Studies at the University of Michigan (where I was a visiting fellow) provided the perfect environment for thinking and writing. Living at Telluride House in Ann Arbor was both intellectually stimulating and incredibly fun. My brother Mauro was kind enough to allow me the use of his apartment in Paris in the spring of 2011 so that I could collect materials on the French Maoists—and enjoy life in the French capital. The archivists at the Wisconsin Historical Society, which hosts the CCAS papers, were extremely helpful and welcoming.

My academic life is split between two colleges and two departments. This can create some minor problems, but I have been blessed with wise chairs (Kevin Gosner and Albert Welter) and friendly colleagues, who have been very supportive of my research and my work.

I presented portions of this project at conferences and invited lectures all over the globe, including at the Center for the Humanities at Tsinghua University, Duke University, the Global Studies Conference in Shanghai, the Berkeley-Stanford Graduate Student Conference in the Modern Chinese Humanities, the Critical China Studies Workshop at the University of Toronto, McGill University, Rice University, the Center for Chinese Studies at the University of Michigan, Nanjing University, the University of Freiburg, the University of Hamburg, the University of Cologne, the University of Colorado–Boulder, and the University of Chicago.

I benefited immensely from the encouragement and the critical eye of many friends and colleagues. Tani Barlow, Paola Iovene, and Alessandro Russo read an earlier version of the manuscript and gave invaluable advice. Aminda (Mindy) Smith read drafts and offered criticism, support, and a healthy dose of irony. The two anonymous readers understood the project and provided very useful suggestions; their reports were a model of how to be encouraging and critical at the same time. I strove to incorporate all of their recommendations. Many others read sections, listened to my presentations, or had engaging conversations on the material: Majed Akther, Gail Bernstein, Pär Cassel, Chris Connery, Susan Crane, Alex Day, Christian Depee, Michael Dutton, Jacob Eyferth, Josh Fogel, Marc Frey, Hai Ren, Dhruv Jain, Matthew Johnson, Joan Judge, Anna Krylova, Ralph Litzinger, Julia Lovell, Federico Marcon, Covell Meyskens, Georgia Mickey, Ian Miller, Alex Mirkovich, Carla Nappi, Jadwiga Pieper-Mooney, Claudia Pozzana, Branislav Radelich, Massimo Raveri, Tang Xiaobing, Sigrid Schmalzer, Nicola Spakowsky, Julia Adeney Thomas, Malcolm Thompson, Daniel Vukovich, Wang Hui, Tim Weston, Wu Yiching, Jake Werner, and Angela Zito. All through my academic career, Rebecca Karl has been an inspiration for her honesty and her scholarship. Hannah Dübgen, Mauro Lanza, Roger Zuccolo, Stacy Scheff, Aengus Anderson, Lauren Dreyfuss, Lucia Carminati, Sebastiano Mussi, Sara Marchetta, Edoardo Chiamenti, Gian Luca De Biasi, and Alain Bullo provided friendship, distraction, and laughter, all of them very much needed. My mom, Anna, reassuringly kept on being my mom.

At Duke University Press, Ken Wissoker shepherded this project with consummate ability, and Elizabeth Ault was incredibly helpful throughout all the phases of the publication process.

Parts of chapter 1 and chapter 2 appeared in my essay "America's Asia? Revolution, Scholarship and Asian Studies," in *Asianisms: Regionalist Interactions and Asian Integration*, edited by Marc Frey and Nicola Spakowski (Singapore: NUS Press, 2016), 134–55. An embryonic version of chapter 2 was published as "Making Sense of 'China' during the Cold War: Global Maoism and Asian Studies," in *De-Centering Cold War History: Local and*

Global Change, edited by Jadwiga Pieper Mooney and Fabio Lanza (New York: Routledge, 2012), 147–66.

Two persons very dear to me passed away while I was working on this manuscript: my father, Flavio, who would have been proud—because he was always proud of his children; and Saundra (Sandy) Sturdevant, whom I had the good fortune to meet because of this project. She was an extraordinary woman, a feminist, an activist, a writer, and an immensely talented photographer. One day, in the last weeks of her life, when I went to visit her in her house in central California, she called me "a good comrade." Coming from her, it was the best compliment possible.

This book is dedicated to Sandy's memory.

INTRODUCTION

OF ENDS AND BEGINNINGS; OR, WHEN CHINA EXISTED

La paura della speranza e l'amore per la disperazione. Non si tratta d'un medesimo sentimento, né si ritrovano nella stessa persona. Non necessariamente. Ma parliamone, perché la "Cina" scatena l'una e l'altra.
—Franco Fortini, "Ancora in Cina"

Ah ça, dit Truptin, mais voulez parler de Mao de la révolution culturelle, *tageming*? . . . Invention, madame mademoiselle, invention de journaliste, tout ça, moi en Chine, jamais rien vu tout ça. Chine, invention française, parisienne même, tous des ignorants, ignorant la langue, l'écriture et ça parle, ça parle puisque ça ne sait pas lire. . . . Permettez-moi de vous dire, madame, permettez mois de vous dire, la Chine n'existe pas.
—Natacha Michel, *La Chine européenne*

As the title of this book suggests, I start from the end. And I don't mean it as a rhetorical ploy or a narrative gimmick; this project originated—in personal, political, and intellectual terms—by taking stock of an ending, by registering an absence, by marking a disappearance. Personally, this happened many years ago, when I was a young undergraduate student at the University of Venice. Browsing through the then-not-particularly expansive collection of Asian studies journals, I encountered a publication that—just by virtue of its name—stood out among the *China Quarterly*, *Modern*

China, and the *Journal of Asian Studies*: the *Bulletin of Concerned Asian Scholars*. To a nineteen-year-old freshman in 1987 Italy, the title sounded curious and, frankly, quite puzzling. *What were these scholars concerned about*, I asked myself, *and what were they concerned about specifically as "Asian" scholars?* While, at that time, my puzzlement was due to my own ignorance, the gap that separated me—an otherwise politically aware young student—and the collective statement of a position of "concern" inscribed in the *Bulletin's* title pointed to a larger set of issues. More than a geographical and generational distance, what was implied in the almost archival separation I felt in picking up the *Bulletin* was a political and intellectual break. This book is, in many ways, an investigation into that break.

A Double Disappearance

The Committee of Concerned Asian Scholars (CCAS) was an organization of young professors and graduate students who were vociferously critical of U.S. policies in Vietnam (and in Asia in general), and of the complicity of the field of Asian studies with these policies. The organization questioned the very intellectual constitution of the field itself. Between 1968 and 1979, the Concerned Asian Scholars (CAS) mounted a sweeping attack on the academic, political, and financial structure of Asian studies in U.S. academia and engaged in some memorable debates with the founding figures of the field. The journal they published—still in existence (albeit under a different name)—the *Bulletin of Concerned Asian Scholars* (BCAS), was radical, vibrant, at times excessive, and always politically minded.[1]

"Concerned" is quite a distinctive characteristic for a scholar to self-define, and even more so for a group of scholars: it implies a subjective, personal commitment, a direct involvement in the issue at stake—and it further implies that there exist scholars who are *not* concerned, but rather indifferent.[2] In the case of the *Bulletin* (and the Committee behind it), it also implied the possibility of a *collective* concern, of a positioning vis-à-vis politics and knowledge, in particular the politics of knowledge embedded in the profession and the field of Asian studies. It implied and even called for a political militancy in—and outside—the arena of intellectual production. This book interrogates how such a militancy could be articulated; how the emergence of a collective political subjectivity called CCAS was possible; and, perhaps more importantly, how it disappeared, how it became de facto impossible, to the point where by 1987 it looked so unusual and out of place to a budding Asia scholar.

The most obvious and obviously recognized factor behind that collective concern was, of course, the Vietnam War, and in that CCAS represented an interesting and distinctive part of the larger antiwar movement.[3] The parable of the organizational fortunes of the Committee coincided in large part with the evolution of the war itself: the end of the American involvement in the conflict and the consequent dissolution of the antiwar élan marked a crisis for the Concerned, who did not endure much longer as a collective. However—and here I admit my own bias as a historian of Modern China—in this book I want to highlight another factor behind the activism of CCAS, one less easily recognized and definitively much more controversial, both at the time and in today's memory: China.

While it included scholars of Japan, Korea, and South and Southeast Asia, CCAS was overwhelmingly a China group, in terms of both membership and readership.[4] But what made China an unmistakable point of reference for CCAS was not just the sheer numbers of China specialists in the ranks; it was also and more significantly how they approached China and what China meant for the organization in general. In Marilyn Young's recollection, "most China people [in CCAS] were attracted not because they had this great love for Chinese civilization but already because of politics." Unlike the Soviet historians of their generation, these young scholars loved the country they studied, and they wrote out of affection for China. And what drew them and motivated that affection was China's "revolutionary situation."[5] The Cultural Revolution, which had exploded in 1966, had captured the attention of the radical Left all over the world, and by 1968—the year of the founding of CCAS—the example of the Red Guards was being invoked globally. While these young scholars could not visit China (there would be no diplomatic relationship between the United States and the PRC until 1972), the political proximity was recognized across the physical distance.

China figured as the necessary "positive" side of the Committee's harsh attack on the Asian studies field and on U.S. imperialism in Asia. Viewed from afar, China offered the possibility of alternative development, a more humane economy, and peaceful policies. It was through their evaluation of the Maoist experiences that the Concerned Asian Scholars were able, for the first time in centuries, to consider "Asia" and "Asian people" as political subjects, capable of original thought and practices. While CCAS was by no means a Maoist organization, much of their intellectual and political endeavor was framed by their confrontation with the existence, the contradictions, the tensions, and the ultimate demise of Maoism.

This ended in 1976, when Mao Zedong died and the Cultural Revolution ended. Between 1976 and 1981, only three or four essays on China were published in the *Bulletin*, and none of them addressed directly the dramatic shift that was taking place in Chinese politics and its potential consequences. In 1972, Richard Nixon's trip to China had already shaken many activists' faith in the PRC, which was perceived as having abandoned Vietnam; by 1980, it was clear that the new regime of Deng Xiaoping was dismantling all the Maoist experiments CCAS had celebrated and moving the country toward some form of capitalist system. In this scenario, China basically disappeared from the journal's pages; it became a conspicuous absence, the veritable elephant in the room. When it reappeared, in a double issue in 1981, the contributors to the *Bulletin* struggled to cope with the new China and the very different image of Maoism it presented. Gone was the optimism toward the Chinese model, gone was the possibility of alternative policies, but also gone was much of the grounding that since 1968 had provided a foundation to the collective subject of the Concerned Asian Scholars.

But there was also another, more painful disappearance. While most of the Concerned Scholars who specialized in Japan or Korea went on to prestigious and well-deserved careers (John Dower, Herbert Bix, and Bruce Cumings, to name a few), the China side of the Concerned Scholars was more seriously affected. By the late 1970s, many of the China scholars dropped out of academia completely, did not get tenure, or suffered more personal losses.[6]

In the following pages I track the role of China in CCAS's political and intellectual enterprise, and I trace the patterns of that double disappearance. I follow in detail the founding and the evolution of the organization, but this is not simply an "institutional" history. Rather, I examine the case of the CCAS to shed some light on a larger moment of transition in Cold War international politics, the history of Asian studies in the United States, and the connections between scholarship and activism. In order to illustrate the larger—and potentially long-lasting—relevance of the issues at stake, throughout the book I deploy references to thinkers and political groups that were active, in the same years, on the other side of the globe, as part of the phenomenon usually labeled "French Maoism."

Distinctly philosophical in tone, French Maoists were drastically different in inspiration, goals, and locations from the Concerned Asian Scholars.[7] Yet "China" and "Maoism" identified themes and practices that were shared across these very diverse situations. First, in both cases, "China" did not name solely a cultural and geographical location, but rather a set of ideas and concerns that had potential worldwide relevance. Attention to and embrace of Maoism therefore represented the first major instance in which people around the world—in Europe, the Americas, Africa, and so forth—approached Asians in a potentially non-orientalist way, as subjects with the right to original thinking and independent political practice. Second, Maoism presented a fundamental alternative both to the capitalist and the Soviet models, precisely at a time when, both in France and in the United States, radical movements had laid bare the profound inequalities that persisted after the postwar economic boom. Third, the crisis of the 1960s invested directly the privileged locations of politics in France as in the United States—the political parties. The Cultural Revolution then appeared as the final attack on the validity of any privileged location for politics and as a declaration of the legitimacy for people to organize independently of the state.[8] Finally, Maoism interpellated intellectuals directly. The Cultural Revolution addressed issues that could not help but call into question the daily experiences of students and teachers everywhere: the division of manual and intellectual labor, the role of science and objectivity, the relationship between politics and knowledge, and the ideological structure of the transmission of learning. All of these were crucial problems for both CCAS and the French Maoists.

While these are two very limited and situated experiences, they provide a glimpse into how Maoism influenced groups and individual activists around the world, from South America to Africa, from U.S. inner cities to Iran. Maoism traversed the sixties not as mimicry, with people parroting the ill-digested stories of exotic Red Guards. Rather, it was the privileged name—resonating differently in different situations—that connected a series of crucial political issues and a set of practices forged specifically to deal with those issues. These were practices that were configured as alternatives to existing models (liberal and Communist), specifically in relation to the issue of equality. Maoism, then, provided U.S. scholars and French radicals—but also Tanzanian farmers and Iranian revolutionaries—with a vocabulary to identify equalitarian practices across the world, practices that were eccentric both to the nation-state and to the leftist parties. Maoism was the grounding to criticize the existent and propose alternatives.

The analysis of these specific cases within a larger context of scholarship and activism offers three distinct but interconnected contributions. First, it provides a new perspective into a unique moment in the fraught history of the idea of "China," inside and outside academia. Today, orientalist tropes of "Asian values" are being reified at the level of a global ideology to articulate differences within a triumphant capitalist modernity.[9] In the long sixties, I argue that Maoist China stood instead as the signifier of global equality in regard to issues of development, ideology, and political power.

Second, my analysis of these specific cases in the context of global Maoism addresses historically the relationship between politics and scholarship, activism, and academia. The comparison between these two cases provides a broader reflection on the politics inherent in the production of knowledge; in France, as in the United States, it was in part through Maoism that a thorough critique of the role of the intellectual, of science, and of ideological reproduction was formulated. Finally, although this is not a research project about Maoism in China, the question of why and how we should study that political experience shadows this entire book. I hope that by examining how the experiments of the Cultural Revolution were reinterpreted in the West, I can contribute to the scholarly effort to clarify the political meanings of this extremely complicated period.[10] While I look at the global sixties from the perspective of China, I also try to rethink the significance of Maoism in light of how it was understood and appropriated outside of China.

Global Maoism

This book moves from a premise that I should not leave unspoken, which is that the sixties took place as a global event—or a globally connected series of events—and that Maoism was a crucial element in that global happening. By that I mean that the existence of the sixties as a period was not just—as Fredric Jameson has argued—in "the sharing of a common objective situation, to which a whole range of varied responses and creative innovations is then possible, but always within the situation's structural limits."[11] Rather, the form, the language, and the significance of those responses and innovations were also shared and translated across borders. Maoism was an essential code for that translation. This is not to say that we can trace easy lines of comparison among different locations, people, and organizations that, in dissimilar ways, appropriated for themselves the term *Maoist* or showed a particular interest for China. I am not arguing that we should look at Indian Naxalites and the French PCML, Sendero Luminoso and the Black Panthers as necessarily and automatically belonging to a presumably interconnected global struggle. Nor do I want to discount how the leftists' fascination with Maoist China—especially in Europe—was marred by orientalist attitudes and fantasies.[12] But it seems to me undeniable—and very important—that the long sixties were the only moment in recent history when China, specifically because of its revolutionary situation, came to constitute a foundation for a transnational discourse of intellectual and political change. This particular discourse did not place at its center ethnic- or culturally based values, nor did it espouse the myth of a "rise of China/Asia" in terms of geopolitical power. Rather, Maoism here was the name of a shift in the political and intellectual frame of reference in the 1960s and 1970s, when what was happening in Asia acquired a new relevance for people all over the world within their own historical circumstances. Maoist China, then, was not the Oriental paradise of Communism realized in material deprivation, but the point of reference of a flawed, incomplete, failed, yet collective search for alternatives to existing developmental models. Understanding that search, in all its limitations, seems to me extremely important even (and especially) in our historical circumstances.[13]

When I presented different sections of this book in meetings, conferences, and roundtables, I often demurely introduced it as my book about "China"—as opposed to my more serious, archival work on China. Thankfully, on more than one occasion, attentive friends and colleagues pointed out the hollowness of that distinction and confronted me about the fact that this project had indeed something to say about China—without quotation marks. They pointed to the fact that I was talking of a China that was no less real—and no more constructed—than the one that I encountered in fragmented pieces of archival material. Because in the sixties, for self-labeled French Maoists, radical black activists, and Concerned Scholars, Maoist China, to paraphrase one of the epigraphic quotes above, *existed*. It existed as an example of what was possible, as the vocabulary to phrase diverse experiences, and yes, as a misunderstood point of reference; it existed differently in each of these cases, but it existed. As Franco Fortini, the author of the other epigraph, wrote after his second trip to the PRC, "now for me China is *true*, because it has its measurable reality. It is part of the world."[14]

One of the goals of this book is precisely to examine the modes and the consequences of that existence, of that accepted reality. If "the perverse legacy of Said's orientalism" has been that Western historians "pay attention to 'the East' primarily as a mirror with which to see the West more clearly,"[15] here I want to twist that mirror and start instead from the premise that Maoist inventions in China had a political reality and a political value per se. It was the recognition of that reality and that value that framed political and intellectual movement elsewhere, including in "the West," and by looking at that recognition as a serious undertaking we might actually discover something about Maoist politics in China and globally. But, in order to do that, we need first to steer away from what seems to me has been the dominant mode of interpretation of the role of Maoism outside China in the long sixties, one that has been at least in part promoted by former Maoists, especially in Europe. Paraphrasing Lenin, we could call this view "Maoism as the infantile stage of liberalism." In this particular pattern, the fascination with China by mostly (but not exclusively) young people is described, in terms borrowed from pop psychology, as an infantile enthrallment, an adolescent phase that, once overcome, led eventually—and thankfully—to a more mature awareness. In the French case, to make an example, the "daft seduction into unreason"[16] that pushed people to frame their activism following the image of faraway Red Guards supposedly evolved into an "acceptable" commitment for gender and LGBT equality, humanitarian enterprises (Doctors Without Borders), and full participation in liberal democracy, finally shed of its childish excesses.[17] According to this analysis, Maoism was "a political learning process via which French youth cured itself of its infantile revolutionary longings in order to focus on more circumscribed tasks pertaining to the transformation of everyday life and the regeneration of civil society."[18]

Then, if China existed, as a former French Maoist famously quipped, it did so only "in our heads,"[19] and as such it was an existence that was easy to overcome once reality (or adulthood, one could say) set in. Individually, some former Maoists, or "China lovers," have described this evolutionary process into and out of a relationship with "China" as a complete break, in which the sudden realization of the true nature of the Maoist experiments leads the former activist to a complete political reversal.[20] Others have instead framed their political evolution as a continuous path in which only the objects of desire and passion are shifting (then the complex political path subsumed under "Maoism," now liberalism, human rights, whatever), while the individual's moral center of gravity remains stable. Perry Link, former CCASer who went on to an illustrious career at Princeton and UC Riverside, provides perhaps the best example of the simplifying rhetorical power of the latter pattern: "In the late 1960s, I admired Mao because I felt strongly about things like peace, freedom, justice, truth, and a fair chance for the little guy. Today I detest Mao and his legacy. Why? Because I am drawn to things like peace, freedom, justice, truth, and a fair chance for the little guy."[21]

I have spent a large part of my intellectual life studying political movements of young people and questioning precisely the uses—and abuses—of categories such as "youth" or "children" in defining and describing politics.[22] I am therefore instinctively wary of any description that deploys metaphors of infantilism or youthful enthusiasm, as it is always a strategy to confine or deny the political meaning of that occurrence. We should seriously interrogate the role of "youth" as a category and a social classification in the long sixties, outside of simple metaphors of adolescent fascination, but this exceeds the scope of this book.[23] I would also agree with Quinn Slobodian that one of the main political effects of the denial of Maoism (often framed in terms of personal repentance) is to prophylactically discipline "any potential future inter-racial and transnational political identifications." If the only legacy of that experience is a conversion to humanitarianism and human rights, this means that "the First World relationship to the Third would now only begin—and usually end—with medication and missiles."[24]

My point here is relatively simple: I take seriously that there were people who, in different locations and within different historical contingencies, took Maoism and Maoist China seriously. And that political choice, no matter how misguided it was, had momentous political and intellectual consequences. Taking Maoism seriously produced real effects for those who did. It shaped practices and debates; it framed organizational structures and conflicts—it was, in a word, a political discovery.

Also, the recognition of the existence of Maoist China was not something we should confine to the imagination of radicals in different countries; it was not, that is, just a mental projection with localized practical effects, a love at first sight that nonetheless produced dramatic changes in the loving one. Rather, that recognition—with all its misjudgments, its contradictions, its massive gaps—was based on the acknowledgment that people in Maoist China were dealing with issues and experimenting with practices that were globally significant and potentially valuable. In that, an analysis of global Maoism writ large might indeed tell us something about China under Mao—if not about the details and the specifics of those practices, at least about their political meaning, about how we approached them then and how we can try to understand them anew now.

The encounter with the Maoist experience—as a global event—defined the intellectual and political path of thinkers as diverse as Louis Althusser, Alain Badiou, and Jacques Rancière: I deploy their work in this book specifically to highlight the significance of the issues that were conjured under the name "China" in the 1960s and, perhaps, more importantly, to highlight how we can still make sense of that project today.

The World, Asia, and China

In this book, I then approach "global Maoism" as a political phenomenon that is valuable in itself—and not just by virtue of the openings its disappearance allowed.[25] I take, as my central and limited case study, a group of activists and radicals who tried to be at the same time also scholars of Asia (often specifically of China). By looking at the tensions produced by that choice, I intend to highlight two other issues that were central in the long sixties but whose relevance extends way beyond that chronological frame.

First, at the very basic level, like many other groups in many different locations, CCAS confronted the dilemma of integrating—in theory and practice—scholarship and activism, academic life and political militancy. Was it enough to be at the same time a detached expert in the classroom and a committed radical outside? How could one challenge the existing state of knowledge without simultaneously destroying the very methods of production of that knowledge—that is, without altering the practices that constituted the functioning of education and research? What were the implications of the attacks on existing power relations for teachers, students, and scholars? These and others were questions at the very foundation of the political configuration we call "the global sixties," and they echoed from Mexico to France, from Turin to Berkeley;[26] the importance of these issues can be viewed as both the reason behind and the effect of the centrality of students in the 1960s. But, in the case of CCAS, these questions acquired an added resonance precisely because "China" was both the name of their chosen area of specialization—the object of their knowledge production—and the name of the politics that authorized a rethinking of the modes of that production. The Cultural Revolution was, if nothing else, perhaps the most sweeping—and yes, at times violent—critique of the school system, including its formalized educational methods, the bureaucratized relationships between teachers and students, the separation between practice and learning, the persistence of intellectual privileges, and so on.[27] It was a critique based on the acknowledgment of the intelligence of the people, of the authority to think and speak of those who, up to that point, had not been recognized for the ability to think, and in that it presented a fundamental challenge to the position of the teacher, the scholar, the educator. And it was a critique that led to interesting, if often failed, experiments. As Sigrid Schmalzer's work on agricultural science shows, the push to be at the same time "red and expert" went beyond the simple rhetorical ploy of indoctrination, but produced specific practices of learning and distribution of knowledge.[28] That is why many students across Europe felt a kinship with the Chinese experiments in alternative forms of education and in their search for egalitarian forms of knowledge production.[29]

For the Concerned Asian Scholars, by virtue of their chosen area of study, that kinship with China and the echoes of the Maoist experiments with their own academic/political conundrum could only be felt even more strongly; as such, their case highlights the crucial elements of the political criticism of academia in the sixties, the challenge presented to intellectuals and scholars by the Maoist experiments, and the tensions produced in the attempts to combine scholarship and activism. These were problems that resonated globally at the time but that should also be vital for intellectuals and activists today, as universities are progressively subsumed under the neoliberal model, with emphasis placed on the function of research and professionalization "to the detriment of the transversal civic and political functions."[30] The question of the separation between the classroom—where we can teach Mao, Marx, or Badiou—and the social practices that dominate our lives, our students' lives, and, ultimately, our very modes of production and transmission of knowledge should still be at the center of our theory and practice. I propose that looking at how other people, decades ago, tried to act on that separation might help us think about it today.

That separation remained, however, unbreachable, as the Concerned Asian Scholars could not fully adopt a model that accepted or celebrated the "intelligence of the people." One of the reasons was that for many within CCAS, it was Americans' lack of knowledge about Asia—promoted by the active misleading of the U.S. government with the assistance of "politically neutral" established Asia scholars—that led directly to the carnage in Vietnam and U.S. policies in the continent. In response to their understanding of the situation, the Concerned tasked themselves primarily with producing more accurate knowledge about Asia and spreading it to "the American people" (via fact sheets, public lectures, and textbook evaluations) with the hope that "the people" would become aware of their misconceptions and act to stop their government. Yet this, in the end, remained very much the project of a scholarly elite teaching "the masses"—rather than the other way around—one that maintained the respective roles of the teacher and the taught.[31] Even if some of the CCASers took the Maoist example to its more far-reaching conclusions and were interested in dismantling the structure of social relationships that shaped academia, the production of knowledge, and the patterns of global dominance, this political push often remained subordinated to the pedagogical need to enlighten the people. That contradiction marked the history and the very existence of the Committee.

Second, CCAS articulated the tension between scholarship and politics within the field of Asian studies, and at a specific moment in the history of that field, but also in U.S. academia in general. Asian studies was constituted, like all area studies, in the immediate postwar, largely through direct government intervention. Money was funneled through private foundations (Ford first and foremost), and centers for the study of Asia were developed in specific universities (Harvard, Columbia, Berkeley, and the University of Washington). For all the exceptional scholars who taught or were formed in those centers, the field itself remained partially defined by the Cold War imperative to "know thy enemy." But, and perhaps more importantly, Asian studies carried other, deeper scars; immediately after its establishment, the field had also been one of the main targets of the McCarthy persecution. One of the very first rounds of attack on academics by the House Un-American Activities Committee (HUAC) was precisely centered on the issue of "the loss of China" and directed against the scholar Owen Lattimore and the Institute of Pacific Relations (IPR).[32] The McCarthy purges had a huge effect on Asian studies, dividing loyalties (with eminent China scholar Karl Wittfogel accusing Lattimore),[33] impacting individual lives, but more than anything silencing—directly or indirectly—an entire generation of scholars, who got used to censoring their own work, especially as it related to contemporary issues. As Ellen Schrecker has argued, there is "considerable speculation that the devastating effects of the IPR hearings on the field of EAS [East Asian studies] made it hard for American policy-makers to get realistic advice about that part of the world."[34] In this, Asian studies is an example of a larger phenomenon, what David Price, in his study on the field of anthropology, calls "the specter of McCarthyism." That specter, Price shows, limited the questions scholars asked and answered; it led them to willfully ignore the connection between the theories they created and "American Cold War policies of dominance and dependency."[35] By the late 1950s, the decline of hearings and firing was due not so much to a calming down of persecution but to the self-imposed quieting down of academics.[36]

The CCAS generation was the first post-McCarthy generation and the one that witnessed—and lived—the effects of that silencing in the connection between academic acquiescence (or, in some cases, vocal support) and the disastrous U.S. policies in East Asia. Their criticism addressed precisely those effects in their complex institutional, political, and intellectual ramifications. Moreover, that criticism came also at a specific moment in the history of many of the disciplines (history, anthropology, literary criticism) that had been channeled into the awkward conglomerates of area studies. By the 1970s, for example in history, in large part as a function of the political critique of the 1960s, social history emerged as the new approach, legitimizing a view that incorporated the voices and stories of "ordinary people" and that often reverted to a language of class. Yet by the 1980s, we see the beginning of another shift, with the introduction of cultural history, gender studies, and eventually the reception of Said's *Orientalism* and the broader phenomenon of "French Theory."[37] The experience of CCAS is chronologically and intellectually framed within these two large shifts in the intellectual episteme; then, through an analysis of this experience, we can also trace how politics influenced the transformation of the academic discourse—as well as the limits of that transformation.

The arch of CCAS history also coincided with a very concrete change in U.S. academia, from the seeming abundance of employment and funding opportunities of the 1960s to the rapidly shrinking job market of the 1970s. As we live today in a period of acute crisis similar to (if not more profound than) that of the 1970s, this parable also hints at the practical conditions and limitations for activism in academia.

This book is not meant in any way to be an exhaustive history of Asian studies in the United States, nor do I dwell much on the construction of area studies other than as reflected in criticism of CCAS. Rather, I aim at discovering the opportunities for thought, interpretation, and action that the particular political situation of the 1960s opened—specifically under the name of "China." I describe how those possibilities were largely foreclosed by the 1980s, but I also question the connections—at a scholarly and political level—between the intellectual perspectives opened during the long sixties, as presented by CCAS, and those that developed with the introduction of new theoretical frameworks after the 1980s. And these connections are often unclear and always contested.

Finally, while I do not use Chinese sources nor really deal with Chinese actors directly, this book claims to say something about China. This is in part because even today, in a completely different political, intellectual, and practical situation, it seems to me that some of the questions that animated the experience of global Maoism and CCAS still stand. For example, can we really make sense of the Cultural Revolution without taking seriously the criticism of the party-state or the Maoist promises of radical equality? Can we think of the history of China and Asia within the framework of expanding imperialism? How do we know China? How is our knowledge shaped by the lingering understanding of China as a "field" to be visited and mined for resources? Why and how should we write about China, and specifically Maoist China? What are the connections between political understanding and scholarly knowledge? The scholars and activists that I describe in this book struggled endlessly with these questions. To even those who could visit China, and perhaps especially to them, it remained multiple and elusive. When the Maoist project was terminated, many among them wondered whether it made sense to keep writing about a China now subtracted from the shared understanding of the long sixties and reduced to another a political-territorial-cultural entity, fully inserted in the path of capitalist development. More recently, we have seen the development of a renewed, and often excellent, scholarly production on the PRC, at times grouped under the label "new PRC history."[38] This is a valuable enterprise, and one to which I contribute myself, but it is also largely based on the recent availability of archival material on the post-1949 years—an availability that, alas, seems now to be progressively diminishing due to government restrictions. This book then also asks what a generation with no access to archives—but with excellent questions—can teach a generation with a (temporary) abundance of sources.

Subjective Positions

All books, even scholarly books, are personal for their authors insofar that, behind the sometimes stiff and controlled academic prose, they carry the weight of days at a desk, dust of the archives, too-often neglected spouses and children, long periods of self-doubt, and the little joys of a sentence well crafted or a problem finally clarified. Yet this book is especially personal, and in more than one sense.

As a scholar, I have almost always written about people who were either long dead or far away in space and time. This project took me for the first time close to people who are not only alive, but also often still active in my own discipline; and, in one case, people who passed away during the time I was writing. With some of these people, I developed cordial, collegial relationships. With one of them, the retelling of the past led to mutual respect and a true friendship, and now to the mourning of a loss.

This is nothing new to anybody who has been even marginally involved in oral history, and if it were just a question of personal experience, it would probably not be worth mentioning. Even if, in the period I investigate, the personal was indeed claimed to be political, I feel confident that, following Michel Foucault, I too could "make of a personal question the absence of a problem" and leave my personal experience unspoken.[39] However, as I mentioned in the beginning, this book (like all historical works, in a sense) measures the distance—and the proximity—between intellectual and political subjectivities, then and now. And I think it is necessary to clarify the subjective positions involved.

There has been a resurgence of scholarly interest in the sixties in recent years. New monographic studies have refocused our attention on groups, organizations, phenomena, and specific figures, mainly in the United States and Europe, but often with an unprecedented attention for global connections.[40] A new journal, devoted explicitly to the history, politics, and culture of the sixties, has been published since 2008.[41] Why this renewed attention? While most of the new scholarship on the subject is indeed excellent and at times groundbreaking, there is always the nagging suspicion that, when one talks about that era, nostalgia lurks in the shadows: nostalgia for political postures now largely impossible, for organizational forms long gone, for global networks seemingly lost. And this applies even to people of my generation (I was born close to the end of the 1960s), who feel nostalgic for things never lived, but rather seen on TV or in movies, or narrated by an older cohort.[42] In this book, I programmatically look at that period with the opposite of nostalgia. I argue instead that we should approach the sixties, and specifically the global sixties, not out of regret for good things gone, but as a way to reflect on the possibilities—in the here and now—for alternative politics and new intellectual concerns. I search, in that moment of high organizational and creative intensity, for undeveloped opportunities, failed attempts, intellectual openings, and political inventions. Not to repeat or recycle the subjective positions of the past, but to think with them in the subjective and objective contingencies of the present.

The End of Concern is also—while not primarily—a history of a moment within Asian studies in the United States, a field with which I have some intellectual and political qualms, but within which I have worked for almost two decades. It traces the history behind some of the intellectual, scholarly, and academic conditions in which my colleagues and I operate today. As such, throughout this project, I have been wary of the danger of writing a "navel gazing" story, an insider's probe into debates that have little interest for people who do not share the same academic affiliations within the American university system. Yet, as I have argued in the rest of this introduction, and as the rest of this volume will hopefully prove, this analysis—while centered on a relatively restricted group of young scholars in a specific academic setting—relates to larger issues, including the global politics of the sixties, the meaning of "Maoism," and the connections between learning and activism. In the end, the details of organizational debates or of the academic confrontations between students and teachers in the 1960s and 1970s seem interesting to me not only and not so much if they speak to the evolution of a field of study, but if they address questions that still remain problematic today, within and without the classroom, within and without the confines of academia.

Finally, I have tried to respect the subjective positions of my actors—and my own—in the way I wrote the following pages. It has been my good fortune that the Concerned Asian Scholars were very prolific in their written production, both as part of organizational practice and in their correspondences as friends, colleagues, and fellow activists.[43] A large collection of documents is preserved at the Wisconsin Historical Society in Madison. In addition, Saundra Sturdevant and Joe Moore were incredibly generous and handed me their personal archives (they are now with the rest of the CCAS documents in Wisconsin). All this material conveys, in a fragmentary but vibrant manner, the voices of many of these young scholars at the time. These are voices rarely subdued, especially in their internal correspondence: the fights were contentious, the arguments loud, the passion and the despair equally high, the intensity at times overwhelming. These are voices that I found difficult to tame within my own narrative and even more difficult to juxtapose—let alone reconcile—with the more cautious, wise, and pensive reflections that came out of the interviews I conducted with former CAs in recent years. In the end, I decided to let these voices speak for themselves as much as possible; if there was a statement that could be made by reporting a direct quote, I did so, even at the risk of producing unresolved cacophonies. Next to those voices I placed my own, with the goal of providing context, highlighting similarities, and, more importantly, inserting the details in a larger theoretical framework. As always, while I tried very hard to be fair to those actors, I have probably made them say things they would not have said at the time and that they would not definitively say now. Like all writers, I constructed a narrative and an argument with their voices, but it is my narrative, my argument.

This is a narrative that might sound, at times, critical, but that comes from a position of sympathy—in the original Greek sense of "feeling together." It comes from the recognition of a common, if differently situated, search. I argue in this book that global Maoism was based on the acknowledgment of Asian people as subjects, geographically distant but politically close; likewise, this work started from the recognition of political and intellectual subjectivities in the not-so-distant past, from which there is both distance and closeness. As probing as it can be, my perspective into the history of CCAS and global Maoism is, as Roland Barthes wrote about his own gazing at China, a "sideways view."

Characters

Many of the names that crowd the pages of this book will be unfamiliar to any reader who does not have intimate knowledge of the field of Asian studies. And yet they include people who provided (and are still providing) crucial contributions to the knowledge of Asia in the United States—in terms of teaching, research, training, and public advocacy. Instead of breaking the narration every time a new character appears—or adding extensive footnotes—I thought I could provide here some minimal background notes for *some* of these figures.

First, the man who was identified by CCAS—not mistakenly—as the very embodiment of (Modern) Chinese studies in the United States, John King Fairbank. Fairbank, a Missouri native, had studied in England and at Harvard, sojourned in China before and during World War II, and then spent the following decades building what would soon become the largest program in Chinese studies in the country, at Harvard University. It is impossible to overestimate the influence Fairbank has had on our understanding of Modern China, an influence that was expressed not so much through his research, but through his teaching and organizational skills: his many textbooks are still printed and used in classrooms to this day, and his students have been prominent in at least two generations of Modern China specialists. The Center for Chinese Studies at Harvard proudly carries his name.

Unsurprisingly, many Harvard grad students were among the founding and early members of CCAS. Marilyn Young was pursuing a PhD in U.S. and Chinese history, and she would go on to teach at Michigan and then at NYU and to publish widely on the Vietnam War and U.S.-Asia relationships. James Peck did not finish his PhD at the time, leaving Harvard for a career in publishing at Pantheon, where he shepherded many notable books on Asia and China; he eventually got his doctorate at NYU and authored two excellent books on U.S. imperialism. John Dower got his degree at Harvard and became one of the leading historians of Modern Japan, teaching at MIT until his recent retirement. Herbert Bix, also a Japan specialist and a Harvard PhD, was a founding member of CCAS; his biography of Emperor Hirohito won the Pulitzer Prize in 2001.

Mark Selden, another one of the founders of CCAS, had received his PhD from Yale; he taught for years at SUNY Binghamton and published the seminal book on the Yan'an period, twice revising it in light of new evidence in the post-Mao period. Selden is also one of the few scholars who has constantly worked on both China and Japan, and he has devoted a large part of his career to helping younger colleagues in publishing. Moss Roberts and Bruce Cumings received their degrees from Columbia University, the former in Early Chinese literature, the latter in Modern Korean history. Roberts is a well-respected translator and literature scholar (at NYU), and Cumings is probably the leading historian of Korea in the United States, teaching at Chicago.

Joseph Esherick was studying at Berkeley at the time of CCAS's inception. He went on to shape, with Paul Pickowicz (a member of the first CCAS delegation to the PRC), one of the most successful programs for Modern Chinese history at the University of California–San Diego. John Berninghausen was a Berkeley graduate too, specializing in Chinese literature and language. He molded and led Middlebury College's famed Chinese language program for over thirty years. Orville Schell completed all but his PhD dissertation at Berkeley; he cofounded (with his teacher Franz Schurmann) Pacific News Service and later became a famous writer and journalist. He served as dean of the UC Berkeley Graduate School of Journalism and is now the Arthur Ross Director of the Center on U.S.-China Relations of the Asia Society.

Structure of the Book

The volume is not organized in a chronological fashion, in part because the period covered is relatively short but also because I found it more useful to devote chapters to specific themes.

Chapter 1, "America's Asia," describes the founding of CCAS in 1968 in Philadelphia and follows the first few years of the organization, paying particular attention to the intellectual and scholarly debates that the committee waged with the main figures of the field at the time (John K. Fairbank above all). I trace the connection between political concern and scholarly production, and I illustrate how CCAS's understanding of the "new things" happening in Asia—and specifically in China—was crucial (but ultimately insufficient) in defining a novel theoretical and scholarly approach. Through a comparison with the role of "China" for some groups of French Maoists, I illustrate how "global Maoism" was the name given to a series of political practices and intellectual attitudes that, while similar and connected to the Chinese experience, were also specifically situated.

To take Maoist China seriously could not but imply a rethinking of the very position of the scholar as an intellectual and political being. The Cultural Revolution had shown that it was impossible to be an intellectual in one's office or classroom and an activist in the streets; politics had to permeate and alter the very fabric of daily life, the structure of the professions, the framing of one's intellectual activity. Chapter 2, "To Be, or Not to Be, a Scholar," examines how the Concerned Asian Scholars strove to integrate their intellectual and political lives, scholarship and activism. I analyze their struggle to be political within academia (in particular, their challenge to the funding of the field), but also their continuous wrangling over the different temporalities of cultural production and activism. It is not surprising that by the mid-1970s, many within CCAS had found this tension insolvable, and they left or were forced to leave academia; some did not get tenure, some did not find a university job, and others simply moved to other ventures. Once again, the French Maoists—who tried repeatedly to breach the separation between manual and intellectual labor—provide a comparative and theoretical perspective.

Chapter 3, "Seeing and Understanding: China as the Place of Desire," deals specifically with the issue of closeness and distance from China. In the summer of 1971, before the Nixon rapprochement, CCAS was the first scholarly organization to be admitted to visit the PRC. A second delegation was invited to China the following year, and both groups met with Zhou Enlai and members of the "Gang of Four." The China trips had very practical effects for the organization, as they shifted the priorities of CCAS toward an almost exclusive focus on the PRC, thus creating massive rifts in the group. But also, and perhaps more significantly, by going to China,

CCAS delegates found themselves in the position of other "fellow travelers," caught in the tension between the desire to understand Chinese socialism politically and the need to explain Chinese realities academically, between friendship and investigation. This tension had huge consequences for the very unity of the Committee, and it is still reflected today in the conflicting memories of those first visits.

The last chapter, "Facing Thermidor: Global Maoism at Its End," follows the dissolution of the Committee in 1979, but also traces the intellectual and political debate within the editorial board of the *Bulletin of Concerned Asian Scholars* leading to the publication of two special issues on post-Mao China in 1981. Specifically I look at how two concepts, "class" and "culture," that had framed the understanding of the Cultural Revolution in the previous years became completely obscure or irrelevant in the early Deng era. The China scholars at the *Bulletin* found themselves in a difficult position as the new Chinese regime dismantled and denied much of the experiment CCAS had supported while simultaneously dismissing the concepts scholars could employ to analyze these shifts. The denial of the Cultural Revolution in the post-Mao era was reflected and refracted in the organizational crisis of CCAS but also in the starkly divergent paths that opened to (or were chosen by) the former Concerned Scholars. This divergence was framed, at the time and afterward, as one between career and commitment, but it was ultimately a crisis—and a choice—over the political confines of the militancy of intellectuals and scholars. Jacques Rancière's analysis of his own experience as a Maoist helps highlight these issues.

The epilogue offers an analysis of the major changes in the field of Asian studies in the 1980s and 1990s and of the role of CCAS in creating the conditions for those changes. In particular, I follow the emergence of more explicitly theoretical approaches and the recovery of a different legacy of the Maoist period. Some former concerned scholars positioned themselves against these shifts in the field, even when they seemed to be congruous with their own past enterprise.

CHAPTER ONE

AMERICA'S ASIA

Discovering China, Rethinking Knowledge

[Established scholars have] been irresponsible because they've demanded they be apolitical, which is a very political action. Inaction is. You're being very political in your inaction, and this is the problem of the field, and this is why the China field is in such a rut, why good scholarship is not being done, why most of the things that appear in the journals are a lot of junk, more they are a lot of shit.
—Jonathan Unger, "Wither Chinese Studies: A Panel at the 1970 Convention in San Francisco"

Learning has to be grasped. As soon as they had grasped the truth the young founders of new schools embarked on discoveries, scorning the old fogeys. Then those with learning oppressed them. Isn't that what history is like? When we started to make revolution, we were mere twenty-year-old boys, while the rulers of that time, like Yuan Shikai and Duan Qirui, were old and experienced. They had more learning, but we had more truth.
—Mao Zedong, "Talks at the Chengdu Conference"

In 1971, Pantheon Books published *America's Asia*, a collection of "dissenting essays on Asian-American relationships."[1] Edward Friedman and Mark Selden, the two editors, explained the title of the volume: "Asia is America's in three important ways," they began. "First, it is America's in the sense that we impose American categories to describe, evaluate and direct Asian experience. Our cultural chauvinism might mainly provide material for humorous self-analysis were it not for the overwhelming explosion of American economic and military might throughout Asia. For Asia is America's in this second tragic sense that American power has channeled, distorted, and suppressed much that is Asia."[2]

This was, at the time, a very powerful statement and one that carried important implications, especially as it was pronounced within—and against—the entire field of Asian studies. *America's Asia* was not just the result of a conference or of a short-term collaboration among academics; it was the second volume to appear under the name of the Committee of Concerned Asian Scholars, an organization of graduate students and young professors who had come together in 1968, united in their opposition to the Vietnam War, American policies in Asia, and the very structure of their field of study. The quote above summarizes well the layered and multifaceted criticism waged by the Committee at the time. The Committee proclaimed not only its unwavering condemnation of the Indochina War but also of the economic and diplomatic strategies of the United States in the entire region; Vietnam was just the most extreme example of policies that ultimately constituted Asia as an extension of America's strategic interests. Those policies, CCAS argued, were made possible and viable through the collaboration of American scholarship on Asia, that is, through the work of their own teachers, who had shaped the categories used to distort, obscure, and suppress the very humanity of Asian people.

In articles, conferences, and debates, the Concerned Asian Scholars described how the field—and all area studies—had come to be established in the period immediately following the war precisely as part of a government project, through grants, fellowships, and foundations; they traced the legacy of the McCarthy purges, which, they argued, had transformed Asian specialists into obedient experts, unable or unwilling to see the moral or political implications of their scholarship; finally, they hinted at the mutual imbrication of this scholarship with the actual genocide of Asians.[3] The field of Asian studies was then directly responsible for the making of America's Asia, for the intellectual, economic, and military appropriation of Asia and Asian people by U.S. interests. As Leigh Kagan averred in the first issue of the *CCAS Newsletter*, "the field of Asian studies, neither as a scapegoat nor as a priesthood, but as part and parcel of American society and politics and of our individual lives, is due for a self-conscious probing, and uncompromising self-examination."[4]

Yet CCAS's devastating critique of U.S. policies and scholarship on Asia had another, more positive goal: to highlight the new Asian realities that those policies and scholarship had made invisible. This was the third and most significant way in which Asia could and should be America's, Friedman and Selden continued: "The essays in this book suggest, moreover, that an Asia conceived in antagonistic or contemptible categories is an Asia where much that is humane, valuable, and worthy of emulation is ignored. This adds a final meaning to America's Asia. If we could change our relation to Asia we would be open to learning much from Asian people that could help us create a more decent and just society in the United States."

Asia was not just a site of oppression, the location of a carnage; rather it was truly "America's Asia" in the sense that it offered viable political alternatives to the United States, and potentially to the world. What was going on in Asia transcended its geographical and historical position, as it posed questions and proposed solutions that challenged the political assumptions of people globally. The very last sentence of the book—found at the end of Stephen Andors's essay on the Maoist factory—makes precisely this case: "Ultimately, however, this process of struggle and development going on in China transcends the Chinese situation, and poses critical questions of action and philosophy for all of us."[5] For these concerned scholars, Asia and Asian people were no longer objects to be studied, but instead subjects with whom experiences could and had to be shared.

This chapter investigates the meanings of "America's Asia" in the early history of the Committee of Concerned Asian Scholars. First of all, Asia here was a political signifier: unlike the "Asianisms" of the late nineteenth or the early twenty-first century,[6] CCAS's discourse did not focus on unchanging ethnic or culturally based values, nor on the awakening of the sleeping giant. Rather, "Asia," and expressly Maoist China, once divested of the culturalist trappings that scholars and political strategists had created, appeared as one of the crucial motors of global change, and Asian peoples were leading the transformation that we now identified with the "global sixties": "national liberation movements against colonialism and imperialism; new extra-party and extra-trade union organizational forms and new forms of political subjectivity; radical critiques of capitalism in politics, activism, cultural production, and life; and radical forms of experimentation in everyday life."[7] In this perspective, CCAS's "Asianism" (or even their Maoism of sorts) throws light onto the more general shift in the global, political, and intellectual frame of reference, the decentering of politics in the 1960s and 1970s,[8] when what was happening in Asia acquired a new centrality for people all over the world. This was a time in which workers in France could call for "Vietnam in Our Factories," and Maoism was a shared, if perhaps misunderstood, reference of German students and Indian revolutionaries.

But CCAS was not just a political organization; it was also and primarily a group of young students of Asia, and such a radical shift in their position vis-à-vis the object of their studies had huge implications for their intellectual and professional lives. Within the field of Asian studies, the concept of "America's Asia," as framed by Selden and Friedman, involved a critique of "orientalism" before *Orientalism*, and without the support of Said's elaboration. But in addition, and more fundamentally, "America's Asia"—at least in its third meaning—suggested the need and the possibility of a post-orientalist praxis, as much in scholarship as in politics. It was not enough to criticize the existing epistemic structure of Asian studies and its very practical connections with U.S. foreign policy and militarism; an indispensable next step was to ask what the recognition of the previously inscrutable "Asian other" as a political subject signified for the academic, intellectual, and political practice in the United States and globally, and to act upon this recognition.[9]

This chapter traces the founding of CCAS in 1968 and its activities of the first few years. I focus on the role that Asia in general, and China in particular, had in shaping and defining the organization's intellectual positions within the field. I show that it was the experience of Maoist China—reinterpreted, filtered, viewed from a distance—that provided the grounding for these scholars' concern but also for their criticism of the dominant scholarly paradigms. "China," and "Asia" in general, did not function as "models" to be replicated, nor did they provide ready-made answers. Rather it was because of the recognition of Asians as subjects capable of political and intellectual discoveries—and in dialogue with their experiences—that the Concerned Asian Scholars could frame their own intellectual and political contributions. In the latter part of the chapter, I trace how these contributions provided both a revisionist take on the major paradigmatic assumptions of Asian studies and original insights into possible new approaches to Asia. But I also highlight the theoretical limitations that confined the scholarly enterprise of the Concerned, which often prevented such insights to develop further, especially after the demise of the Asian subjectivities that guaranteed their political grounding.

These limitations can be connected in part to the peculiar character of global Maoism and specifically the ways in which the Chinese experience functioned outside China. As I show in the following pages, to both concerned scholars and French radicals, Maoism had configured itself as a theory that found expression and realization in localized practice, not as a set of rules to follow, nor as a model that could be exported and replicated. This was echoed in the famous dialogue between Michel Foucault and Gilles Deleuze in 1972, when the two philosophers (who had both looked closely at the Maoist movement in France) argued forcefully for a new understanding of theory *as practice*. In the words of Foucault, the intellectual's role was no longer to set himself aside and reveal truth to the benighted masses, but to join in the fight "against the forms of power that transform him into its object." In that, theory was part of a larger struggle: "This is a struggle against power, a struggle aimed at revealing and undermining power where it is most invisible and insidious. It is not to 'awaken consciousness' that we struggle (the masses have been aware for some time that consciousness is a form of knowledge; and consciousness as the basis of subjectivity is a prerogative of the bourgeoisie), but to sap power, to take power; it is an activity conducted alongside those who struggle for power, and not their illumination from a safe distance. A 'theory' is the regional system of this struggle."[10]

By the mid-1970s, because of a series of historical and political shifts of which China was a crucial part, we witness the demise of the larger struggle, the loss of a movement alongside which to fight, and the consequent reseparation of theory and practice. Then, without further rethinking, the radical practices that Maoism had animated could not be redeemed, repurposed, or reignited.

"Gentlemen, Shut up!" Speaking for Asia Scholars

In the 1960s, the centrality of Asia in political discourse and policymaking was reflected in the growth of Asian studies as an academic field. This was fueled by the mounting interest about that part of the world among

Americans,[11] but it was practically made possible by an unprecedented deployment of funds from the U.S. government (as well as from private donors). Crucial was the approval of the National Defense Education Act (NDEA) in 1958, which "authorized a steady flow of federal funds into fellowships, instructional programs, library expansion, summer institutes and workshops, and research projects relating to language and area studies of the less well-studied regions of the world, particularly Asia."[12] It is difficult to collect comprehensive data, but it seems that the NDEA (and specifically Title VI) funded a majority of doctoral students working on "critical languages" (such as Chinese, Hindi, or Japanese).[13] The funding was allegedly very good, and promising scholars of Asia seem to have been comparatively well off: John Berninghausen recalls that he "could not afford to stop studying during the summer," as the fellowship money provided a living stipend way higher than what he could make at a temporary full-time job.[14] Graduate students specializing in Asia constituted a small but rapidly growing cohort, and in the 1960s it probably looked possible that the expansion of the field would continue unabated, opening up plenty of possibilities for employment. Membership of the Association for Asian Studies more than quadrupled between 1958 and 1970 (from 1,022 to 4,708).[15] One of the ironies behind the radicalization of graduate students working on Asia was that the relative safety of their funding might very well be one of the factors that allowed for the time and space for political activism, something largely unthinkable in today's academia.

The Vietnam War irrupted into this relatively rosy situation, and it was obviously the crucial factor behind the activism of the young scholars of Asia who gave birth to CCAS. "Vietnam was what did everything," Tom Engelhardt recalled.[16] The war was a felt, lived presence on campuses and in communities, where young men were drafted or saw the draft as a very real possibility (a failed course, a lottery number). Male graduate students were thus strongly motivated to stay in school until age twenty-six, when "vulnerability to the draft became moot."[17] But unlike other groups, the soon-to-be concerned Asian scholars had a different, more complex framework in which to express and channel their antiwar activism. For them, Asia was not just a real battlefield and the crucial hub of U.S. military and foreign policy; it was also their field of investigation. Moreover, the American discourse on Asia was partly shaped by their teachers and future colleagues, and within their professional organizations. It is precisely in the attempt to change the posture of the main professional group for Asia scholars (the Association for Asian Studies [AAS]) that we can locate part of the originating impulse behind the founding of CCAS.

In April 1966, about a dozen American graduate students and scholars studying in Taiwan sent a letter to the secretary and president of AAS expressing their "concern" and their "frustration with the persistent ignorance and lack of understanding throughout the United States concerning Asia." The signatories called for AAS to assume an active role in producing and disseminating information about Asia both to the government—for example, by providing "systematic and independent assessments of current and alternative Asia-related policies"—and, more importantly, as a substitute to the government. They recommended that AAS set up procedures so that the organization "could take a collective stand on public issues when it appeared such a stand might be a vital and constructive addition to public discussion." They called AAS to issue "authoritative background statements" on Asian-related problems and to critically evaluate teaching about Asian matters (textbooks, curricula, etc.).[18] In the summer, they mailed the proposal to close to two hundred AAS members and an additional forty specifically to China specialists.

The responses from AAS leaders and other prominent scholars were generally not supportive and often outright dismissive. Charles Hucker and Karl Pelzer (respectively secretary and president of AAS) both objected to proposals that would, in their opinion, push AAS toward direct or indirect political action, leading to internal dissension and disruption, and, more significantly, to a possible loss of the association's tax-exempt status. This was not an unfounded fear, especially in the mind of scholars who had witnessed—in some cases, from the inside—the Institute of Pacific Relations being destroyed in part because of the revocation of its tax-exempt status in the McCarthy era.[19] These were deep wounds that made anything which had even a remote echo of political advocacy unpalatable. The unfortunate implication was that this fear, however justified, de facto silenced any criticism of government policy and politics.[20]

The group in Taiwan shifted their strategy accordingly and decided instead to propose a panel on "Responsibilities of a Professional Organization" at the annual meeting of the AAS: the three suggested presentations were to have dealt, and not by chance, with the history of the IPR, the role of intellectuals in society, and "public affairs and professional organizations."[21] The proposed panel was rejected. Robert Sakai, chairman of the 1967 AAS meeting, ruled against the inclusion on technical grounds—late submission—but also, and more significantly, because of fear of prejudicing the integrity of AAS as a nonpartisan, scholarly organization by sponsoring a panel that "might be more political-action oriented than scholarly in nature."[22] In a letter to Edward Friedman, Sakai accused the group of trying to mobilize AAS for "other purposes," with the intention of making it into a "political pressure group"; he went on to suggest that they direct their energies not to the leadership of AAS but to its membership. On the margins of Sakai's letter, somebody (Friedman?) scribbled ironically their deep appreciation for the advice: "Some of my colleagues and I thought we might do just that through a panel at the AAS convention. Robert Sakai stands in the way of this."[23]

The effort of organizing against AAS was eventually taken over in the following year by a group of graduate students at Harvard, which had the largest graduate program on Asia in the country.[24] In Marilyn Young's recollection, she met with James Peck and Tom Engelhardt (all Harvard grad students), and they decided to change strategy: "Let's do what the MLA [Modern Language Association] does, let's create a caucus," they decided, in order to secure the benefit of association with the larger organization without AAS being able to complain.[25] On March 23, 1968, at the AAS meeting in Philadelphia, these young scholars did indeed direct their energies to the AAS membership. Four hundred scholars, one-third of those gathered for the conference, formed a "Vietnam Caucus," chaired by John K. Fairbank, to present, discuss, and vote on different resolutions concerning the Vietnam conflict. As the *Harvard Crimson* remarked, the political discussion was heated, an unprecedented occurrence "among students of Asian affairs, usually noted for their moderation and restraint. For the first time, a large portion of American students of the Far East took a stand against the Vietnam war." Fairbank had to intervene to restrain people who wanted to shut down the caucus, and when violent exchanges erupted, he apparently calmed down the audience by stating calmly, "Gentlemen, shut up."[26] Four resolutions were presented, and the one that received most votes unequivocally condemned U.S. policies in Vietnam, declared the war a "failure," and called for immediate and sustained de-escalation leading to rapid withdrawal.[27]

The Vietnam Caucus also marked a significant (if temporary) break in terms of professional organizations. While in 1966, American scholars in Taiwan had still been trying to address AAS from the inside, reshaping its strategies and actions, by 1968 they had decided that their goals should be pursued through an independent group, one explicitly political *and* scholarly. In Philadelphia, representatives from twenty-five schools met to form a Committee of Concerned Asian Scholars; they decided to publish a newsletter, draft a statement, disseminate information (to the government and the public), and generally "start publicizing the growing concern over Asian affairs and make ourselves known as consultants on current Asian issues."[28]

The Committee explicitly posited itself in opposition to the "rational," "moderate" opinion vis-à-vis the U.S.-Asia relationship, one expressed more cogently in the so-called Tuxedo Statement of December 1967. In a meeting held in Tuxedo Park, New York, fourteen eminent Asia scholars had drafted a statement largely uncritical of the U.S. enterprise in Asia, supportive of deterrence of China, and surprisingly cavalier on the Vietnam carnage. "On balance," the fourteen had assessed, America's record in Asia since World War II had been "a remarkably good one, worthy of support." Accordingly, there was no call for major revision of military policies, no moral or political outrage, just the considerate advice for patience and the careful evaluation of complexities. More importantly, this pro-government statement was extolled as particularly valuable because it came from moderate scholars, thoughtful experts detached from the passions of the "New Left and the Old Right." Because, that is, while the statement was expressly supportive of existing policies, it was still presented as the product of scholarly, nonpolitical reflection.[29] Not surprisingly, the self-declared apolitical moderation of Tuxedo stood as a clear reference at the very founding of CCAS. The CCAS statement was programmatically supposed to be a response to the moderates' argument and the expression of hitherto silenced voices in the field. As one of the participants in the Vietnam Caucus commented, "in the past it's been the Milton Sacks and those who signed the Tuxedo Statement who have spoken for Asian scholars. We're changing all that."[30]

Since its founding, CCAS also positioned itself as an "alternative to the AAS as a professional organization."[31] While the latter was staunchly sticking to an attitude of declared political neutrality, the new group promised to be "fundamentally dedicated to the integration of political and scholarly efforts."[32] The difference and separation between the two organizations was glaringly and spatially evident the following year when, as a *Newsweek* reporter noted, "while the Association for Asian Studies met in Boston to discuss topics such as 'Eroticism in India' and 'The Tea-Horse Trade with Inner Asia During the Ming Period,' a younger group of AAS members met two blocks away to talk about Vietnam."[33] These young scholars firmly declared the separation in terms of politics, goals, and strategies between CCAS and AAS, yet the relationship between the two remained a controversial issue for the entire existence of the Committee. Not only was there overlapping membership, but one of the central goals of CCAS was also to change the profession—while being antiprofessional and in opposition to the main professional organization. Since the very first few weeks of their existence as a collective, the Concerned Asian Scholars oscillated between, on the one hand, a complete break with AAS and the cultivation of an independent sphere of action, and, on the other hand, the perspective of acting as "a dynamic lobby within the existing Asian studies establishment" in order to "foster a steady re-structuring of that establishment, and ultimately help create new institutions responsive to fundamental human concerns."[34] This was an ambitious project, but, in 1968–69, there seemed to be a real chance that, as Dick Wilson forecasted in the *Far Eastern Economic Review*, this younger generation of radical scholars would "gradually extend their influence over American opinion and policy in the years to come—unless," he added, more cautiously, "like the Red Guards in China, they in turn succumb to the subtle subversion of their own academic establishment."[35]

Such a "subtle subversion" was to become a topic of heated debate (and an acknowledged reality) later in the history of the Committee, but the year between the Philadelphia (1968) and the Boston (1969) meetings was occupied by discussions among the CCAS members on how to organize such a group, how to frame a coherent yet open statement, and how to define and pursue its goals. Since the beginning, there were at least two contradictory views of what CCAS could be. One prefigured a loose "umbrella" organization, inclusive of the larger antiwar/anti-imperialist spectrum, and the other a leftist, ideologically coherent group, centralized and efficient.[36] The first option won. The Committee was to be programmatically decentered, with local chapters (in various university campuses) having complete autonomy in deciding their own educational and political programs.[37] The bare-bones central structure of the Committee was supposed to provide coordination and support as well as to manage the publication of a newsletter (later to become a newsletter and a journal), which would host views that could not find a place in any other scholarly venue.[38] In all this, CCAS remained unabashedly political, and politics figured in their discourse not as an accessory, a complement to scholarship, but instead as an integral and legitimate part of the work of the scholar. Political action was needed "to inject new ideas into both the academic and the public consciousness," and CCAS members were expected to pursue new research but also to relate "this research to the realization of changes in the institutions of the Asian studies profession, in public attitudes, and in government policy."[39]

These positions found a concise—if somewhat open-ended—expression in the CCAS Statement of Purpose, which was formally adopted at the Boston convention in 1969.[40] Still reprinted today in every issue of *Critical Asian Studies* (formerly the *Bulletin of Concerned Asian Scholars*), the statement began with an indictment of the U.S. "brutal aggression" in Vietnam and "the complicity or silence of our profession with regard to that policy." It declared concern for the unwillingness of specialists to speak against "an Asian policy committed to ensuring American domination of much of Asia." But silence and accommodation were only the passive manifestations of a field whose prevailing trends in scholarship "too often spring from a parochial cultural perspective and *serve selfish interests and expansionism*."[41] The field of Asian studies was not only guilty of omission, of lack of concern; rather the lack of concern produced, in the name of neutrality, intellectual positions that actively supported the brutality of U.S. aggression and scholarship that was functional and integral to U.S. foreign policy. The response to that, therefore, could not be a more "objective" and neutral stand, but a declaredly political one, a completely new understanding of Asia—and of America: "The Committee of Concerned Asian Scholars seeks to develop a humane and knowledgeable understanding of Asian societies and their efforts to maintain cultural integrity and to confront such problems as poverty, oppression, and imperialism. We realize that to be students of other peoples, we must first understand our relations to them."[42]

New Things, New Thoughts

The essays collected in *America's Asia* took shape in part during a summer seminar at Harvard University in 1968,[43] where several members of the newly minted CCAS discussed the status of existing scholarship on Asia, the framework of academic knowledge and their role in changing both, as well as the structure and goals of the new organization. While the participants did not agree on everything, including the very idea of producing a book out of that summer discussion, they were conscious that there was something major and novel in their considering Asia as a source of ideas, rather than the target of disdain for its backwardness or the object of technocratic manipulation. The closest model they could muster for their approach dated two centuries earlier: "The philosophers of the Age of Enlightenment believed there was much to learn from China about social organization. But as the nineteenth-century West turned to massive imperialist assault on China, the Chinese people became, to our 'practical' men, objects of ridicule and contempt, not alternative models to be contemplated, criticized, and, where fitting, emulated. A century later, American social scientists, generals, and politicians continue to see Asian needs in terms of American advice and aid."[44]

There was obviously a need to unpack, expose, and dissolve the accumulated layers of two hundred years of scholarship, policy, and opinion before one could tackle and accept the new lessons coming from Asia—or even the simple fact that Asia had anything to teach. The first two sections of *America's Asia* appropriately deal directly with the ideological premises of Asian studies, the optics distorting not just the perception of Asia, but also the practice of U.S. foreign policy and military intervention, thus tracing a direct line of responsibility between Asia scholars and invading troops. It is only the last section of the volume—the three essays by Selden, Gurley, and Andors—that moves away from that critique and proposes instead a new model of scholarship, one that does not dissect or demolish, but rather aims at creating "a new Asia for America. It is one that can be approached hopefully and critically, not condescendingly and destructively. Focusing on the *humanity* of their subject, they [the authors of the last three essays] find inspiration and application to general *human* problems, to problems Americans as well as citizens of Third World nations face here and now."[45]

I return later to the references to "humanity," "human," and "humane," which pervade this and other texts by the Concerned Asian Scholars, but first it is worth pointing out how the structure of the edited volume, while it makes sense to the reader, is intellectually and politically in reverse order. It was the revolutionary experience of Asian nations that made it even possible to expose the encrusted ideological blinders of the profession. Asian revolutions came first; they were the necessary precondition for the scholarly and intellectual shift of CCAS. If power produces realities and is exercised through regimes of knowledge, then, in this case, one can argue that it was the Asian attempts to fundamentally alter the structure of power (down to its dispersed manifestations) that allowed the existent regime of truth production to be challenged.[46]

Asia itself could exist as a point of reference only in light of the new revolutionary experiences of the twentieth century: people's wars of liberation (from China to Vietnam) and especially the economic and social experiments of the Great Leap and the Cultural Revolution. The simple acknowledgment of the existence of the Maoist economic experiments, land redistribution in liberated Vietnam, Indian peasant rebellions, Japanese pacifists, and Okinawan activists forced a reconsideration of one's position as an Asia scholar, of one's relationship to Asia, and of the structure of the field itself; because the field could not even see—let alone study or examine—these phenomena. What made Asia change from an object into a subject was the recognition that Asian peoples had already become subjects of their own politics, and by so doing they had stated the possibility of alternative solutions to issues not confined to Asia.[47] Accordingly, in order to start correcting the compromised position of the field, one had to start from "a commitment to the need for revolutionary change in Asian land, and a concomittant [sic] re-orientation of the scholarship and teaching in the field."[48]

In this sense, the last three essays of *America's Asia*, which describe the universal value of these revolutionary "new things," constitute the logical and political premise of the entire book, and, possibly, of the entire CCAS enterprise. For example, in his analysis of the People's War, Selden argued that from the protracted wars of liberation in China and Vietnam "emerged a radically new vision of man and society and a concrete approach to development."[49] In the liberated areas Selden saw, in embryo, the possibility of new forms of society antithetical to the anarchist struggle of "atomized individuals" fighting for private end—a not-so-subtle reference to his own capitalist society. Rather, Selden concluded, they embodied "the freedom of all continually redefined by an accepted and cherished community."[50]

Asia stood as a referent for the possibilities of alternative social constructs, but I would argue that, in the discourse of the concerned scholars, "Asia" was often deployed as a metonymy for China (and vice versa, China as a synecdoche for Asia). It was in China that those possibilities could be more easily located, articulated, and defined. Japan, while home to a vibrant pacifist and antiwar movement, was often described as akin to a client-state shaped by postwar U.S. occupation; South Korea was an even more glaring example of dictatorial subservience; India stood as a memento of missed revolutionary opportunities; and Vietnam, while embodying the promises of anticolonial liberation, was first and foremost the location of a massacre that had to be stopped. In China, on the other hand, liberation had succeeded and the long-term experience of Communist society was now being rethought and reevaluated—against other, discredited socialist models—through the upheaval of the Cultural Revolution. A majority of CCAS members were China scholars, and the reevaluation and reassessment of Maoist China and, in particular, of the politics and policies of the Cultural Revolution was one of the central tenets of the group. As Edward Friedman succinctly summarized, "the experience and creations of some 700 million Chinese this century provides a basis for asking and probing the most pressing human questions."[51]

What did China offer to CCAS? In a world torn by a cold and a very hot war, China presented the case for a nonexpansive, nonaggressive foreign policy. Despite the irrational U.S. fear of a communist expansion in Asia, it was China that, in the eyes of CCAS, had a very rational and motivated fear of U.S. imperialism in the region. "Many of us," Selden recalled, "were drawn to the fact that the U.S. was essentially at war with China from the Korean War and Vietnam War."[52] Yet, in the words of Zhou Enlai, China pursued opposition to any aggression policy by the United States as part and parcel of its "opposition to any policy of aggression of any country of the world."[53] China was therefore an inspiration for those in CCAS as they were developing "anti-imperialist perspectives," and CCAS pressed for normalization of relations with the PRC "as a key to solving problems of ongoing wars."[54] When this normalization eventually happened, in 1972, however, it was under the auspices of Richard Nixon, who was at the time pursuing massive bombing campaigns in Indochina. Then China's abrupt turn in its foreign policy—largely justified by fear of the Soviet Union—was perceived by many activists as an abandonment of Vietnam (and of all anticolonial and liberation movements), and that broke the suture between the antiwar and the pro-China positions.[55]

Maoist China also stood alone in Asia as a seemingly successful model of economic change, one that did not follow the prescribed patterns of "rational development" but that nonetheless "brought an unmistakable improvement in living standards,"[56] especially for the poorest. Yet, as Victor Lippit contended on the pages of the *Bulletin*, the great "improvement in social welfare wrought by the Chinese revolution" had been ignored or misrepresented in orthodox analyses.[57] In his essay in *America's Asia*, John Gurley claimed that China had "outperformed every underdeveloped country in the world." "The basic, overriding economic fact about people in China," he continued, "is that for twenty years they have all been fed, clothed, and housed, have kept themselves healthy, and have educated most. Millions have not starved; sidewalks and streets have not been covered with multitudes of sleeping, begging, hungry and illiterate human beings; millions are not disease-ridden."[58] In the face of such a rosy statement, the question looms of what will happen when this empirical evidence will be proven to be at least partially false, when it will be revealed that millions had indeed starved.

But, in the long sixties, it was not only that the economic success of the Chinese revolution still looked more unequivocal; it was also that its nature was perceived to be unique, and uniquely different, an alternative both to capitalist modernization and Soviet dirigisme. Noam Chomsky wrote on how Walt Rostow (modernization theorist and Lyndon Johnson's national security advisor) was terrified by "the possibility that the Chinese Communists can prove to Asians by progress in China that Communist methods are better and faster than democratic methods."[59] Both the Soviets and the Americans saw the central characteristic of the Chinese revolution in "the stubborn, irrational, and ultimately doomed resistance to the bureaucratic, elitist, technocratic urban life of advanced society." Yet, argued CCAS member Stephen Andors, "it is precisely such resistance that gives to China's modernization both its unique and its universal character."[60]

China, in this sense, proposed a completely different vision of society, one that challenged entrenched assumptions about politics and economics. Such a vision brought to the fore issues of democracy in the workplace, "worker participation in management, cadre participation in labor, and incentives for working," as well as new relationships between work and leisure, industry and agriculture, urban and rural. These were questions that Western modernization theory considered to be settled but that were at that very time being disputed in practice in schools, factories, and streets in the United States and Europe. To this challenge, the Chinese process of development—which Andors described as "the reverse of how the concentration of population and the division of social labor have proceeded thus far in other modern societies"—provided, if not a model, certainly an inspiration.[61]

Discovering Humanity in Asia

In order to accept the "reality" of the Chinese experience, one had to start from evaluating the PRC in terms of its own goals and methods for attaining those goals, and from recognizing the validity of those goals.[62] As I mentioned earlier, the CAS stressed repeatedly the need for a more "humane" approach to Asia, a concern that was inscribed in their statement of purpose. I was at first a bit puzzled by the insistence on this term, by the extent to which these scholars felt compelled to show that "the Chinese are human too."[63] It seemed at the same time excessive and vague; what was to be gained by stressing a shared "humanity"? Was that really necessary? This insistence makes more sense if we once again reverse the perspective: "humanity" was not just lacking in the eye of the Western beholder; rather, "humane" was the defining characteristic of the Asian revolutions, which, as such, required a humane approach to be understood. The participatory model of Vietnam and especially China, Mark Selden wrote, offered "hope of more *humane* forms of development and of effectively overcoming the formidable barriers to the transformation of peasant societies."[64] Similarly, John Gurley described the Cultural Revolution as "perhaps the most interesting economic and social experiment ever attempted, in which tremendous efforts are being made to achieve an egalitarian development, an industrial development *without dehumanization*, one that involves everyone and affects everyone."[65]

Here "humane" marks the stark opposition to models (first and foremost those imposed by U.S. planners, but also Soviet technocracy) that were considered inhumane, in the sense that they erased the human costs of development under the mask of scientificity and rationality. "Humane" stands in as a reference to the radical equality of the Asian revolutions, as exemplified at the time by the Chinese experiments of the Cultural Revolution—cadres' participation in manual labor, workers' participation in management, attempts at reducing differences in salaries, a combination of mental and manual work, workers' universities, and so forth. The reference to "humanity" also expressed a frontal attack on modernization theory, which dominated both U.S. state policy and academia. As the understanding of societies in terms of modernization levels and stages of development was connected with a foreign policy that imposed these models onto other nations, then those Asian revolutions that presented alternative practices could only be understood through a more humane scholarly approach, one that abdicated the technocratic/culturalistic framework of the existing social sciences. Producing new scholarship devoted to China was therefore inseparable from a fundamental rethinking of the cultural and political assumption of the field, as well as of America's role in the world.[66] Accepting the "humanity" of Asian revolutions required first and foremost a drastic shift in the very structure of academia and the intellectual world. In that, CCAS was part of a larger movement of dissent within the academe, which was often framed around the same terms. One can cite, for example, Christian Bay's 1968 criticism of the field of political science: "I am convinced that our profession will never help us to advance from our wasteful, cruel, pluralist pseudopolitics in the direction of justice and *humane* politics until we replace political systems with concepts of *human* need and *human* development as the ultimate value framework for our political analysis."[67]

I analyze later in the chapter how the experience of the Chinese (and Asian) revolutions allowed for many of the exceptional scholarly contributions in the early period of CCAS. But first I want to highlight how the recognition that something unprecedented was happening in Asia—yet something that was not exclusively Asian nor was confined by culture and geography—made possible a political shift of perspective, one in which Asian and specifically Chinese people became the inventive producers of political experiences that had potential value outside of their original location.

What I find perhaps more interesting is how the acknowledgment of the extraordinary significance of Asian revolutions allowed CCAS to expand connections and spaces of comparisons, based on the assumption that "Asia" truly had something to teach America and the world. This was visible, for example, in the attention devoted to Asian Americans and the issues of migration, racism, and activism within that community (in its relations to Asia).[68] It led CCAS to try to identify "Asian models" for agrarian revolution in Latin America.[69] And it also justified a new understanding of Asia, this time one not filtered through colonial or neocolonial discourse, but rather viewed through the lens of hope for more dramatic transformations. The Committee discussed whether there was something called "Asian socialism" that connected China, Korea, Vietnam, but also potentially India and South Asia. China and Vietnam shifted from being simply "America's problem" to embodying the focal point for a series of Asian connections, a network of activism for which they represented a possible reference.[70] This was evident, for example, in CCAS's relationship with the pacifist movement Beheiren in Japan and the journal *Ampo*.[71]

"America's Asia" was first and foremost a subject worthy of attention and possibly of emulation for the United States. In the introduction to *America's Asia*, Selden and Friedman mention the Chinese educational system, which had moved away from a strictly meritocratic basis, "because it was unjust to the majority of economically poor and culturally disadvantaged." China scholars had ridiculed the move, only to find that the American system, faced "with the demand of Black America for justice," was now challenged by identical problems. "How is America doing by comparison? Is there anything worth learning from China? Is anybody looking?" Friedman and Selden asked rhetorically.[72] The same questions could be repeated in the case of other Chinese "new things," from health care (was the attempt to provide health care in rural China useful for poor inner city areas?) to gender equality and elder care. Similarly, Selden's analysis of the People's War in Vietnam suggested insights "not only for nations struggling with problems of foreign domination and economic stagnation but also for a highly atomized, individuated, and alienated society like America."[73]

Even more stunning was the degree to which the Chinese experience of peasant revolution made it possible for South Asianists within CCAS to rethink agricultural policies and peasant rebellions in the Indian continent. "India," argued Gail Omvedt, "might be used as a negative case to prove that without socialism there is no economic development. India needs what China had: a revolution. And to some extent, the Indian problems enable one to understand what happened in China."[74] "The successes of agrarian production in China and north Korea," Omvedt asserted, "contrasted with their failures in nonsocialist countries (including south Korea), especially India, forces [sic] the conclusion: there is no revolution in production without a revolution in the relations of production."[75] It was through the comparison with the PRC's success and by highlighting the practical achievement of Chinese farmers, organized in communes, that, for example, Richard Franke could expose the political and ideological character of the supposedly technologically driven Green Revolution.[76] South Asianists in CCAS chided their unconcerned colleagues for their cultural assumptions that denied the "castebound Hindus" the propensity for peasant war, which they reserved for East Asian people, the Chinese, and the Vietnamese. They called instead for "the building up of mass organizations of the poor, or workers and peasants and oppressed sections of society, organizations which alone are capable of resolving the crisis of development."[77]

Finally, China was mobilized as an argumentative foil in addressing the failure of Gandhi and the nonviolent movement in providing true relief from poverty and caste degradation. While the violent revolutions in China, through the bottom-up mobilization of the peasant masses, had produced "an undeniable social and moral advance over the prerevolutionary situation," the Gandhian nonviolent movement had been inherently conservative in that it had purposely prevented social change by pacifying the Indian revolution from the top down.[78] In their deployment of the Maoist example to rediscover and reaffirm the revolutionary potential (and the revolutionary needs) of Indians, I see in the CCAS South Asia scholarship a forerunner of the analysis that, with deeper theoretical foundations, the Subaltern Studies collective was going to produce in the 1980s.[79]

The scope of political rethinking that was connected to the discovery and acceptance of the Asian and Chinese inventions was therefore potentially truly global. This scope, I argue, was founded on the awareness of new political subjectivities, new political thinking and experiences, which pressed those who recognized and took them seriously to drastically alter their view of the world. These were outspoken subjectivities, claimed through revolution and war, which did not ask but rather forced the interlocutors to recognize them.

"What Do You Want?" Taking Maoism Seriously

In a piece for the *Bulletin* (later to be developed into a monograph), Tom Engelhardt eviscerated the racist and dehumanizing character of Hollywood portrayals of the Other (especially the Asian Other) while highlighting Gillo Pontecorvo's *The Battle of Algiers* as an alternative depiction.[80] The reference is revealing. Pontecorvo's film describes the activities of the Algerian National Liberation Front (FLN) between 1954 and 1957 and the brutal (yet temporarily successful) repression of the movement by French paratroopers. The movie ends, however, in December 1960, when massive demonstrations in the Algerian capital opened the way for the country's independence. One scene is especially iconic: on the last day of the demonstrations (December 21, 1960), we see a French soldier wielding a megaphone asking the assembled and unrelenting crowd one final question: "Qu'est ce que vous voulez?"—"What do you want?" Through the entire movie, there is no recognition from the French side of the desires of Algerians, or that those desires had to be listened to.[81] It is only at the end that, through the force of an anticolonial revolution, the colonized Other is recognized as capable of speech, of will, of political subjectivity.

It is the appearance of the self-affirmed subjectivity of the oppressed—through revolution, national liberation, and decolonization—that shifts the perspective, laying bare the global mechanisms of oppression and, potentially, presenting the possibility of radical alternative for the world at large. It is in this "awakening sense of global possibility, of a different future," that, following Christopher Connery, I locate the worlded characters of "Asia" and "China" in the long sixties, a worldedness of "links and co-presence." For example, Connery argues that, despite the unprecedented isolation of China during the Cultural Revolution, "Cultural Revolution Maoism was a fully worlded presence, and not only to those outside China."[82] Similarly, beyond Vietnam's revolutionary practice, it was the actuality of its existence against a globalized U.S. power that made it truly relevant across the globe. "Vietnamese communism was overwhelmingly national in its orientation, but the force of its oppositional power, its actualization of the Great Refusal, had a significance that was international, and multiple. If the United States could be resisted in that place, it could be resisted elsewhere."[83] Thus, the Cultural Revolution and Vietnam's war of liberation affirmed the possibility of engaging *everywhere* in a struggle against oppression and for equality. Clearly, that possibility resonated with and reinforced the efforts of many within CCAS who, in Mark Selden's words, were trying "to develop global perspectives that located Asia and the Pacific within frameworks of capitalism, empire, war, and revolution, which transcended area studies approaches that looked deeply in many cases into a specific nation and its experience."[84] However, those global perspectives could be imagined and developed only after people in Asia had vocally and practically affirmed their political existence.

It is crucial to stress that, in this view, Asia, and especially China, prefigured an opening; they did not present a foreclosed model to be adopted, copied, or transported. Too often—but often not without reason—the sixties' interest in Maoism and specifically in the Cultural Revolution is viewed today with skepticism and uneasiness (especially from the point of view of the contemporary Left). It is usually and safely disposed of as an infantile mimicry, based on the idea that a misunderstood model of peasant revolution and youthful rebellion could be transplanted in the streets of Paris or in the urban ghettos of America's big cities. Trips to China of "fellow travellers" are then described as visits to a realized utopia and the obsequious reprinting of Mao's Little Red Book as a new form of blind faith, all embodying a form of "radical orientalism" that idealized the East and denigrated the West—while reaffirming the binary opposition of the two.[85]

However, as I highlighted earlier, for CCAS, Maoist China did not function as the end point of a developmental trajectory to be followed, but rather as the precondition for thinking alternative political praxes. Victor Nee and Jim Peck argued that one should not use "Maoism" but rather the proper term "Mao Zedong Thought," which "offers foreigners not a body of doctrine or a blueprint for their own societies but a model for thinking. . . . Despite the strident calls at certain times by some Chinese to make Mao's thought into a doctrine or a 'recipe for revolution' throughout the world, the primary emphasis in Mao Tsetung [Zedong] Thought is on fundamental theory, which is always rooted in specific situations. Understanding its implications requires experimentation and the initiative of the observer or nation involved."[86] It was not a question of marching behind a North Vietnamese or Chinese flag, as Judy Perrolle remarked in an epistolary exchange with John Berninghausen; rather, the very existence of revolutionary China was a reminder "that people can stand up against all the odds. China is very important to lots of us," Perrolle added, "for just that reason, not to be confused with a 'China, right or wrong' policy."[87] Even Zhou Enlai, in his interview with the CCAS delegation in 1971, pointed to the impossibility of "mechanically" importing the Chinese experience. Rather, he extolled Maoism (or Mao Zedong thought) as a theory of localized practice: "We have only our experience, but we are not at all well acquainted with your situation. So that must depend upon your own efforts," Zhou advised.[88]

The example of Maoist China resonated in very similar ways in the completely different context of 1960s France. French Maoists are usually depicted as the textbook case of the adolescent fascination with the revolutionary East. Yet they too strove to avoid any silly imitation and stated repeatedly that theirs was not a wholesale transplant. At his trial, Alain Geismar, one of the leaders of the Gauche Prolétarienne (the largest and most prominent Maoist organization), defended the indigenous French tradition of struggle and revolution and denied categorically any intention of "transposing mechanically what other people have realized," or of "rebuilding China in France."[89] And while Geismar repeated over and over the refrain "as in China today" (comme en Chine aujourd'hui), talking about either the students involved in production or breaking the urban-rural divide, his was not the faithful adoption of a model, but rather the statement of a coeval struggle for a "new and bright world," a struggle that unified, each in their own historical contingencies, French university students, Vietnamese anticolonial fighters, and Chinese peasants.[90]

It was often the specific character of Maoism as "praxis," its continuous reference to a localized experience, that stood out in the discourse of the French Maoists: Maoism here was first and foremost a method of analysis of reality.[91] As Georges, a young member of the Gauche Prolétarienne (GP), maintained, the issue was not "to apply directly the thought of a Chinese leader to the reality of a French factory."[92] Rather, he concluded in much more direct language, "We don't really give a fuck about China" (la Chine, on s'en fout).[93] "We take stock of it," he continued, "but only as an experiment which has succeeded and from which we can learn something if we study it." The lesson of Maoism was not one of certitudes and easily transferrable programs; it was one of lived and shared experience—"Chinese yes, but still experience."[94] This was described, once again, as a more humane experience. The Cultural Revolution was viewed as a reaction against a tendency to value productivity over people, and it was this aspect that, in the words of two miners from the North, resonated with the lived practice in France, where too the worker was "like an animal" (il est comme une bête). It was in the light of this shared experience of debasement and of the need "to put man first" that what was good for China could be "good for us too."[95] It did not matter that, as another GP member lamented, her fellow workers did not accept the Maoists because "it was a Chinese thing." So, she continued, "let's leave Mao to the Chinese. There must be somebody here with a name from here to wage our own revolution. . . . If what they told me about Maoism is correct, we are all Maoists." Maoism was, in the end, "largely open," she concluded.[96]

For CCAS, as well for the French activists, "China," therefore, and specifically the China of the Cultural Revolution, did not function as a model to be exported nor Maoism as an ideology to be adopted and followed. Rather the Cultural Revolution proposed a series of theoretical and philosophical lessons that could be borrowed and explored,[97] but whose crucial character was always a "specific, situated practice." In this sense Maoism was globalized, without being universalized, as a theory "whose effectivity was a praxis,"[98] as a call to extend and expand the limits of what was not simply politically conceivable but also practically possible.

In the discourse of modernization theory, "Asia" and "China" could exist as unities only as the vaguely geographically identifiable repository of ahistorical cultural values, removed from the universal normality of natural development. Even when brought back (through colonial force) into the "normal" path of history, Asia, as Dipesh Chakrabarty synthesized, remained the realm of the "not yet," endlessly catching up and endlessly lacking.[99] Through the paradigmatic shift of the sixties, in CCAS critique, however, this "not yet," the space between Western normativity and Asian exceptionalism, instead of a lack, of a failure, becomes an opening, a space of experimentation. Here lies possibly the most important legacy of CCAS to students of Asia of the following generations: the ability to see their chosen locations of study not as exceptions, but as part of a global, coeval, and always incomplete political and intellectual undertaking. That is, to see "Asia" as "an unfinished project, whose truth is not in a new and emergent dominant, but in the end of the very logic of domination."[100] In the best of CCAS analysis and practice, "America's Asia" then prefigured the historical universality of equalitarian and emancipatory politics. At the time, rather than reproducing an orientalist gaze in other forms, Maoism seemed to provide a possible solution for the still-ongoing quest of "provincializing Europe," for displacing the centrality of the West and Western paradigms, not in order to privilege new forms of exceptionalism but to push forward the project of a global insurgent equality. In this sense, it is not surprising that the trajectory of subaltern studies started from a very close and passionate engagement with Maoist ideas and vocabulary, which was progressively reframed through the prism of European theory.[101]

"Oh Say Can't You See?" The Rational Blinders of the Profession

In June 1967, John K. Fairbank and Edwin Reischauer, the two most eminent East Asia scholars in the United States, gave a public talk at Harvard University titled "East Asia and Our Future." Viewed today, the lectures, especially Fairbank's, are revealing of the contradictions and the problems of the field of Asian studies at the time of the Vietnam War, a field of which the two scholars were in many ways the personification.[102] At the beginning of his talk, Fairbank described the magnitude of the transformations that had happened to China in the last century:

> Over there, the Chinese have been going through and are still going through the biggest revolution that any people have ever experienced. Of course, the Chinese people are the most numerous, the biggest single block, but they are also the most distinctively separate from the rest of us, the most different. Their writing system is different, you know how different they are. Even though as individuals we invariably find that Chinese are wonderful people, still their society is set up in a different way, it's put together in a different way. And the Chinese revolution has been a century-long process of that society coming apart, being torn down, because of the fact that the outside world, which we now represent particularly, was so different and it had come from such a different basis in Western history. So we have

to begin with the size of this revolutionary change and try to imagine what it is like to live through the last phase of it.[103]

Two things are notable about Fairbank's *incipit*: no real explanation was needed of the obvious fact of Chinese difference, of the total incommensurability of China. Second, dramatic change came to China almost in the form of a physics experiment, where the Asian "matter" was placed next to the Western "anti-matter," as per the impact-response paradigm. There was no agency involved in the process, and, significantly, Fairbank never uttered the words "colonialism" and "imperialism."[104] Fairbank then described the century-long process of the Chinese revolution as profoundly traumatic—the "strangulation of an entire civilization," with the 1911 revolution "decapitating" society. But he argued that this process was also marked by seemingly unchanging continuities: the modern parties existed only as substitutes for the deposed emperor, and change, even revolutionary change, proceeded always from above. This view allowed Fairbank to discount Communism as largely irrelevant, an epiphenomenon at best ("sort of a second-rate variation on statism, coming from our own western society"). Maoism represented then just the last step in the long and tragic path of China's modernization, one destined to produce the same results as those state forms that came before it: "The problems of the Chinese revolution are insoluble, for Mao as they have been for everybody before. . . . Everybody has failed in dealing with the Chinese revolution, the problem is too big. And now Mao Zedong is failing before our eyes."

Having quite summarily dismissed contemporary China, Fairbank moved on to Vietnam, and the war about which he had clearly been having some doubts. He described the failure in Vietnam as a failure of culture. It was because of their entrenched cultural norms that Ho Chi-min and the North Vietnamese were not responsive to U.S. "selective bombing" (we "bomb this and bomb that, not people but just your communication routes, your logistic supply," Fairbank described matter-of-factly). Asia, according to Fairbank, was not under a structure of law, but rather was organized around power and reputation, that is, face. The West was rational; the East was ritualistic and culturalistic. In order to achieve some success in Vietnam, Johnson needed almost literally to kowtow; he needed to cater to the ritual needs of the Vietnamese leaders, and then to adapt his approach to their form of thinking. Fairbank could not condemn the U.S. policies and politics in East Asia as wrong per se. They were wrong only in so far as they were going to be misunderstood, because they were framed in rational terms to irrational people.[105]

Fairbank was not what we would call a hawk, and his talk tried to strike an affable, at times awkwardly funny, middle ground. He was very consciously embodying a liberal, moderate position. Less than a year later, and largely speaking from the same position of moderation and equanimity, Fairbank was going to chair the meeting of the Vietnam Caucus in Philadelphia, where CCAS was founded.[106] He was neither a declared standard bearer for U.S. government policy nor a prominent advocate of any specific theoretical approach, including the one dominant in the social sciences at the time, modernization theory. He looked stubbornly measured, alien to ideologies and metanarratives.[107] Yet precisely because of Fairbank's character as a consciously moderate bridge builder and his role as the founder of modern Chinese studies in the United States, his arguments—and slips of the tongue—are revealing of assumptions deeply embedded in, or rather constitutive of, the field. His 1967 talk is therefore a good starting point to illustrate some of the crucial issues that shaped the concern of his young radical students and that were at the center of CCAS's sweeping criticism of the field of Asian studies.

If, as I previously discussed, it was the discovery of "America's Asia" and the actuality of the Chinese revolutions that produced the grounding for this critique, then Fairbank's talk pointed first and foremost to what the dominant view of the field—even in its most benevolent manifestation—made invisible. Fairbank's discussion of the Vietnam War glossed over death, destruction, and the very reasons for U.S. presence in Indochina. He reduced the incredible Vietnamese resistance, geopolitically, to a "problem for America," and he chalked it up to a set of traditional attitudes, largely obscure and impenetrable to us "moderns." Similarly, Fairbank embodied the field's blindness concerning Maoist China: he described the Chinese revolution as imposed from above, largely in continuity with what the Guomindang had done; he dismissed Communism as a relatively irrelevant detail in the scope of the modern transformation of China; and he proclaimed the Cultural Revolution to be the outward demonstration of Maoism's failure. There was, in the end, nothing to see in Maoist China, or at least nothing worth seeing. Move along, young fellas.

The "blindness" of the field was one of the most prominent targets of CCAS's attack precisely because it was proof of the limitations in the theoretical trappings of existing academic knowledge. The Concerned Asian Scholars pointed out, for example, that the field was incapable of producing an analysis of Maoist socioeconomic change that exceeded the narrow attention to economic growth. In such a perspective, Charles Cell noted, experiments such as the Great Leap Forward appeared as a "silly tangent," because it was not going to do anything for economic growth. The established "brand of thinking" was incapable of viewing that socialist human relations were compatible with economic growth. Therefore economic growth itself had to explained away, so that no credit could possibly be given to Communists "for dealing with human inequalities in a positive vein."[108]

Economics was of course an extremely important part of the Chinese revolution, but social development, CCAS members in Berkeley argued, was equally central in Maoist revolutionary strategy. "Unless a student is able to evaluate the collectivization, communization, or the hsia-fang [xiafang] movement (in which city people were sent into the countryside to work, where no doubt they were not always paradigms of competence) as goals in themselves, much of the Chinese revolution will not make sense."[109] The problem of "liberal scholarship," Richard Pfeffer elaborated in a review of Ezra Vogel's book *Canton under Communism*, was not one of scholarly "execution," of poorly deployed tools or methodological flaws; it was one of paralyzing and blinding theoretical presuppositions. Even a skillfully crafted and well-researched volume such as Vogel's, Pfeffer continued, could contribute only a surface analysis of bureaucratic forms. Vogel showed no interest in, let alone commitment to, the content of the revolution, because, in the perspective of liberal sociology, there was no qualitative difference between revolutionary and nonrevolutionary rule.[110] Thus, the very existence of revolutionary agency or revolutionary subjects was a moot issue, and the Chinese people appeared "almost exclusively as objects to be administered."[111]

If the innovative and inspirational character of the Chinese revolution — the revolutionary potential of the peasants, and the oppressed in general — was so easily discarded, then change could happen only from the top down, with elites manipulating the masses. "This belief," members of the Berkeley CCAS accused, "is translated into research interests such as 'elite studies' and more directly into research projects aimed at providing information helpful for the suppression of 'elite-inspired' insurgencies throughout Asia. Yet these actions are wrapped in the mantle of American idealism, of self-determination for peoples, of protecting freedom around the world. But this rhetoric is uneasily familiar." "The disaster of the war in Vietnam," they concluded somberly, had "its scholarly counterpart."[112]

A case study of the theoretical blinders of "liberal" scholarship was Chalmers Johnson's influential *Peasant Nationalism*, whose stated aim was "the exploration of the nature of mass mobilization" but which, in Elinor Lerner's detailed assessment published in the *Bulletin*, ended up being just "a description of a change in elites." Allegedly an analysis of peasant participation in the Communist revolution, Johnson's study, Lerner explained, was "actually oriented around the standard questions of elite theory: how does an elite gain power and how does it legitimate its rule, quite different considerations from those involved in studying popular resistance movements!"[113] In Lerner's critique, elite theory reduces the relationship of the base to the elite as one of consent and views change only in terms of substitution of one elite for another, of loss and gain of authority. In the case of China, an outside event—the Japanese invasion—displaced the existing elite, the GMD, creating an opening for a new elite, the CCP, whom the peasants desperately needed. The CCP reinforced its legitimacy by appealing to the nationalist feelings of the peasants. In Johnson's book, there was no understanding of social change as a long-term process, grounded in internal contradictions, "involving the active, conscious, deliberate rationality of people." By adopting this framework, Johnson could blissfully gloss over descriptions "of peasant life, the mode of agricultural production, rural economic and power relationships, village social and class structure,"[114] because they were ultimately irrelevant, as were the different practices and policies of different elites. There was no real need to confront the CCP's program of rent reduction, for example, with the situation under the Nationalists. "One does not evaluate elites in terms of the quality of their rule; one merely notes their comings and goings,"[115] Lerner noted, not without sarcasm. In Johnson's "elitist" explanation, history is largely outside the control of the people, political planning of revolutionary movements is largely illusory, and there is no real hope of changing the relationship of power between the elite and the masses.

For CCAS, such blindness toward Asian revolutionary realities was a manifestation of much more pervasive theoretical issues that shaped Western academia—and, in turn, American policy and public opinion. A crucial issue was the assumption of Western rationality and Eastern irrationality, and the consequent abstraction of Western historical contingencies to a role of absolute and self-evident objective truth. Fairbank touched on that in an attempt to explain away Vietnamese resistance to the occupation of their country. He joked awkwardly that Johnson's "targeted bombing campaigns" would work as a strategy to bring people to the negotiating table "in Oklahoma and Texas and Massachusetts." Not in Vietnam. In the United States, Fairbank went on, society is organized around a structure of law and the lawyer is really the "top man" ("Dick Nixon is a lawyer," he added, to the audience's delight). Not in Asia, which is instead dominated by "traditional" concerns over face, rituality, and form.[116] Here too Fairbank's good-tempered witticism is symptomatic of a deeper bias within the field (and the social sciences in general), one that the CCAS skewered mercilessly.

James Peck examined the pervasiveness of psychocultural tropes that animated modernization theory, framing the United States as the rational side and therefore labeling any opposition to U.S. policies, methods, and strategies as inherently irrational. America presented itself as the achieved dream of the capitalist world, its methods *the methods* of successful modernity. "No Chinese ever meant quite so much when speaking of China as the Middle Kingdom," Peck quipped, quite effectively.[117] The very people who accused the Chinese of being trapped by their own culture were effectively enclosed within a system that took an idealized version of present-day America as the yardstick for all the social sciences.[118] Moreover, Peck continued, this self-referential focus on the alleged rational and scientific character of Western modernity led scholars to compare China "with a theory (of bureaucratic rationality, of modernization) rather than with its concrete historical reality." Andrew Walder has described this attitude as a form of "unwitting 'occidentalism,' an orientation that led us *implicitly* to compare what we observed in China with a stereotyped textbook image of 'the West'—our bureaucracies are models of Weberian impersonalism, our political systems actually operate according to the principles of our written constitutions, people advance primarily according to merit, objectively judged, and we are a society of rugged, self-reliant, socially isolated individualists."[119]

Doing otherwise would have challenged the very assumptions behind modernization theory, revealing how this allegedly "objective" view takes the "most painful and exploitative characteristics" of industrialization and makes them into "rational progress," how it extrapolates what is good for one class, the bourgeoisie, and makes it into progress for everybody.[120] The Chinese experiments of the 1960s and 1970s attacked many features of Western industrialization, and therefore, Peck reproached, they "must ultimately be judged by American observers as utopian, ideological, and abstract because they challenge what modernization theorists insist is the ahistorical essence of rationalization and the division of labor. Ironically, looked at from the perspective of the classic British example of industrialization, such views of rationality and modernization appear intricately interwoven with violence. It is not only the rational which is real in the history of Western capitalism, but the violent which is rational."[121] It was not so much the Chinese, but rather the allegedly rational American social scientists and China scholars, who were trapped in culturalistic and psychological delusions about themselves and their own theories.

Accordingly, Lucien Pye, who had pioneered the psychoanalytic approach in the study of Chinese politics, was one of the first targets of CCAS's criticism—and, at times, ridicule. In an early issue of the *Bulletin*, Cheryl Goodman chided Pye for feeling no need to analyze the psychocultural tropes behind American policy. It was, in his mind, obviously rational, and the psychoanalytic method is proper only "when a society behaves in a way that is patently irrational and unnecessarily self-destructive." Yet, Goodman argued, Chinese political behavior looked irrational only because Pye measured the goal of the Chinese leadership "by his own image of development," and by social science concepts whose usefulness had "never been more than tentatively established" but that he nonetheless considered universal and absolute.[122] Or, to put it in the harsh words of Berkeley members of CCAS, "Asian acts are contrasted with Asian idealism to reveal hypocrisy and deceit while Western idealistic goals are taken as reality and used to justify almost any behavior by Western powers."[123]

Looking at the broader picture, one can see in CCAS's critique the beginning of the larger academic and intellectual change taking place in the long sixties. In history, for example, a shift took place moving the discipline toward "the social," toward a renewed attention on the activity of the people "without a voice." In the social sciences, we witness the temporary demise of studies that focused exclusively on the elites or that presupposed the universal power of technocratic solutions and a unified model of development. Similarly, in France, the late 1960s saw the emergence of theories that challenged the stability of concepts such as class, ideology, power, science, and, finally, revolution itself. The recognition of new political subjects, in China specifically but also in the various mass movements of the long sixties, was crucial for this epistemic shift. It was the irruption of people challenging the authority of the party, the intellectual, the colonizer, and assuming the ability to think and act without representation that fractured the epistemic coherence of existing knowledge.

The (Political) Subject of Objectivity

Starting from an obviously and outwardly political disagreement (over the U.S. policies in Asia and the evaluation of the Chinese revolutionary experience), CCAS criticism moved to an academic—but no less political—denunciation of the ideological discourse that allowed those policies and that evaluation to remain dominant. Crucial for CCAS was the revelation that, beyond the orientalist perspective that framed the West as rational, scientific, and progressive and the East as irrational, culturalistic, and traditional, it was the very character of scientificity and objectivity attributed to Western knowledge of the Other—as of itself—that was eminently problematic. Western academia reproduced and reinforced the relations of power under which it existed not just by the content of the knowledge it created but also and perhaps primarily by accepting the implicit assumptions about its form, its character, its epistemic conditions of existence.

For CCAS, this meant that a new intellectual production based on a humane approach to Asian people (i.e. on the political foundation of equality) required also the dismantling of the assumption of objectivity and neutrality behind the existing structure of learning and the unveiling of the political character of that assumption, in the name of a different politics. The "rubric of 'value-free social science' and 'scientific' objectivity," Cornell members of CCAS highlighted, masks the theoretical biases of the field and "submerges crucial moral and theoretical problems.... Uncritically accepting these preconceptions, scholars have evaded the consideration of necessary ethical and theoretical questions."[124]

The "sacred principle" of objectivity made it unprofessional for scholars to get involved in the problems of the world, and that, Orville Schell commented, had made academia into an alienating place: "Unfortunately most scholars of Asia have either retreated into a world of self-generating and ornate irrelevancy by choosing to anchor themselves so firmly in the past that they can deny all pretensions to relevancy, or by pretending to deal with the modern Asia much the way a doctor treats a plague patient; by protecting themselves with an impervious layer of theoretical armour, jargon and scholarly detachment."[125] The purposeful and systematic elimination of passion, of feelings, of involvement in the real world, Schell continued, also meant that any moral concern for justice or injustice, any conviction about right or wrong, any ethical measure of truth and falsity become excluded from academic practice. Personal involvement with the subject matter becomes an obstacle, rather than a prerequisite. So, in a paradoxical turn, "sinophobes study China, reactionaries construct elaborate models of revolution, while geriatrics make pronouncements on the student movement in Japan. Detachment becomes the summum bonum of study."[126]

Even more perniciously, objectivity and neutrality not only were producing alienation and blindness to ethical questions; they were in themselves political attitudes. In his reflections on the implications of the Vietnam Caucus, James Peck recalled how "time and again, 'youth' was reminded of its lack of the training and experience which had made their elders such models of moderation and reason, such paragons of political effectiveness and neutrality." But the Vietnam Caucus and the founding of the CCAS reversed this position, by stating loudly that neutrality was already a political and moral stance, one framed as a posture of acquiescence to "a policy and a situation."[127] A year later, CCAS members at Columbia University made an even stronger case: phrases such as "value-free research," "objective scholarship," and "free exchange of ideas" were not just excuses for passive compliance with power. Rather, they were used actively "either to serve as cover for the involvement of individuals in the University with the continual manipulation and oppression of third world peoples, or to mesmerize us into a false belief in the autonomy and independence of the University in our society."[128] Being "neutral" and "objective" was being political, because it meant embracing the fiction of the apolitical scholar while reinforcing and supporting specific political assumptions. Neutrality was a ruse: being neutral was not a question of keeping a distance from all political convictions; it was rather that certain convictions were seen as beneficial to scholarship and others were seen as "interfering with it." As Jesse Lemisch pointed out in his 1975 indictment of the historical profession, the field endorsed and admired the activism of somebody like Arthur Schlesinger, who had worked for the government and the war, yet it was not even close to tolerating the activism of those who criticized wars and governments.[129]

The Concerned Scholars did not stop at the unveiling of neutrality and objectivity as convenient disguises masking a particular kind of political attitude. They also traced the origins and the emergence of this academic discourse through two different but interconnected paths: a historical analysis of the field and a theoretical challenge to modernization theory. The field of Asian studies had been built in the United States as part of a government effort to shape the study of the enemy (real or potential). As such—and as a specific portion of academia directly connected to areas open to the "Communist menace"—it had been particularly and tragically affected by the McCarthy witch hunts, with the case of Owen Lattimore and the IPR standing as powerful reminders of the danger of perceived involvement.[130]

The effects of the McCarthy era on the field of China studies had been devastating, yet they had been largely ignored by younger generations of scholars, for whom "China was just another dusty attic available for scholarly rummaging." Few among the teachers and the graduate students "cared to remind their classes, or themselves, that the work being done and the ideas being set forth were largely the products of men who had either survived or missed a purge." And those who survived, in the words of Orville Schell, were either cold warriors who faithfully believed in the Communist conspiracy or "those who retreated into a kind of academic senility or liberal limbo land where value-free truth was found equidistant between any two current extremes."[131] Neither group offered any hope for political and intellectual awakening. Between the mid-1950s and the mid-1960s, there had been no real opposition to U.S. foreign policy within academia, and anti-Communism was an unquestioned assumption among most intellectuals. In such a situation, it is not strange that intellectuals, who "accept and ratify a society's power structure," would willingly and autonomously "employ their talents and energies to forward the objectives" of the authorities.[132]

McCarthyism and the Cold War did not only chill (or rather freeze) the political climate of Asian studies, according to CCAS criticism; they inscribed in the field the assumption that the American way was the norm, thus shaping American scholarship into serving, openly or not, to justify American policy abroad.[133] Judith Coburn's essay in *America's Asia* illustrated the evolving connection between the academe and the government, one shaped by funding, institutional restructuring, access to Asia, and so on. But she also highlighted the crucial role of the Kennedy administration, when, with the rejuvenation of the liberal idea of public service, "the most 'enlightened' and heretofore most critical members of the Academy" came to be integrated into the dominant discourse.[134] And, within that discourse, "even critics of the war," another concerned scholar remarked, "have often been trapped in the posture of criticizing it, while never doubting our right to interfere in the Vietnamese efforts at self-determination."[135] Even critics of the war, such as Fairbank and John Lewis,[136] then could justify continuing to work as government consultants. Even critics of the war, that is, shared "an interest in implementing rather than substantially changing the operation of the American political system."[137] This was the maddening crux of the academic consensus.

Living in the academic consensus also implied accepting—overtly or by omission—the tenets of the dominant methodologies with which Western scholars had analyzed Asia up until that point. In the social sciences (but one could argue for a broader influence), that meant Modernization Theory (MT). In his study of the rise and fall of behavioral sciences, a branch of Cold War social sciences particularly shaped by MT, Ron Robin highlights how MT derived much of its widespread appeal precisely from its consolatory psychological and justificatory character. "Given the ability to develop without artificial hindrance—the intervention of subversive, foreign ideologies such as communism, for example—modernization theorists assumed that all societies would eventually converge" toward a format of development similar to the one that the United States was the first to complete.[138] Modernization was therefore uniquely "American," and thus it allowed a separation between the current practices of the U.S. government and the legacy of European powers. It could, then, be portrayed as inherently noncolonial (or even anticolonial), precisely because it did not share the history of European colonialism. Modernization Theory was, finally and more importantly, assumed to be "natural," in two senses. First, the process of development was presupposed to be based on universal rules of social organization and a unified code of human behavior; underdevelopment or failure to develop following the prescribed pattern were due to "'tradition' or mental processes, rather than the legacy of colonialism or material factors."[139] Second, the political premises behind this process had been "naturalized" as scientific common sense, as the unquestioned ideological background of the field. Modernization was, as Michael Latham has shown, a form of ideology. As such, it reflected a worldview "through which America's strategic needs and political options were articulated, evaluated, and understood."[140] But also, and more powerfully, modernization was a cognitive framework, one that allowed scholars, often unconsciously, to shape facts, data, information, and ideas into knowledge functional to the perceived role of the United States in the world.[141]

The Committee of Concerned Asian Scholars pointedly highlighted the unspoken and biased postulations behind that approach. They showed how MT reflected a predisposition toward "gradualistic, peaceful and technical changes rather than fundamental (or revolutionary) changes in social structure"; this led to an excessive emphasis on stability justified by an ingrained fear of violent change.[142] It projected Western and specifically American models of modernization on Asian situations to which they might not be applicable,[143] as humorously summarized in Senator Kenneth Wherry's 1940 comment, "With God's grace we will lift Shanghai up and up, ever up, until it is just like Kansas City."[144] But more importantly, CCAS attacked MT's upholding of a path of development "which Asian nations will naturally follow."[145]

James Peck, in what was a merciless assault on China watchers' ideological blinders, remarked how this idea of a "natural path" of development was conveniently suited to defend and guarantee American presence in Asia. U.S. "protection" was necessary to assure that these countries could proceed toward maturity without the risk of being perturbed by chaotic social change or, worse, being led down a pathological revolutionary course. If modernization was a natural and unavoidable process, then the roles of imperialism, colonialism, and the continuing presence of the United States could be also discounted as irrelevant. In the analysis of people like Fairbank, "imperialism," Peck commented, was just the name given by the Communists (and others) to the "modern world's dynamic expansion."[146] It was described as a psychologically consolatory way for a failed nation to frame its own inability to keep up with the rest of the world, a way to shift the blame for its own lack of modernity onto other, largely well-meaning, nations. It was indeed time, Peck rebutted, to look at the reality of colonialism and imperialism while disclosing America's own sources of psychological comfort: "For though American China watchers have sought to explain how and why the theories of American imperialism and revolutionary Marxism were so emotionally satisfying to the Chinese, it is our theory of modernization which could be understood as a 'psychologically' comforting rationalization of America's imperial role and its consequences."[147]

It was the implicit (and at times explicit) adoption of the premises of modernization theory that has thus made all "neutral" scholars—the CAS's teachers—instrumental in justifying America's policy, even when they did not actually work for the government and had indeed suffered from purges. "This was not because many approved of the actual course of American policy toward China after 1949, but because by the work they did not do they upheld significant portions of the official definition of reality and, by the work they did, even elaborated upon it."[148]

Fairbank reacted to Peck's characterization in what became a famous and heated exchange on the pages of the *Bulletin*. He defended the neutrality of academia and rejected the idea that modernization could be in any way construed as a "political" perspective. Unlike revolutionary Marxism, it was essentially academic, largely meaningless outside the social sciences and the intellectual speculation of "ivory tower contemplation." He called his interlocutors in the United States to devote themselves to try to understand what was going on "rather than trying to take an active role in someone else's revolution."[149] Peck's reply was trenchant—surprisingly so, given that this was a dialogue between a graduate student and his very famous teacher. Fairbank's reaction confirmed the unquestioned, almost repressed, character of the theoretical framing of the field. The leaders of the China field, Peck argued, "did not withdraw from political involvement"; they chose a different mode of involvement by internalizing the "rightist world view." This was the pernicious and hidden legacy of McCarthyism.[150] China scholars had accepted the basic premises of the anti-Communist perspective, with its bipolar and moralistic view of the world, which de facto idealized American power and its global role (the good guys). Once that premise was internalized, Peck continued, any conflict was reduced to disagreements "over the techniques for implementing a fundamentally rightist world view."[151] Asian scholars already agreed on the strategy of containment vis-à-vis the Communist menace, on the role of the United States in nation building, and on an understanding of the Chinese revolution based on the concept of totalitarianism. The distinctions among them were then limited to a little more or a little less bombing, a little more or a little less targeted killing, a little more or a little less cultural influence.

Academic consensus and the shared acceptance of the premises of MT disproved, according to Peck, that the university was a "marketplace of ideas" that needed to be sheltered from outside political influence. Rather, Peck averred, the existence of a group like CCAS was predicated and dependent on the outside pressure of the larger antiwar movement and, even more, on the liberation efforts of American blacks and the Vietnamese. Without their successes, there would have been no hope for critical ideas to be heard within academia. "It is not, then," Peck concluded, "the image of a 'neutral' university that provides a model, but rather the mutually reinforcing intellectual and political forces of the Chinese May 4th Movement."[152]

In order to escape from the trap of consensus, it was not enough to claim access to a different and better objectivity or a more perfect neutrality. What was needed was instead embracing different politics. The Committee of Concerned Asian Scholars admitted that their concern with Asia was of political nature and that they were ready "to accept (in fact, seek out) its political consequences, and then act." What was needed was, in the end, "to redefine the whole notion of 'Asian expert.'"[153] Mark Selden celebrated the early work of CCAS precisely as part of a long-term political involvement:

> There are signs that CCAS is beginning to emerge as a significant focal point in the intellectual ferment that is taking place in America. With the bankruptcy of the essential paradigms which have held undisputed sway for two decades—Cold War scholarship and its offshoot

models of modernization, totalitarianism, American innocence etc.—it has become possible to rethink the entire basis of a worldview which for many seemed truth itself prior to Vietnam. We have begun to pierce the mask of 'objectivity' to reveal precisely whose interests have been shored up by the work of a generation of scholars, journalists and writers. We have begun to replace narrow nationalism and the rationale for neo-colonialism with perspectives that point toward a humanist, anti-imperialist and internationalist scholarship. We have begun, but only barely begun, to make our work available to the anti-war movement, to the general public and to Asian specialists. Yet already it seems clear that CCAS has an important intellectual role to play both in long and short range terms in its immediate support for the peace movement and in participating in a generation long effort to redefine perspectives on Asia and ourselves.[154]

The Committee was not to be another "sinological preserve." Rather, it configured an attempt to shape a new generation of scholars, not just to rethink the premises of their profession, and to write and read accordingly, but also to implement their work and thought in practice, "accepting the involvement and commitment to political causes that all of this entails."[155]

I devote the following chapter to the tensions between the thought and the practice, the scholarly and the political. But I want first to highlight the original scholarly insights that this political rethinking allowed. What were the new perspectives within the field of Asian studies that were being shaped in the early years of CCAS?

Rethinking and the Limits of Theory

For an organization that had "scholars" in its very name, CCAS was troubled by tensions about what being a "scholar" meant and about what counted as "concerned," "radical" (or even just plain "good") scholarship. In 1969, the Berkeley and Stanford chapters proposed a panel for the annual conference precisely about the question of CCAS scholarship: "Is CCAS just a vehicle for the expression of our political concerns, or can it help encourage new approaches in our respective disciplines?" they asked.[156] It was, in many ways, a legitimate question, and one that plagued the editors of the *Bulletin* and many CCAS members throughout the years.

That was specifically the case with China studies, in which, Mark Selden gloomily remarked, BCAS had produced a fair amount of very sharp critique but "disastrously little in the way of positive contribution."[157] And yes, Selden was probably right, the most notable portion of CCAS scholarly work in relation to China was criticism of the existing *doxa*, a dismantling of assumptions and cognitive blinders. But the concerned scholars did produce original insights on China, which sometimes remained at an embryonic level but were often confirmed by further developments in the field in the later years. It is difficult to assess the intellectual production of such a varied and scattered group over ten years and a long list of publications (including a few multiauthored books),[158] but there are at least three areas in which I think the contributions of the CAS were particularly notable.

First, scholars like Carl Riskin and Stephen Andors brought CCAS political reappraisal of the Maoist experiments into the field of economics to supplement and rethink theories of motivation, growth, and efficiency. Riskin challenged the separation operated by most China economic experts between "ideology" and "economic, managerial, and technical rationality." An unrefined and restricted concept of "work incentives" as exclusively material—or worse, monetary—made Maoist economic policies completely obscure. Rather, the Chinese approach to productivity, Riskin argued, required a new consideration of motivation, a variable usually neglected by economists, as well as of "its links with other variables, such as organization, leadership, and the distribution of political power."[159] Moral incentives, Riskin continued, were not only effective and important and should be evaluated as part of a study of motivation; they were also still means to produce socially desirable behaviors and as such, a measure of the distance that Maoist China still had to travel to achieve a true form of "Communist labor," a concept that economic experts could not even consider.[160] In another essay, Riskin challenged the relevance of standardized growth rates in assessing "real" economic development, as growth can be achieved on the basis of "mushrooming bordellos and American bases" or of increasing class stratification.[161] As John Gurley had also written, understanding Maoist China called for the revision of the concept of "growth" into something that had less to do with GDP numbers and more to do with the potential of creating a socialist system in which people would collectively accept heavy sacrifices in the present for equally distributed material results in the future.[162]

The experiments of the 1960s were similarly redefining the function and meaning of the "enterprise," Stephen Andors explained. The Maoist factory had to cease to be "part of a vertically integrated economic system whose purposes are maximizing production and profits on the one hand, and providing work for wages on the other."[163] Rather, while it continued to serve production purposes, it was supposed to also assume educational and social roles, to serve as a health clinic, a social center, and "*a center for the mass training of people.*"[164] If Maoism forced experts to reinterpret the very location of production in the light of factors and variables that were not strictly "economic," then the idea of "efficiency," Andors suggested, had to be rethought as well. All the Maoist experiments since the Great Leap Forward aimed at solving major economic issues, but these problems were defined and could only be understood politically. The Great Leap Forward and the Cultural Revolution were then not simply (misguided) attempts to achieve speedy technological development, but they also aimed at "redefining some of the principal relationships and crucial institutions in 'modern' society."[165] Maoism questioned, in a confusing and at times confused struggle, the political, economic, social, and organizational consequences of technology and modernization, consequences that were then assumed to be "a universal given" both in the West and the Soviet Union.[166] In Maoist discourse, "efficiency" included "both political and social priorities as well as the calculation of economic costs."[167] Then, taking Maoist China seriously required a complete revision of the disciplinary episteme, down to its organizing concepts.[168]

Second, the scholarly work of CCAS was central—while certainly not unique—in placing imperialism and colonialism back at the center of the debate on modern Chinese history. While there was a long tradition of Marxist-inflected analysis that focused on imperialism and the violent expansion of capitalism,[169] CCAS felt that modern Chinese history in the United States was being dominated by the "response to the West" trope (promoted by the so-called Harvard school). The most direct attack to this approach came in the December 1972 issue of the *Bulletin*, and specifically in Joseph Esherick's contribution to a special section devoted to imperialism in China. Esherick curtly but comprehensively dismissed the "response to the West" approach as internally contradictory. The "West" indeed presented China with a problem in the form of "the political and military incursions of imperialism"; it also provided model solutions in the form of "economic and political modernization." Yet it was the very existence of imperialism that prevented China from successfully adopting this model. Esherick pointed out the contradictions inherent in a structure of knowledge that tried to explain China's modern history as a failure of understanding the rise of Euro-American power and of adopting Western ways, while at the same time eliding colonialism and imperialism as the defining factors both in the West's rise and China's "failure." In the end, without imperialism, the issue of a "response to the West" did not exist.

But, more interestingly, it was once again the particular revolutionary path that Maoist China took that directly framed and justified not just the negative attack on the Harvard interpretation but also a positive alternative historical—and political—reappraisal. In light of the revolution, Esherick concluded, China did not really fail to respond to the West.

> That proposition is true only if Japan's imitation of Western finance capitalism and economic and military imperialism is to be the model of 'success.' What the Chinese case implies is that any Victim nation's attempt to collaborate or coexist with imperialism is destined to failure. Imperialism, in effect, eliminates for its victims the possibility of a bourgeois-democratic road to development. However, in China the very struggle to eliminate the economic, political, social and psychological vestiges of imperialism produced the basis of sustained, self-reliant economic and political growth. Maoism, it is safe to say, is inconceivable in the absence of imperialism, and China's decision to follow a Maoist path to development can hardly be judged a 'failure.'[170]

Third, as I briefly highlighted earlier in the chapter, CCAS strove to reveal and revise the orientalist biases in the profession. This happened in part through an attempt to rescue the rationality of Chinese foreign policy—and Vietnamese resistance—vis-à-vis a field that framed them as determined historically by a persecution complex (due to their mistaken obsession with imperialism), cultural blinders, and totalitarian pathologies. In this view, the Chinese leaders were irrational, illogical, and prone to violence; their use of imperialism denoted the need for psychological comfort; they were maladjusted, unfit for the modern world. From highlighting the contemporary political use of these tropes, CCAS moved to produce a counterargument to the theory of "China's world order." By revealing how the idea of a ritualistic China was a construction of the policy needs and the colonial tropes of the Western nations, the Concerned Scholars produced, without the support of Said's Orientalism or Foucault's notions of power, an argument that predates more sophisticated analyses by about twenty years.[171]

The lack of supporting "theories" and, more importantly, the absence of a significant theoretical engagement was, however, not a minor issue. And it was recognized as such by many within CCAS. The idea that "America's Asia" posed a need for a totally new approach, that America (and the world) needed to think through "theories" in order to appraise, understand, and help realize the emancipatory experiences of Asia, came to the fore repeatedly in the discussion within the organization. In 1970, for example, Ric Pfeffer stated the need for "more grand theories" on China: "We're going to get a lot of people doing the fact-grubbing and lots of people doing kind of middle-level analysis. We have to go to a lot of new approaches to China in terms of grand theories, like Chinese visions of modernization or Chinese visions of anti-modernization."[172] In the same year, at the 1970 Eastern Regional Conference, a speaker called for CCAS to develop a counterimperialist ideology: "This ideology would be the foundation of a lasting CCAS organization and should get at the roots of the whole system we are fighting; it should, for example, concern itself with the basic causes of the American destruction of Vietnam's and its own ecology: capitalism and imperialism, rather than with the destruction itself. Our opponents know what they're at—they live in and manipulate the system every day. The questions are: Where are we? What do we believe in?"[173]

These questions still loomed large in the following years. Even as late as 1975, Bryant Avery, then editor of the *Bulletin*, asked whether it was not the time to study Marx, Lenin, and others "in order to better understand Asian socialist movements within the larger international capitalist structure."[174] In October 1972, the *Newsletter* had encouraged—apparently without much success—local chapters of CCAS to form study groups on basic Marxist theory. The Committee had developed a basic consciousness of anti-imperialism, yet "people felt that we have never systematically developed an understanding of the origins of capitalism, or an understanding of the origins of the Marxist movement. People recognize that there is a basic difference between simply opposing imperialism, and really understanding its causes and effects."[175] Indeed, while CCAS produced an impressive scholarly critique of U.S. imperialist ventures and of orientalism in Asian studies, it did it seemingly without a direct or deep engagement with Marxism, Leninism, or any theory of imperialism. The Committee produced excellent analyses of Maoist economy, People's War, and revolutionary strategy, as well as a trenchant critique of Asian studies, but largely gave up any attempt to conceptualize the political and intellectual issues in universal theoretical terms. They recognized the universality of "America's Asia" but too often refused to confront it in those terms. Harry Harootunian points to a similar problem in the reappropriation of Japan historian E. H. Norman by radical scholars, especially following the publication of his selected writings, edited by CCAS member John Dower. "Even though 'new left' critics declared their kinship with the discredited Norman in the late 1960s and 1970s," Harootunian writes, "the problematic that had prompted his own project demanded a theoretical grasp of Marxism that many of his later supporters discounted out of hand as unnecessary. Their easy dismissal of theory, that is, often risked making the 'new left' critics sound very much like the people they were trying to criticize."[176]

This dismissal had major consequences, especially in the long term. If we consider modernization theory, and in general any epistemic arrangement of knowledge, as ideology,[177] then unveiling its biases and mistakes was not enough to displace its lingering power. Nor was it possible to displace it by an appeal to "true" real science. As Jacques Rancière argued in his criticism of Althusser (produced precisely at the same time in which CCAS was putting forward its critique of the field), there was no science separate from ideology. "What the university teaches is not 'science,' in the mythical purity of its essence, but a selection of scientific knowledges that have been articulated into *objects of knowledge*."[178] And it is in the forms of dominant ideology that scientific knowledge becomes an object of knowledge; it is in a set of institutions framed by the dominant ideology that these objects are transmitted, and the forms of this transmission are themselves ideological. This was evident to many within CCAS, but for various reasons—their residual faith in empiricism, a certain diffidence toward "theory," and the very pragmatic need to respond to political contingencies, among others—they never formulated a criticism of knowledge production that could challenge the existent structure at its deepest core. And over time, this tested the limits of their own knowledge production.

But there is another not-less-important form of criticism and rethinking in which the Concerned Scholars engaged, which I believe is related on a more complex understanding of how ideology works. Ideology, following Slavoj Žižek, is not a misrecognition of reality; rather, it structures social reality through our practices, through "what we do." "Ideology is not an illusion masking the real state of things," one that can be dismantled by lifting the curtain and exposing the truth of its hidden workings. The illusion is not on the side of knowledge, but embedded and inscribed in reality; therefore, critical distance and intellectual exposure leave that reality unaffected.[179] Thus, when CCAS argued the epistemic structure of the field was ideological, they also understood—even if they did not fully theorize that understanding—that the struggle could not be conducted solely in the realm of intellectual production. It affected the very forms of production, their locations, the roles of students and teachers, and the daily existence of the scholars. Ideology penetrated and shaped the practices of scholarship, the scholar's everyday life, and the social relationship of intellectuals; therefore, it had to be fought and challenged in those realms as well. In this too the inspiration of the Cultural Revolution was crucial.

CHAPTER TWO

TO BE, OR NOT TO BE, A SCHOLAR

The Praxis of Radicalism in Academia

It seems to me as I come here today that a lot of people are terribly concerned and perhaps most of you shouldn't be scholars. You should be activists, revolutionaries, politicians.
—**David Keightley, "Wither Chinese Studies" panel**

By acting politically in accordance with our consciences, we may not survive in American academia, but if we surrender this principle we cannot survive as people.
—**"Ramblings of a Berkeley Chapter, CCAS, Member"**

In what is still arguably her most widely read and quoted essay, Gayatri Spivak launched her inquiry on whether the subaltern can speak by taking apart a famous dialogue between two revered French intellectuals, Gilles Deleuze and Michel Foucault. Meeting in 1972, when the political parable initiated by the events of 1968 was showing signs of dissolution, the two philosophers amiably discussed the new conditions of existence for intellectuals and the new relationships between theory, practice, and power as they had been reshaped by the upheaval of the previous years. In the course of their brief conversation, Foucault and Deleuze listed a series of political subjects—workers, prisoners, women, homosexuals, "a Maoist," "Vietnam"—which had emerged, had claimed for themselves the authority to speak without mediation, and had proven that they were capable not just of practices but of theory. The emergence of these new "subjects-in-revolution" in turn had dramatically altered the role of the intellectual: "The masses no longer need him to gain knowledge: they know perfectly well, without illusion; they know far better than he and they are certainly capable of expressing themselves," Foucault declared.[1] It is precisely this perceived immediacy of the voices and practices of the oppressed that Spivak found problematic. Foucault and Deleuze's acceptance of the presumed transparency of the reality of the subaltern—the concrete experience of the factory, the prison, the school—could only lead, Spivak argued, to a form of uncritical representational realism, to the acceptance at face value of the experience of the oppressed. What's worse, this acceptance signaled the abdication of the main task of the counterhegemonic intellectual, the critique of subject formation under capitalist ideology.[2] Beyond that, Spivak chided, Foucault and Deleuze were dangerously naive about their own subject position: in their view, the intellectual was not supposed to represent (speak for) the newly vocal—yet always generic and anonymous—subjects, but he could re-present (describe, present) them by virtue of their self-declared concrete existence. "The banality of leftist intellectuals' lists of self-knowing, politically canny subalterns stands revealed; representing them, the intellectuals represent themselves as transparent," Spivak concluded.[3]

The criticism of Foucault and Deleuze was for Spivak just the initial stepping stone toward elaborating her complex and very famous argument on the representability of the subaltern. When I picked up this essay again, many years after first reading it in graduate school, I realized I had completely forgotten this polemical incipit, and it struck me with renewed force. It struck me precisely because Spivak took as the target of her critique an intellectual position that was unequivocally the product of the late sixties and specifically correlated to global Maoism. Maoism appears directly on the second page of Spivak's essay, as one of the exemplary cases of the fallacy of transparency, in the form of Foucault's reference to "a Maoist" as the anonymous yet self-evident revolutionary subject. By appropriating "Maoism" as the name of their own eccentric Maoism, Spivak mentioned in passing, French intellectuals rendered Asia seemingly transparent and representable, thus disguising the fact that it was, to quote Derrida, only a "European hallucination."[4]

Spivak's criticism of the transparency of Asia and Maoism in the French intellectual scene is, of course, very much to the point, and I have no intention of downplaying the complex issue of the immediate translatability of political subjects. It is also essential to remember that Spivak's problem, in that essay and in her overall critical trajectory, is "women," and specifically the question of female subaltern consciousness. The blindness to that issue was the central focus of her criticism of the Subaltern Studies Collective precisely because the silence about and of subaltern female subjects presented a structural challenge to the entire project.[5] This is another crucial point that I don't want to minimize, especially because the Chinese Revolution put the question of "women" at the center and because the very issue of gender politics was an important factor of crisis within the groups I am analyzing in this book. As I show later, a certain inability to fully account for the presence of the gendered (and racialized) subalterns was one of the factors that limited the political horizon of many CCAS members. Spivak's admonition should therefore remain a central source of analytical doubt.[6]

Yet I have argued so far against the risk of falling into the opposite extreme, where we end up denying the possibility of recognition of political subjectivities and of shared political experiences across different locations. In chapter 1, I showed that alternative intellectual and political positions in the United States and France were predicated precisely on the recognition of Asian and Chinese people as subjects—albeit never transparent ones—who could and did act and speak for themselves. And it is the recognition (or maybe the productive misrecognition) of the possibility of speech and action that Spivak's critique runs the risk of eliding completely.

Foucault and Deleuze might have been temporarily blinded to the hidden ideological reproduction of their oppressed subjects, and they were definitively blind to the gendered structure of their own discourse. But they were also discussing at a time and place where it seemed undeniable that subalterns had indeed spoken and were still speaking—against their oppression and the mechanism of its reproduction, and often against those who claimed to speak for them. They were the workers of Paris and Shanghai against the Communist Party and the trade unions, students all over Europe and Asia against their teachers, fighters in Vietnam and other colonies against imperialists and corrupt governments. Everywhere, speech had been captured through very visible actions.

The political connections among these different events were much more complex than they looked at a first glance, and the transparency of the subaltern's voice was indeed going to be a crucial issue. Yet I think we cannot gloss over what was one of the perceived, declared, and probably unrealized possibilities of the 1960s: the capacity of the oppressed to speak for themselves, denounce their oppression, and subvert the mechanism of domination. And in declaring that capacity, Maoism and China constituted a crucial location, beyond any simple appropriation. One of the challenges that Maoism posed to those who were willing to look at the Chinese experience with open, if perhaps too credulous, eyes was that of rethinking the relationship between those who work with their hands and those who work with their brains. Maoism (and specifically the "high Maoism" of the Cultural Revolution) affirmed the competence of the masses to speak and subvert their domination without—and often against—the wise guide of the philosopher/scientist/party leader. To use the words of Jacques Rancière's critique of his teacher Althusser, Maoism proclaimed a double superiority, "that of the people's fighters over imperialist and feudal armies and that of the peasant of Tathai [Dazhai], the workers of Shanghai and the students at Tsinghua University over the specialists who want to teach them the art of leading the class struggle, of producing, of cultivating the land and of studying Marxism."[7]

This chapter deals with the potential and the limits of that rethinking, with the attempts and the failures by these young scholars to integrate their intellectual and political lives. I first illustrate how the contradiction between politics and scholarship was present at the very founding of CCAS and how it was articulated since the inception of the group. I then highlight a couple of cases that underscore the practical ramifications of this issue, with particular reference to the founding of the journal *Modern China* and the debate over the funding of the profession. Last, I show how this tension was embedded in the everyday life of the "radical intellectual," how it manifested itself in seemingly endless discussions on the nature of the organization, and how it remained unsolved until the dissolution of CCAS.

Once again, I propose this case as a way to identify the profound challenge posed by the sixties and by global Maoism. The subaltern subjects of the revolution might have still been anonymous in Foucault and Deleuze's descriptions, but it was their loud presence (in speech and actions, in

France and China) that forced a rethinking, albeit temporary, of these intellectuals' position and, more importantly, of the question of equality in relation to scholarly and political practices.

The Intelligence of the People

Before tackling the first few months of CCAS's existence and the first major debate about the nature of intellectuals' activism, let us go back to France. Not to Foucault and Deleuze, but to another theorist whose trajectory was critically shaped by 1968 and by his encounter with those emergent revolutionary subjects, some of them Asian. I find the work of Jacques Rancière particularly useful in identifying the theoretical and political implications of Maoism and of the Cultural Revolution—or at least of their global perception. Rancière has placed at the center of his work the question of equality, and specifically of equality as "self-emancipation."[8] His basic assumption is, quite simply, that everyone thinks and everyone speaks, yet "the prevailing division of labour and configuration of society ensures that only certain classes of people are *authorized* to think."[9] And here originates Rancière's incessant investigation—waged through history, philosophy, and aesthetics—into how and under what conditions those whose business is *not* to speak and think can assume the authority to do so and therefore constitute themselves as thinking and speaking subjects, that is, as political subjects. That is, how can proletarians, workers, and peasants speak with a voice that is not just the expression of the misery of labor and oppression, but that instead adopts the self-proclaimed authority of a thinker?

Rancière himself acknowledged the role that Maoism and the mass politics of May '68 played in shaping his perspective, when the former prized student of Althusser was confronted with "the capacity of the dominated," in the form of a "Cultural Revolution on a global scale, and students who contest the authority of knowledge on a local scale."[10] Because, and that's part of my argument, what justified both the Cultural Revolution and the upheaval of '68 was precisely the assumption that workers, peasants, and young students could speak and did speak, and that they did not simply speak as workers, peasants, or students, as the embodiment of the wisdom of the oppressed. Rather, peasants could invade the territory of agricultural scientists,[11] of artists (as in the famed and partly misunderstood case of Huxian),[12] and even of philosophers. When the entire country of China was called to debate whether the one divides into two or the two unite into one, it was an explicit recognition that the masses had the capacity to engage in the previously forbidden task of the philosopher—thought.[13] Similarly, for all the mechanical and dogmatic recitation associated with it, the Little Red Book could be viewed—and was viewed—not so much as a perverse instrument of mass indoctrination but rather as the physical embodiment of shared equality by way of the text, on the basis of which the poor farmer could potentially produce deeper insights than the cadre and on whose authority new behaviors could be invented, often against the sanctioned authority of the party.[14] In this perspective, then, here emancipation, to use Rancière's words, is not a matter of making labor the "new founding principle of the new society." It is rather workers emerging from their status as exclusively people who labor, proving through their actions "that they are not merely creatures of need, of complaint and protests, but creatures of discourse or reason, that they are capable of opposing reason with reason and of giving their action a demonstrative form."[15]

Now, the history of the Cultural Revolution shows that the Maoist quest for equality was contradictory and marred by individual and collective tragedies, and the authority of the oppressed to speak for themselves was often more a theoretical presupposition than a practical reality. Also, we should highlight a couple of blind spots in Rancière's own reading of the Cultural Revolution. First, going back to Spivak's criticism, there is here a deafening silence over "women," a silence made even louder by the centrality of that category (together with the ones that Rancière duly mentions: worker, peasant, student, etc.) in the history of the Chinese Revolution.[16] Secondly, by stressing the ideological construct of the separation between thinking and working—even with the explicit goal of overcoming it—we run the risk of reifying it. One of the major frustrations for many in CCAS was that, despite their very real and intense search for new roles for the radical intellectuals, the very assumption of a stark dichotomy between the classroom and the street, between activism and scholarly impotence made it more difficult for them to see the existing possibilities for alternative forms of political engagements. The Maoism of the Cultural Revolution did not simply aim at breaking the distance between those who work with their hands and those who work with their brains.[17] Rather, it aimed at reframing the very meaning and practices of labor and of the production of knowledge.

Yet, these problems notwithstanding, I argue that if the capacity of masses to speak and think is taken seriously—and I assume that my actors, both in France and in the United States, did so—then that recognition could be the grounding for the potential ultimate subversion of the social and political structure. First and foremost, it subverted the position of the intellectual, be it the Platonic philosopher, the Marxist scientist, or the modern sociologist. The assertion by the revolutionary masses of their right to speak against the authority of their teachers and masters during the Cultural Revolution or May '68 was the manifestation, according to Rancière, of "a new intelligence—the intelligence formed in the struggle, the knowledge reclaimed from the hands of the exploiters." He continued, "This new intelligence, forged *over there*, obliges every 'Marxist philosopher' *over here* to rethink the question of its practice and its knowledge; it obliges him to reconsider his place in the distribution of spaces of power and knowledge that reproduces bourgeois domination."[18]

If other people could think and were thinking, then the intellectuals lost their privileged access to theory and pedagogy. Maoism, in this perspective, reaffirmed that workers did not need "our science, but our revolt," and, as such, "the Cultural Revolution destroyed the very place of the educator,"[19] be it the philosopher or the Party itself. As Alain Badiou reminds us, not without a certain glee, the high tide of Maoism in France—when the masses took front stage—coincided with "the silence of the garrulous philosopher, of separated philosophy."[20]

To this invasion of their proper field of operation, the intellectuals could react in different ways. They could join the choir of "the so-called specialists, engineers, politicians, economists, revisionists" who brutally reaffirmed their own knowledge and the ignorance of the oppressed, telling them, as Alain Geismar ironically mocked, "Tu ne sais rien, tu n'as droit à rien. Travaille, tais-toi, on pense pour toi" (You don't know anything, you have no right to anything. Work, shut up, we think for you).[21] More subtly, the intellectuals could celebrate work as the "true culture of the poor,"[22] indirectly condemning again those who work to their cultural limitations and reimposing the hierarchy between worlds. Finally, they could more simply separate themselves (and their theoretical musings) from what was going on in the streets, something epitomized perfectly by old Theodor Adorno, who, clearly without any sense of the ironic, called the police when Parisian students occupied the building where he was teaching Marxist theory in 1968.[23]

But there was also always the possibility of a completely different reaction to this invasion, one that did not simply accept and recognize the existence of the thinking Other and the shared equality with regard to thinking, but that also reflexively interrogated what that equality meant for the scholar. Because, if other people can think, then maybe intellectuals can and should do something else besides thinking; they could and should act. But in what guise, and under which relationship to their own thinking and that of others? And even more, under which relationship to the political conditions that the recognition of the thinking of others produced? This was, in part, the reaction of the Concerned Asian Scholars, and these were some of the crucial questions that preoccupied the Committee throughout its relatively short existence. For many in CCAS, there was clearly a parallel between the emergence of Asia and China as sources of alternative politics on the one hand and the new authority of the powerless to speak for themselves on the other. It was the struggle of the "lower ranked" within China (and in the decolonizing world) to act as self-authorized political and intellectual subjects that made "China" and "Asia" the referents for emancipatory politics worldwide. As the students wrested from the master, the teacher, the pedagogue the authority of explanation, thus destroying the obstacle to the always deferred equality vis-à-vis the truth, so too did China and Asia displace the "not-yet" of an always deferred development with the possibility of a different present. The two processes could only be inseparably intertwined for self-defined "radical Asia scholars."

Living an Integrated Life

In this context, the role of the radical intellectual—and even more of the "concerned" scholar of Asia—was extremely problematic, and CCAS members did not reach any definitive or even shared conclusions about it. Actually, the search for new intellectual practices remained a source of tension within the group and of personal angst for individual members. But the debate around these issues highlights both the political possibilities and the political crisis that "taking China seriously" implied. That debate was coincident and coeval with the foundation of the Committee. In the summer of 1968, just a few months after the March meeting in Philadelphia, several members met in Cambridge, Massachusetts, for the self-organized "CCAS Harvard seminar"—where the volume *America's Asia* was formulated. Many afternoons and evenings were spent dealing precisely with the self-definition of these young scholars and their relations to politics.

The meetings at Cambridge were intense and the discussion was always passionate, with numerous points of contention. Many hours, it seems, were devoted to a serious (if inconclusive) reflection on what the group was, what it was supposed to be, who its enemies and friends were, and, most importantly, who *they* were—as intellectuals, scholars, and political actors. They were, at least the people in the room, declaredly *not* liberals. They were unabashedly "radicals." But there was very little clarity of what that term meant, especially in the case of people whose present and potential future lay within a set of academic institutions that were, by their own nature, repressing radical politics and radical intellectual endeavors. In the end, the entire discussion can be summarized as "an attempt to formulate a definition of a radical," and their relations to the political and academic context.[24]

"Concerned" scholars, it was argued at the beginning of the discussion, should be concerned about criticism *and* creation "of a better social order." This entailed going "beyond *ad hoc criticism* to the posing of alternatives," which in turn implied moving away from strictly professional boundaries. With a clear reference to the Maoist lingo, the CAS argued that it was necessary to repudiate the concept of "expert"; "rather, one should consider oneself as a radical working within a profession," they declared.[25] That entailed, in the first instance, a willingness to change not just the rules of the game but the game itself, by transforming the objectives of the profession. They tried to define "a radical" first by what it was not: a radical was not just "critical," a radical was not just a muckraker. And what differentiated radicals was the posing of alternatives and, significantly, "the creation of a new vocabulary in the description of what is." This idea of a new vocabulary, a new form of conceiving and describing reality, was mentioned only in passing, but it was directly connected to the political changes happening globally, in which the current protests were described precisely as introducing a new form of speech, a new lexicon.[26]

It was the emergence of this new speech—the recognition of the other's ability to speak—that required a total break with the past embodied in the radical position. However, the tension between radicalism and the profession, between scholarship and politics, and, eventually, between career and activism remained an unsolved conundrum that affected the daily praxis of the concerned life. The formulation that the peculiar social responsibility of intellectuals was to engage in politically relevant analysis and discussion—which made them automatically political acts—was clearly not satisfying to these people, whose area of study was beset by a much more essential challenge to the task of the scholar.[27] As Orville Schell lamented, in a different venue, it was impossible to continue to study the China of the Cultural Revolution and yet "eschew all responsibility for being actors in those social and political consequences."[28]

The dichotomy between scholarship and politics was unacceptable to all who met in Cambridge, but the group split over the possible modes of integration between the two. As I have shown in chapter 1, CCAS's criticism of the field was based on the recognition, the acceptance, and even the need for a political point of view in scholarship, so it was obvious that, at a very basic level, a radical would relate one's political goals to scholarship and would be driven to choose "a radical subject by political awareness."[29] But that was, at the time, a minimal requirement, one that remained largely restricted within each individual scholar's activity and that could not really provide any exhaustive prescriptive definition for a collective organization. Also, the very hypothesis that scholarship—even politically infused scholarship—could be enough was at the root of the debate. Yet participants in the seminar, by their own admission, found it extremely problematic to go beyond that "personal fusion of scholarship and politics," and they strove instead to stretch the realm of the political so to make scholarship itself politically subversive. The concluding paragraph of the August 1 meeting is worth quoting:

> It is no accident that politics was central to our discussion, for there lies the power to effect change. At the same time we proposed to extend scholarship as another sphere in which one could act radi-

cally. Scholarship can be subversive of accepted thought and assumptions as working towards a critical political order can be of legitimate political modes and styles. For lack of close delineation we again seem to rely on an emphasis of self-image and style. Politics tended to be considered mainly in a Platonic sense of actualizing the ideal. Opposition, whether in scholarship or politics, was conceived as values conflicts. At the same time the way was prepared for substituting for the distinctiveness of the political sphere the political dimension or aspect of all that we do.[30]

In an attempt to synthesize what had been a complex and divisive debate, the language of the report above ends up taking a quite cryptic slant, but I think it is fair to assess that these young scholars identified a two-step process in what we could call the displacement of the political. First, there was the aforementioned reevaluation of critical scholarship as parallel to a political attack on established orders and modes of thought/action. But then, and here is the more far-reaching move, they advocated for the expansion of the political into every realm of activity, the elimination of a confined place for political action. If a radical is "dedicated to change," as members claimed in Cambridge, their objectives can only be defined within a "total approach," "one which views the relatedness of things."[31]

Here we can see already a division within CCAS—and one that possibly affected intellectuals in general, when they had to account for the challenge of the suddenly vocal and thoughtful masses.[32] The split was between those who aimed at a "radical scholarship"—in terms of categories, contents, and political bias—and others who were proposing a complete redefinition of what "scholarly" meant, a theoretical rethinking of the profession and a practical remaking of the life of the intellectual. The latter maintained that radicalism could not involve just the content of one's publications, but it also required a reconceptualization of how scholarship was produced and what the scholars themselves were. In the words of Mark Selden, more was needed "than incremental additions to the prevailing model." There was, he argued, "the perceived need for being radical with a vision of enlarging human potentiality. The need to lead unified lives, whereby scholarship and being radical come together."[33]

The former, less "totalizing" position was presented more clearly—and quite surprisingly—by Noam Chomsky, who joined at least one meeting of the Cambridge seminar and whose main contribution to the discussion was the oft-cited refrain that objective truth is by its own nature radical.[34] Chomsky argued for an almost unquestionable connection between being radical and being a good scholar, in that objective truth is firmly on one political side, and, as such, "being a hawk and a good scholar are incompatible."[35] In an essay for the *Bulletin*, Chomsky displayed all his faith in the simplistic power of "objective scholarship" as a tool of activism. First, he argued, such scholarship could demolish the psychological support for imperialistic policies by assuaging paranoid fears and undermining the belief in American benevolence. Second, it could be subversive by revealing the underbelly of U.S. ideology, thus demystifying the system.[36] This was a notion of activism as education that, in Steve Andors's recollection, was based on the idea "that you can educate people, and convey factual information, or at least factual information in so far as it can be known, and then people would rationally consider it, take it into account, and then change their behavior according to the information they have received."[37]

Yet Chomsky's position, while respected and often cited, was never truly accepted by the radicals within CCAS. Tactically, they questioned the idea that truth could really win, in the end, and wondered whether a focus on research and documentation was not simply a guarantee of political impotence and a way to avoid getting involved in social action.[38] At a deeper level, the critique of "objective scholarship," as we have seen in chapter 1, was at the center of CCAS's attack on the Asian studies establishment; they were therefore very aware that the concept was functional to patrolling disciplinary borders and ensuring the distance between supposedly "neutral" academic production and political participation. If the task of the radical scholar was just to dismantle a previously accepted set of "truths" and substitute for it new "real," "more objective" truths, that, in the end, had no effect on the ideological and institutional structure that allowed for these alternative versions of truth to be formulated.[39] And, more importantly, such a perspective ultimately restricted once again the capacity of thought and speech to the intellectuals, revealers of truth, and denied the capacity of the masses to see it by themselves. It re-enclosed scholars within the walls of thoughtful (if politicized) reflection, thus reinforcing a separation that the capture of speech by the masses had made de facto untenable.

Being radical, in the end, could only mean exceeding the confines of radical scholarship, precisely because the political upheaval that we identify with the "global sixties"—and specifically with China—also took the form of the disruption of the boundary between knowledge and action, between those who speak and those who are spoken of, between the philosopher and the poor, red and expert. The fracturing of those boundaries by political movements in Asia and worldwide meant that those who wanted to be radicals in the university had to live, in the words of Ric Pfeffer, "a very schizophrenic life, really schizophrenic." Even the simple requirement to produce a minimum amount of academically viable knowledge posed enormous problems, if one really wanted to create scholarship that reflected one's values.[40] But the schizophrenia extended far beyond scholarly production and invested the entire life of the radical intellectuals, a life that seemed endlessly splintered in an unsustainable dichotomy between thinking and acting, where people were forced to have "minds pickled in jars operating without arms and legs."[41] At the Cambridge seminar, the idea of being radical as a "total view," an all-encompassing practice, was voiced precisely against the idea that one could "fracture one's life into discrete compartments" (here scholarship, there activism).[42] Yet "the problems entailed in adhering to one's values in every aspect of life" seemed intimidating at a personal level, let alone at the collective level of a new organization trying to define a shared path forward.[43]

This difficulty was compounded by the fact that the main models of activist scholarship available at the time in the United States—or rather the ones the CAS made reference to—were not really either useful or satisfactory. Noam Chomsky, Howard Zinn, and Staughton Lynd were among the few public intellectuals in recent U.S. history who were examples of personal activism, but they were also intellectuals whose main body of scholarship was critique, not conceptualization—or, in the case of Chomsky, whose main body of scholarship was separated from his political production. Their personal and professional experience could exemplify the tension between scholarship and politics, but, as we saw earlier, they had very little to say about it, at least in the terms that many within CCAS aspired to achieve. There were very few attempts by CCASers to directly deploy theoretical approaches to the issue of intellectuals' role in a revolutionary period. One of the few was Ed Hammond from the Berkeley chapter, who invited his fellow concerned scholars to adopt the role of Gramsci's organic intellectuals, establishing the cultural hegemony of the Left both within academia and "among the broad masses of the people." To be red and expert, "to learn from and serve the people" while also dealing with the highest academic circle was, Hammond argued, the distinctive mission of CCAS, its specific form of radical politics.[44] Yet the practical and theoretical contours of that mission remained very obscure. How could one unify the two sides while remaining within a university system, which, as Alain Geismar had denounced, was predicated on the dictatorship of knowledge, reproduced in schools that were firmly separated from life and inaccessible to the oppressed?[45]

In the end, the integration of the intellectual and the political in the life of the radical scholar required more than a simple cry for a more "contemporary" scholarship; it was "a quest for a new conception of academic life in which social and political actions have a legitimate role."[46] If so, that implied the obvious possibility that the two sides (activism and scholarship) could not be reconciled in the end—or that they should not, if the system remained unchanged. That is, it implied the real risk of curtailing one's life within academia: as poignantly put by an anonymous member of Berkeley CCAS, "by acting politically in accordance with our consciences, we may not survive in American academia, but if we surrender this principle we cannot survive as people."[47] This warning loomed over the discussion at the Cambridge seminar, with repeated calls to reject "the success-achievement theme."[48] Just before Chomsky's arrival at the meeting on July 29, 1968, Tom Engelhardt had presented the strongest position in dealing with this contradiction. He voiced the complete incommensurability of an academic career with the embrace of political radicalism, calling for "a group of people willing to forego acquisition of the Ph.D." He argued that a seemingly critical but academic activity like presenting a counter-course was in reality a direct attack to "the structure and organization (and supporting theory) of the university," and that this conflict could only produce a split, a crisis in one's life. In the end, abandoning the academe was the only possible solution for the radical intellectual.[49]

How to Be Scholarly

There is, however, a discordant and somewhat hollow note in Engelhardt's call to leave academia and forgo a PhD as the ultimate option for activist intellectuals: it was pronounced (by a white male in an Ivy League institution) precisely at the time when some of "the others," the previously excluded (Geismar's "oppressed"), specifically women and minorities, were entering academia—especially public universities—in much larger numbers and struggling to get their voices heard. This discordance and misrecognition is revelatory of a certain rigidity and blindness that marred the CAS's attempts to unify politics and scholarship and that eventually made dealing with that tension even more complicated.

Most people in CCAS wanted to be radicals *and* scholars, yet they were very continuously reminded by "people who are sitting in the professorial seat" of the "bleak future of any attempt to work within the academic structures." So they were presented with a choice: in the words of John Berninghausen, they either could get out, or, if academia was where they intended to make their bed, they could strive for "a real transformation of academic institutions, academic mores, the, uhh, point system, the, uhh, career goals, career expectations, the whole shmeer that we all live in if we're academically oriented." Radicals, that is, needed to seize control of the profession and its institutions, at least "enough control that you can break what's going on now."[50] Yet what seemed to go unnoticed in this discussion was that the transformation was happening already, with issues of gender and race entering the hallowed halls through the presence and actions of women and people of color. In this sense, CCAS's perspective on academia (and the possibilities of activism within it) was restricted by the perception of it as unchanging, at the exact time when it was changing.

The Concerned had been faced since their coming together with questions that had political, intellectual, and practical implications: what kind of scholars did they want to be, not just in terms of content but also of the mode and conditions of their production? And even more essentially, could they really pursue any form of radical endeavor in the institutional setting of U.S. academia and, if so, under what relationship with the rest of the field? These questions were already voiced, in blurred, conflicting, and inchoate ways, during the Cambridge seminar in 1968. The debate about the Concerned Scholars' role within the profession sounded very similar to the discussions on the relationship between teachers and students that were being waged, often in a very practical fashion, from Paris to Beijing, from New York to Berlin. The more moderate requests about "democratizing the profession" and investigating the administration of funding within Asian studies were often viewed as a limited and ultimately insufficient tactic for a group that wanted to become an alternative to the profession itself. And while they could not agree on whether the university should be fully under student control, the members in Cambridge seemed ready to abandon the old model where "old professors teach us what there is to know." Rather "the old folks need to be taught," Ed Friedman concluded,[51] echoing inadvertently one of the famous slogans of Paris '68: "Tout enseignant est enseigné. Tout enseigné est enseignant" (All those who teach are taught; all those who are taught teach).[52]

This was a tall order indeed, especially for a small group of young professors and graduate students whose entire careers rested within the very institutions that they wanted to fundamentally reshape. And the relationship between a radical stance and institutional environment was at the center of some of the most divisive confrontations within the organization. I mentioned the complex relation CCAS had with AAS in the previous chapter, but here I just want to highlight how it embodied the problematic coordination of scholarship and radicalism in the praxis of young academics. In October 1969, John Berninghausen voiced skepticism of the simple aspiration to just be "the radical caucus" of AAS, or even to supplant the current rightist elite of the Association with a new, younger "leftist elite." That would not change in any way what it meant to be an Asian scholar with a "unified human/intellectual/political existence." He also strongly condemned an attitude apparently common among some CCAS members of "getting out on the pond with a foot in each boat," taking "CCAS for politics, AAS for scholarship" or "CCAS for intellectual/political fun and games, AAS for career building."[53]

Yet the very split between politics and career that the radical scholars aimed at overcoming was instead easily reified precisely by stressing the institutional divide between the field (and its organizations) and the potential alternative presented by CCAS, especially when the Committee tried to impose or suggest policies and strategies that prevented collaboration with the "non-concerned." Marilyn Young, who was chastised in 1970 for her decision to deliver a paper at the AAS annual meeting, responded quite forcefully to the accusation of doing "their work" and argued instead that CCAS was actually reinforcing and solidifying the split in the life of the scholar: "I reject the notion that I do 'their' work when I talk to 'them' or that, in fact, my life is divided in the way the CCAS statement suggests," she averred. "I do not change what I say for anyone—CCAS or AAS—and somehow I find the suggestion that I (or anyone else for that matter) do insulting."[54] Affirming an unbreachable opposition between radical politics and establishment scholarship had the unwanted effect of preventing or obstructing ongoing efforts to practically change the dominant male, white, upper-class academic establishment.

This became a much more divisive issue between 1972 and 1974, when CCAS tried to enforce a boycott of JCCC (the Joint Committee on Contemporary China), and indirectly of some of the major funding organizations in the field (SSRC, the Ford Foundation). The decision of the boycott came after the *Bulletin* published its exposé of the structure and funding of the China field,[55] which had shown how, since 1959, control of the field had been taken "by groups primarily responsible to external interests such as the Ford Foundation, and various governmental agencies, whose mission is above all political service to an imperial power."[56] The CCAS requested that the funding of the field be put under AAS control and that documentation concerning JCCC's "secretive projects" be made public. Despite divisions and disagreements concerning the wisdom—and even the legitimacy—of the boycott, the policy was adopted in 1972 and upheld twice in 1973, but always by the small minority of members who attended the national convention or the summer retreat.[57] It is difficult to assess the advisability and the success of the boycott. It was introduced at a particularly bad time, when financial support of the field was being drastically reduced, and to voluntarily give up even the possibility of external funding was a major blow to the career and the research potential of any young scholar. The boycott tested the limits of the organizational cohesiveness of the Committee, which, as a poorly coordinated and dispersed organization, was not the best vehicle for what was essentially a "union-style" move. The tension over the boycott exploded in 1973, when Marilyn Young was kicked off the list of participants to the third CCAS trip to China (see chapter 3) because she had taken part in an SSRC-sponsored conference in Berkeley. Young recalled the incident with a certain amount of disdain for the modus operandi of the Committee: "They were behaving like fucking party functionaries," she quipped.[58] As for results, in 1974, JCCC agreed to have a three-member committee (Carl Riskin, Ezra Vogel, and Samuel Chu) look into its archives.[59]

Between the Establishment and the Movement

The questions brought forth by the JCCC boycott and the investigation on the founding of Asia studies were not simply organizational or practical, in the sense that they did not just highlight the limited ability of CCAS to require members' compliance or the contradictions between criticism and career. Rather, they involved the very possibilities of radical scholarship, the modes, locations, and content of alternative scholarly production, as well as its connection with and dependence on a larger political environment. In the end, the battles with AAS and the obstinacy of defending a tiny ethical turf against professional pressure would have been quite petty had they not been set in the context of a larger commitment to radical politics.

As an anonymous CCASer wrote, it was indeed necessary for these scholars to "question sources of funding, methodology, and decision-making,"[60] working at "purifying the profession."[61] But that was still an elitist approach to political action, replicating the elitism that pervaded "the very structure of our profession." The only way to overcome those limitations was to go outside the ivory towers and connect with the community at large;[62] the only way to escape the impotence of professional structures was to embrace social action. But, as a seemingly exasperated Felicia Oldfather asked, "what does that mean?"[63] Or, to put it in a slightly more verbose way, how could a scholarly group like CCAS shape the form, context, and content of its production to fit the needs of a political movement within and without the university?

These questions affected directly the main scholarly outlet of CCAS, the *Bulletin*, whose identity remained, in a sense, contested and open for many years (see chapter 4). The first decade of the BCAS was marked by a certain amount of ambivalence, not only about the kind of scholarship to be published, but also about the audience of the journal, the political strategies behind the choices of material, and its place in the profession and in the larger landscape. In 1970, in a letter to Al McCoy, Mark Selden, member of the *Bulletin* editorial board since its creation, stated the goals and commitment for the journal: "The Bulletin, like the overall CCAS program, must be committed to furthering the unity of our thought and action, of our scholarship and a (growing) political movement of which CCAS chapters and individuals (both as individuals and chapters) are an integral part, a movement that is committed to a fundamental social change in the United States, toward fundamental overhaul of our foreign policy, that is solidly anti-imperialist and is open to the revolutionary winds sweeping the world."[64]

Yet how to practically articulate an integral relationship with the larger movement from the perspective of what was, in the end, just a journal of young Asia scholars was clearly an extremely daunting task. Selden's own writings offer a sample of the struggle to find always-incomplete formulations of the role of the *Bulletin*. At times, he articulated something akin to Chomsky's interpretation. The scholar was essentially a social critic, Selden wrote to his fellow "concerned" in 1969; he noted that the main contribution of CCAS lay "pre-eminently in exposing the turgid underbelly of American Asian policy and developing an intellectually compelling critique of its ideology and scholarly underpinnings."[65] Besides being a position that had proven unsatisfactory to many CCASers since the inception of the group, this view left open the issue of the audience: to whom was the criticism of the young, radical Asia scholars addressed? Selden recognized the tension between existing as "the house organ for a tiny corps of specialists" and writing for a larger group of informed citizens and movement activists. Again, he cited Chomsky, Zinn, and Lynd as models, but he also implied that the very nature of the profession had to be transformed (was being transformed?) to bring these different roles closer together.[66] Yet the very potential of that transformation resided outside academia. It was only Vietnam and the antiwar movement that made CCAS's ideas "significant though not respectable," and in the absence of that movement, there was no doubt, Selden prophesized, that "CCAS would at best continue as an intellectual anachronism or more likely succumb to political and professional pressures leaving the field once again to the AAS."[67] So, the very existence of CCAS and BCAS, the very possibility of changing the conditions of scholarly production was predicated on the permanence of a larger (global but ill-defined) political movement. The Committee strove to find practical ways to integrate itself with this movement. Members were active in public lectures to nonacademic audiences, they wrote reviews of textbooks on Asia, they provided fact sheets on the main topics concerning contemporary Asia, and they worked on educating teachers about alternative perspectives on Vietnam and China.[68]

Yet these efforts, obviously, remained within the confines of a pedagogical role of the intellectual, and they did not prospect or configure a satisfyingly new relationship with global activism—as well as with the profession. By 1973, it seemed apparent that, as Jon Livingston remarked, CCAS was activist only in a very broad sense: they could not serve "the Movement" "in any direct means whatsoever," because they could not decide research priorities or issues to be covered.[69] Those decisions remained outside their control. In a sense, this perceived powerlessness can be viewed as the reflection of the "elitist" attitude that, according to some within the Committee, still framed the activism of CCAS. It was extremely difficult for a group of young scholars trained in the best universities in the country to envision (and, more importantly, to follow) strategies other than the control of the profession and its research priorities, or, at the opposite end of the spectrum, the dissemination of better information to the unenlightened masses.

Here it seems to me that CCAS's efforts and political contributions were limited precisely by their insistence on—and reification of—the separation between inside and outside academia, between scholarship and activism. Despite efforts to identify specific subjects and groups for possible collaboration, the CAS often seemed to evoke "the movement" (sometimes capitalized as "the Movement") as the amorphous signifier of "real" activism—something that sounded more like a state of mind than a set of actual organizations and political positions. This might be one of the reasons for their failure to think or recognize other models that, while still antagonistic to the academic establishment, potentially proposed a more complete integration of teaching, research, and politics. In the same years, intellectuals like Angela Davis and Kate Millet were, from their positions within academia, breaking the boundaries between scholarship and politics with modalities very different from—and one could argue more radical than—those of Howard Zinn and Chomsky.[70] Yet those coeval examples left no trace in the recorded debate within CCAS. In this sense, it seems to me that the conundrum of CCAS, which was often framed as the choice between career and activism, lay instead in the inability or impossibility to identify a proper space of political action for these intellectuals—a space that was not bound to an inside-outside binary perspective, that truly recognized the voice and practices of the "others" within and without academia, and that, in turn, allowed to theorize ways to be truly political as an academic. Of course, identifying that space was by no means an easy task, and as I show in the next few pages, failure was not because of lack of trying.

So, while the scholarly production of CCAS configured a crucial critical intervention in the field of Asian studies (see chapter 1), many of the Concerned continued to voice their discomfort for their collective inability to define precisely a mode of action and a set of theoretical foundations that would assure the position of the group both within "the movement" and vis-à-vis the profession. Without those foundations, the risk of a conservative drift remained looming, and the impact of the scholarship seemed confined to the level of surface criticism. As it was argued during a summer retreat in 1972, "if the Bulletin lacks theoretical depth, and tends toward 'interpretative journalism' does this cause an anomalous situation where people are activists in the streets but establishmentarians in the classroom?"[71]

These contradictions came violently to the fore in 1973–74. It was, as we will see later, a time of political "slump," when the waning of the antiwar movement posed more urgently the question of the goals, missions, and functions of CCAS "in a new and changing political and intellectual context." The "twin commitment to scholarship and political activism," Steve Andors remarked, was not so easily understood without the focal point of the Vietnam War.[72] Or, to put it in different words, what could be the scholarly production of a group of radical activists once a larger context for activism had dissipated?

In coincidence with this larger—possibly global—crisis of activism, CCAS was faced with what they perceived as a challenge to their role from within the profession. In 1973, Philip Huang and Edward Friedman (one of the early members of CCAS) proposed to Sage Publications a new academic journal, originally named *Contemporary China* but later to see the light as *Modern China*. The first proposal for the new journal started with a long, explicit reference to the experience and contributions of CCAS. After praising the *Bulletin* for having shown the interconnectedness of China scholarship with the policy assumptions of "the *now bygone Cold War era*," it lamented how the Committee's promises for a renewed intellectual production remained practically unfulfilled: "The Concerned Asian Scholars pointed the way toward new inquiries which would be more objective and more humanistic but *little substantial scholarship* has yet emerged from this new direction."[73]

This proposal—which had the added ironic touch of coming from a CCAS member—generated a huge debate, and the massive epistolary exchange was then partially published in a special supplement to the CCAS Newsletter in February 1974. In many ways, Huang and Friedman had struck a nerve, because there was already dissatisfaction among the Concerned with the quality and modes of their scholarship. Yet the reaction to the new journal was vehement, because Modern China presented itself explicitly as a place for "radical" essays that, however, could also be acceptable to the profession. In a long letter to Friedman, Steve Andors made clear that it was not just a question of competition or rivalry, but of the larger political implications that the new project conveyed. The creation of the new journal, Andors wrote, took "the power to define a 'legitimate radical' approach from 'irresponsible radical propaganda' out of the hands of radical intellectuals" and put it back "in the hands of those who already hold positions of organizational and ideological hegemony in our field, and in the social sciences generally." The new journal claimed a separation between legitimate scholars and the "activist-oriented," and defined legitimacy "as the categories of inquiries and elitist, non-activist modes of behavior of established tradition."[74] By so doing, it implicitly confined on the fringe of academia those who did not accept that definition of legitimacy, those who strove for a real combination of activism and scholarship. In short, those like many within CCAS.

The issue with Modern China, Andors continued, was that it represented a de facto retreat from what had been the project of the Concerned, that is, to change the functioning of the field, of the profession itself, the modes of intellectual production. And while, Andors conceded, there was indeed a distinction between "legitimate scholarship and trash," Modern China did not address the question of "who is defining that distinction, and what criteria and methods are used in the process."[75]

To Andors and others in CCAS, the creation of Modern China was in itself a conservative—or, literally, reactionary—move, because it represented a surrender *of* the praxis of combining scholarship and activism as well as a surrender *to* the field's requests (better footnotes, "serious scholarship," etc.).[76] And by using the Bulletin's name as a stepping-stone, the new enterprise presented itself as overcoming CCAS and implicitly proclaiming its futility. Nina Adams, one of the Southeast Asia specialists in CCAS, connected this move to a retrenchment in the profession, an attempt to "give young radical scholars struggling for tenure in Establishment institutions a more respectable outlet for their work."[77] It was therefore a concession to the requirements of the academic career. In the same vein, separating once again China from Asia implicitly brought back narrowness and specialization, in contradiction with CCAS's politically global perspective. For Adams, it was obvious to see in this case a reflection of another form of dissolution, one that mirrored the divisions within CCAS in the previous years. The Committee, she argued, "was to be an organization whose members tried to combine radical politics with scholarly endeavor in teaching, writing, and personal lifestyle. The aims of the organization included breaking down the artificial barriers between area studies and among disciplines. It hoped to bring the insights of anti-imperialist students into the conservative curricula of colleges and secondary schools, to introduce communities as well as colleges to the study of Asia in a humanistic radical way, and to provide an alternative written outlet for those whose work on Asia was unacceptable to the Establishment journals."[78]

Yet, she went on, the habits and requirements of scholarly production, the necessity of separating subfields and areas of expertise, continued to exercise a strong pull among some in the Committee, and that got exacerbated "in a period when the Movement is dying, CCAS is shrinking, and the overall American framework for radical scholarship is in trouble."[79] She questioned the advisability of separating the study of China from the study of Asia, but she noticed that that too was a trend within CCAS, where "we, and the Japan and South Asia people must take account of China while China types seem immune from curiosity about other areas."[80] In the end, the creation of a publication entirely devoted to the China niche, she wrote to Friedman, "a separate, supposedly 'academic,' journal is a logical outcome of this division of thinking. Do you honestly expect me to salute it?"[81]

What Are We?

The reestablishment of the forced separation between scholarship and activism—of which *Modern China* looked like the harbinger—appeared as a particularly dangerous retreat because it challenged one of the crucial elements that defined the politics of the long sixties, and one that was intimately connected with Maoism and the Cultural Revolution. To sympathetic eyes, the Cultural Revolution had identified in ideology the cause for the persistence of social inequalities, and in the minute gestures of the everyday the location where ideology subsisted, was reproduced, and could therefore be challenged, *in practice*. In her essay on French Maoism, Camille Robcis proposes a different interpretation of the infamous (and dismissive) accusation that the young French leftists had no knowledge of China and knew only the "China in their heads." Instead of naive ignorance, that motto could identify the call for a "revolution in ideology, a revolution in 'our heads,' the only revolution possible."[82] And, maybe, I would add, the one revolution necessary. For example, in a tract titled "We Hold the Power: Let's Change Life," the Gauche Prolétarienne contrasted the authoritarian practice of French school where the teacher speaks and the students listen to the nonauthoritarian example of the Cultural Revolution where "students and professors can mutually instruct each other." And the model of the Cultural Revolution was deployed for all possible areas of concern of the French Left, from feminism to education, from smoking to authority in general, but always in relation to a reinvented praxis.[83]

Similarly, in his critique of Althusser, Jacques Rancière identified the main blind spot of the Maoist group of Althusserian students in Rue d'Ulm in their dismissal of the concerns of French students ("the petty academic, financial or sexual grievances") as "that realm of illusion known in our discourse by the term *lived experience (le vécu)*."[84] And it was the irruption of the lived experience at the center of the political struggle in 1968—an irruption declined under the category of the "Cultural Revolution"—that made that position indefensible. To New Leftists all over the world, the "permanently mobilized Red Guard . . . seemed to embody the unity of politics and everyday life. . . . Creative reworkings of Maoism and the Chinese Cultural Revolution helped New Leftists understand culture as the site where the perpetuation of systematized oppression was enabled and where it could be opposed."[85]

Surprisingly, it was Althusser himself who provided one of the earliest descriptions of the relevance—for Marxists all over the world—of the Cultural Revolution specifically as a practical intervention that illuminates and produces theoretical knowledge about how ideology works. Modifying the old architectural metaphor of base and superstructure, Althusser argued that ideology works not like a floor or a roof in a building, but like cement itself: "The ideological seeps, in fact, into all the rooms of the building: in *individuals*' relation to all their practices, to all of their objects, in their relations to science, to technology, to the arts, in their relations to economic practice and political practice, into their 'personal' relations, etc. The ideological is what, in a society, *distinguishes and cements*, whether it be technical or class distinctions."[86] As such, the ideological is based on and informs objective social relationships, and therefore it does not only include systems of ideas, it is not confined to the level of "ideologies" in a strict sense, but it involves also a "system of practices of conduct-behavior."[87] If ideology regulates all the practices in a given society, the contribution of the Cultural Revolution was to reveal the ways in which this happened and to put into action multiple interventions that, by changing practices, aimed at radically transforming ideology.[88]

If one takes the challenge of a revolution in ideology seriously, then radical politics was not simply a question of new organization or new ideas. It had to do with reforming practices—sometimes minute, negligible, commonsense practices—that marked the reproduction of social roles, including that of the scholar, concerned or not. While CCASers continued to reaffirm "the legitimacy of a scholar being *both* a thinker *and* an actor" and indicted the ideology that lay "masked beneath a veneer of pseudo-objectivity,"[89] over the years they became more and more frustrated with their inability to produce alternative scholarly, institutional, and political praxes—to embed political change in lived experience. The Concerned Scholars did not approach this issue with the theoretical slant of the Althusserian group or the French Maoists, and they often struggled to clearly articulate the problems at hand. Yet the conundrum resonated in the very practical choices of their lives as scholars, actors, organizers, teachers, and students. And it is in this search that they formulated some of the most interesting (if ultimately unexplored) insights on the possibilities for new intellectual practices. This took the form of a question that resurfaced in members' correspondence, public statements, and declarations of intent: what are we?

The question was asked at different levels of intensity and elaboration over the years, but it was always a question about how to act politically and how to overcome the limitations imposed by the professional practices of the scholar.[90] For example, at Columbia University, during the 1970 antiwar strike, the faculty at the East Asia Institute expressed support for the notion that Asia scholars should direct their efforts within the profession. The call to professionalism, however, CCASers argued, sounded hollow when faced with the Columbia black students' position that pointed at "the connection between racist oppression at home against minority groups and abroad against the peoples of Asia," "between 'gooks' and 'niggers.'"[91] Professional practices were not only constraining but had become completely absurd, precisely because what was happening in Asia revealed the truth of a system of oppression and of social reproduction embedded in those very practices.[92]

Members of CCAS questioned their role and their position in different ways, first and foremost by calling their colleagues and comrades to merge with the larger movement outside the university. In the *Newsletter*, Joseph Esherick celebrated "China Week" in Ann Arbor, where scholars discussed the example of China with local activists, members of the White Panthers, and the League of Revolutionary Workers, and drew explicit connections between barefoot doctors and Black Panthers' clinics in the inner city.[93] In the end, being a scholar seemed to have become an obstacle to overcome in order to achieve real political involvement. As Orville Schell commented from a Berkeley shaken by the protests at People's Park, "many of us find it harder and harder to stay with the Ch'ing [Qing] Dynasty or the Communist movement in China when revolution seems to have come so close to our community and university."[94]

In other cases, the discomfort with institutionally inscribed practices led to a call for the adoption of a clearly defined (and narrowly meant) "ideology." The adoption of a radical "counter-ideology" was viewed as a way to counteract the decline of CCAS into a "liberal pressure group" within the profession, what one could call the ideological conformity of scholarly practices.[95] In 1973, members on the East and West Coasts were polled in a long survey that included one question about individual political self-definition (Are you a liberal? An anarchist? A Marxist?) and another about the political definition of the group itself and its relationship to research.[96]

The most interesting and most revealing contributions in this debate on the identity of CCAS addressed directly the issue of practices as shaped by and shaping ideological reproduction—as well as the inherent need to change them in order to revolutionize the social role of the scholar. Academic liberals, Steve Andors trenchantly commented, were not committed so much to an abstract ideology or to particular principle but "to the life of the academic liberal." It was in the name and through that commitment that they were prone to separate their job (their profession) from the political relationships that made that job possible. And that, in turn, had a political effect, as it made those relationships palatable.[97] In 1971, at their annual meeting, and facing the first retaliations of the profession toward the radicals, CCASers discussed whether they should "reform their lifestyle." This was a vague notion, but members suggested alternative practices, ranging from politicizing graduate seminars and refusing to write narrow papers to teaching outside the university and even "building our own university."[98]

Perhaps the best synthesis of the CCAS's conundrum concerning the necessity to change the practices, the everyday, the very life of the radical scholar in view of what was happening in Asia (and in the world) came from Orville Schell. In the January 1970 issue of the CCAS Newsletter, Schell published a lament on the condition of the Asia scholars, split between the study of revolutionary politics and the academic practices that denied the very meaning of those politics. "If one becomes a scholar of Asia," Schell wrote, "and if one has strong feelings and convictions about what has happened and is happening in Asia, one ends up with a severe case of schizophrenia; one's life becomes divided between two essential human functions, namely thinking and acting. . . . Rapidly the world divides into scholars (the researchers) and the actors (the political men). Each side deprives the other of an essential part of its being. Each accuses the other of being misled."[99] This was an impossible separation to sustain precisely because, over there, in the field of study of the Asia scholar, that division was being challenged by workers and peasants who allowed themselves the authority to work and think.

In *The Philosopher and His Poor*, Jacques Rancière identified in Plato's separation between the philosopher-king and the artisan the origin for the prohibition of thinking for those who work. Surprisingly, Schell too went back to Plato and twisted the myth of the philosopher-king into the new reality of the Maoist intellectual: "Learning and scholarship must join the world of activity, so that activists are scholars and scholars are activists. As Plato pointed out, only after philosophers are kings will there be justice. Only after the scholars are driven from their libraries into the streets and political life of the nation, will politics reflect sanity. . . . For the reality of a revolution is not always to be found in a library or a reprinted journal article. It is more often than not found in the experience of involvement. As Mao said, one must learn through doing."[100] "Maoism" and "China" here are the names given to the break in the structure of society and the disruption of the order of learning, which allowed not only for the right of the workers to philosophize, but required the philosopher to do, to act, to change, through practice, their own self-conception.

Schell concluded his essay with a dire forecast. If the breach between studying and living is not compounded, he foretold, then we will lose the finest members of academia, and worst of all, the pointless division in the lives of scholars will continue. "Universities will become the refuge of those who escape from reality and real knowledge into the world of theory and magnificent irrelevance. And finally, Asian scholars will have no alternative but to sit in their offices studying the second hand shadows of revolutions that others make."[101]

The Cultural Revolution had shown that it was impossible to be an intellectual in one's office or classroom and an activist in the streets: politics had to permeate and alter the very fabric of daily life, the structure of the professions, the framing of one's intellectual activity. It was in this particular aspect (the inseparability of politics from culture) that the example of the Cultural Revolution resonated deeply within the experience of the CCAS. The debates and discussions within CCAS, their continuous wrangling over the different requirements and temporalities of cultural production and political activism, and even the organizational tensions that fractured the Committee show the enormous difficulties implicit in the particular position that these young scholars had taken. Rebecca Karl has suggested that central to the (failed) project of the Cultural Revolution was "the attempt to reconcile and bring coherence to the asymmetries between and within politics and culture, understood in their revolutionary forms as mass activity transformed into and actualized through individuals' everyday life."[102] In other words, the Cultural Revolution represented the attempt to actualize in the now of the transformed everyday (in the breaking of boundaries between the manual and the intellectual, the scholarly and the practical) the political promises of the future, always displaced by a lagging cultural change. From this perspective, then, the difficulties and divisions within CCAS reflect their commitment (and ultimate failure) to make the issue at the center of the

Cultural Revolution a principle of everyday practice. In that, they reflect a much more complex understanding of the role of Maoist China for the global activism of the 1960s and 1970s, a role that goes way beyond the promise of a Communist Shangri-La.

Back to the Classroom?

By 1973, the separation that, following Schell, condemned the China scholar to a life of schizophrenia did not seem to be on the mend; quite the contrary. Or rather the division between the intellectual and the actor seemed to have shifted from one within each individual's soul to one between different members within the Committee. This shift was probably related to two external factors: the pull of professionalism and career on the one hand, and the waning of the larger antiwar and radical movement on the other. In any case, by 1973 the split was evident, even if it was assessed differently, and with different degrees of angst.

John Berninghausen, while recognizing that the organization contained individuals whose focus was only on the professional side and others who worked exclusively on projects that related to popular or movement action—rather than people who wanted and could work in both areas—accepted it as a distinctive and positive characteristic of CCAS.[103] On the other end of the spectrum, Jon Livingston reacted with unmitigated fury to the debate hosted in the *Newsletter* (a "pile of shit," in Livingston's words) over the nature of CCAS in light of the China trips and the JCCC boycott.[104] He was appalled by the contention, voiced by some fellow Concerned Scholars, that CCAS was not a "political group." Livingston was adamant on the explicitly and essentially political mission of CCAS since its founding in 1968. "If things have gotten to the point where the word 'political' has bad connotations," Livingston concluded, "perhaps CCAS should sink back to the muck of imbecility of Asian Studies from which it miraculously came. Anybody who finds politics hard to take makes me queasy and I have better things to do with my time than hold their hands. End of sermon."[105] Yet, despite Livingston's exasperation, a certain uneasiness toward politics, or at least different definitions of the political, had existed since the very foundation of CCAS, as we have seen. It was, in the words of Nina Adams, a divergence "between those who value radical scholarship as scholarship, with all appurtenances and without nontraditional personal styles, and those whose definition of radical scholarship comprises personal change, personal political involvement and a desire to innovate in more than written hypotheses."[106] The latter, those who believed that change came in the form of lived practices and who had searched for those practices, found themselves orphans of a movement to serve, and, in that situation, the reductive seduction of radicalism as scholarship became more difficult to resist.

In the face of a political movement that was not moving anymore, when "the great sense of urgency that made people neglect their papers, classes, jobs and families to ACT on the war" was fading fast, the logical choice for the survival of the organization was to "make CCAS more relevant to scholars."[107] If one accepted the fracture between scholarship and politics, then, Chris [White?], another CCAS member, argued, there were plenty of respectable venues for scholarly production (like the *Journal of Asian Studies*) as well as sources for leftist engagements (*Monthly Review, Ramparts*); the middle position occupied by CCAS and the *Bulletin* seemed useless. In the end, she objected, it was time to go back to catering to Asian scholars as scholars: "One gets the impression from the newsletter sometimes that 'scholars' is a dirty word, that being an Asian scholar is an illegitimate occupation, and that only by engaging in political activity *other than* leftist scholarship can one attone [sic] for the sin of being a 'scholar'; and that only by giving money to 'real' movement causes such as the GI movement can CCAS attone [sic] for the sin of being an organization of Asian scholars."[108]

The recognition of a political lack of focus, of a dissolution became clearer with the passing months. This was in part a reflection of events that had taken place in Asia: the end of the Vietnam War and the normalization of the relationship with China meant that the two focal sources of political inspiration had become much less accessible, and a vague call for anti-imperialism was a poor substitute.[109] What, then, was left? In 1974, Andrea Faste, pondering on the need to disband the national structure of CCAS, provided a somber but accurate description

> Perhaps we should look realistically at what CCAS has become. It has become to most of us a state of mind, a radical perspective towards our scholarly work, a sensitivity toward the activism of others (but how many of us are boldly involved with that activism?) and a feeling that somehow there are likeminded people in the profession around the world . . . ok, what do we do with this cerebral condition?[110]

By that time, there was also a shared assessment that "professionalization" had won. Carl Jacobson, editor of the *Newsletter*, wrote a frank and quite gloomy description of the situation in 1974. The end of the war and the rapprochement with China had coincided with many CCASers becoming "junior professors or aspirants to such position," which had altered the focus of the organization and had increased professional pressure. Jacobson added the poignant detail of the Boston annual conference "where conversations were cut short by scrambles for the attention of senior AAS people." The Committee of Concerned Asian Scholars had become a "shred of an organization," one in which the only shared activity was writing. Perhaps, Jacobson concluded dourly, "we don't need an organization—we need a publisher."[111] With the end of outward political involvement, it was easy for scholars to backslide into activities strictly confined to the classroom and the office; the requirements of "professionalism" had triumphed and CCAS seemed to have reverted to the "the same academic workstyles and habits" they earlier abhorred in conservative colleagues.[112]

The last years of CCAS's existence were occupied with the same questions, the same dissatisfaction with the existing situation, and a similar admission of defeat. Throughout 1976, some among the younger CCAS members continued to ask themselves and each other how to combine "theory and practice"; they kept contending that it was vacuous and impossible to make a revolution only in the realm of ideas; they highlighted again and again the inherent limitations of classroom teaching and learning; they interrogated the "old-timers" in CCAS on their own ability—or rather, their continued struggle—to be, at the same time, scholars and activists.[113] But the questions remained unanswered, and these attempts to revive the debate produced no significant result.

In 1977, the CCAS *Newsletter* issued one last call to arms before the annual convention, focusing the members' attention once again on the issues of organizational isolation, separation of intellectual and political life, and the pull of academia. The assessment of the current situation was dire:

> CCAS is approaching dangerously close to the point of becoming a new establishment—a settled, disunified organization of *scholars* (as our name implies) *not* founded upon struggle and change; *not* serving

as the powerful unified force it has the potential to be; *not* speaking to the American people but speaking among ourselves. As the *scholars* we designate ourselves to be today (and I admit I dislike the word), we are forgetting that we do not own the knowledge we seek in our daily work. Every minute of our research will serve its purpose *only* if applied in practice—that is, to bring about goals that, as of now, are poorly defined in our statement of purpose.[114]

"Due to the changing political situation nationally and world-wide," the Concerned Scholars had progressively gone back to being just scholars confined to "progressive teaching and research."[115] They did not need to be just that, the CCAS coordinators argued, and once again they justified their call to activism within and without academia on the basis of Asian models: "Are we going to take the opportunities offered us (to educate Americans in their imperial present) by the Koreans, Thais, Indians, Malaysians, Filipinos and Taiwanese in their fight to emerge from a decadent reactionary past? And by the Chinese, Indochinese, and Koreans in their drive for a socialist future?"[116] Yet, one cannot escape the feeling that, in 1977, the power of those examples had been hollowed out.

The last issue of the *CCAS Newsletter* (May 1979) hosted a short piece by Bryant Avery, highlighting the fight against overspecialization as one of the central themes of the now defunct CCAS. Interestingly, Avery, writing at the end of the turbulent decade-long experience of the Committee, reverted again to the example of Noam Chomsky, who, as a scholar of linguistics, had continued to write widely about matters of politics and empire, transgressing geographical and disciplinary limitations. "He presents us with a clear living lesson," Avery contended: "Don't let the bastards ever tell you, a student of Japan or India, that you can't understand what's happening in Thailand or Korea."[117] Yet, if in the end one does not need to be a student of a specific region or discipline to produce politically based scholarship in that area, what need was there for Asia Scholars, concerned or not? And perhaps even more importantly, what was left of the huge effort to combine scholarship and activism, to heal the fracture at the center of academic life?

The experience of CCAS—and of other organizations—shows that one of the crucial elements of politicization in the long sixties had to do with the recognition of the voice and practices of the people. Leaving aside the issue of whether subalterns can speak, one of the central challenges of this period came from the assumption—misguided or not—that they could, and that they were actually speaking and acting: in movements for decolonization and race equality, wars of liberation, peasant rebellions, and, most evidently, in the experiments of the Cultural Revolution. The case of CCAS, I have argued, shows that that assumption, that recognition had consequences in terms of political and intellectual praxis, in a feverish effort to inscribe—in the lives and production of the radical scholars—the consequences of that recognition. The fact that it was an inconclusive search, that it was probably based on a limited understanding of the Asian examples, and that roles were fully reestablished and the position of academia renormalized does not diminish its value.

CHAPTER THREE

SEEING AND UNDERSTANDING

China as the Place of Desire

I feel that I won't be able to shed light on them in the least—just shed light on us by means of them. So, what needs to be written isn't *So, what about China?*, but *So, what about France?*
—**Roland Barthes,** *Travels in China*

That first visit left an indelible stamp on each of us in the course of lives substantially devoted to writing about China. Indelible . . . but in multiple and diverse ways, including not only our perceptions of China, but also of America.
—**Mark Selden, "Understanding China and Ourselves"**

While China was crucial in defining the intellectual issues and the specific forms of activism within CCAS, it also continuously presented an implicit paradox, an unresolved tension that agitated the individual paths of the China specialists and the collective enterprise of the Asia scholars/activists. For China specialists in the United States, China was an object of study, a vocation, and probably, to a certain extent, a "career." For many China scholars within CCAS, the People's Republic of China was also a subject of politics and a potential inspiration for action and thinking. Yet for all, China's contemporary existence remained physically unreachable. Although they wrote extensively about the PRC, restraints imposed by the Cold War meant that U.S. China scholars had no realistic chance of ever crossing its borders. This intellectual, political, and psychological conundrum was described in a short, humorous text, "The China Scholar as a Legume," published in the April 1973 issue of the CCAS *Newsletter*.

> In Laymens [sic] terms schizofrenia [sic] can be defined as a type of psychosis characterized by a loss of contact with the environment, with the here and now. What better way to describe a China scholar, lost as he is in a fiction, a dream which bears no fruit in the Americo-Nightmare machine. We all know that true knowledge can only be gotten via experience, thru practice (see Mao). But where does his knowledge come from. Intuition, history, politics and all that, but no experience—there is no true carnality in his existence. He is imprisoned then, lost in a false world of kung-fu movies and take out noodle shops where the help only speak Cantonese. He lives in the Middle Kingdom between his ears, a dreamer with an empire to manipulate, but an empire of smoke and kingdom of phantoms—all second or third rate reality—he must be a madman . . . too bad.[1]

Not all CCASers took this little jab at the crucial conundrum of the profession with humor; Vivienne Shue wrote a curt and sharp rejoinder in the *Newsletter*, chastising the piece as "unsubstantiated rhetoric."[2] The issue of China's very practical elusiveness clearly touched some raw nerves, and that was especially the case within CCAS, which in 1973 was still being ravaged by a two-year-long debate about real and potential trips to China. They had all lived "in the Middle Kingdom between their ears" until the summer of 1971, when a delegation of Concerned Scholars studying in Hong Kong had been invited to visit the PRC, the first trip of this kind for a U.S. scholarly organization. The elation, the sense of liberation, the excitement of finally, if briefly, overcoming the separation between "us" and "China" transpires in the first line of the instant book CCAS published to recount the experience of the trip: "We are Americans. We too have been shut off from China for most of our lives . . . until this summer, 1971."[3] The trip was justifiably heralded by some members as a major event, one that could possibly make CCAS—*because of its political leanings*—the central conduit for exchanges with China. A second, larger delegation visited China the following year, and one more trip was being planned for 1973.

The Nixon rapprochement quashed these dreams of grandeur, and the third trip never saw fruition. Yet the planning of the visits and especially the selection of who, among CCAS members, should be given "the honor" of visiting China divided the group and sparked major internal fights.[4] An enormous amount of time and energy, as well as personal and political angst, was devoted to this issue, so much so that many members complained of what they perceived as an exclusive focus on China to the detriment of the antiwar movement and the other areas of concern. The China trips, then, stood at the intersection of scholarly need, political passion, international diplomacy, and the very meaning of the organization at a time when the balance of Cold War diplomacy was shifting. The simple possibility of going to China put the CAS in a unsolvable bind: the emotional need to see the land they had studied and the political system they had supported conflicted with the risk of damaging their long-term political efforts. In all these ways the China trips uncovered some of the hidden contradictions and tensions within the group: between being antiwar and embracing socialism, between individual pursuit and collective loyalty, between oriental elusiveness and subjective proximity, between foreign relations and organizational choices, and between scholarly knowledge and political understanding.

This chapter analyzes these contradictions and the role that the China trips played in the evolution (and devolution) of CCAS, in part through a comparison with trips by other fellow travelers. But first I think it is necessary to address the recent resurfacing of the memories and personal narratives associated with the first encounter with "real China" by a generation of radical scholars. This was spurred in part by Richard Bernstein's farewell article as the China correspondent for the *New York Times*, in which he identified the first twenty-four hours of his visit to China as part of the 1972 CCAS delegation as the turning point in his political formation, the moment that changed him from a Mao sympathizer into "a lifelong anti-communist and devotee of liberal democracy."[5] Bernstein's recollection was followed by those of other former CCASers, who joined him down the memory lane of crushed hopes, crafted coherence, and acceptable revisionism with various degrees of conviction and enthusiasm. These short pieces were published first in an online Hong Kong magazine and then collected in a slim volume, *My First Trip to China*.[6] I have no intention or desire to look at these stories for the psychological insights they could offer (China as the return of the repressed?),[7] nor do I want to challenge the truthfulness or even the verisimilitude of these recollections. Rather I believe that the distances and differences among these accounts echo and reproduce issues and contradictions that existed forty years ago and that marked the very experience of visiting Maoist China, not just for CCASers but also for scholars, scientists, intellectuals, and politicians from other parts of the world. In the end, I would argue, behind the conflicting recollections of today lies the same question posited on the back cover of CCAS's first enthusiastic eyewitness report: "What is 'China?' Can it be understood?"[8]

In this sense, the CCAS China trips—as well as the whole phenomenon of the "pilgrimage to China"—are interesting beyond what they meant for the organization's future. They are a specific instance of larger and deeper tensions, between the desire for factual certainty and impossibility of true knowledge, between what an event can mean to people in different circumstances and to what it "actually" is, between what we share politically and what we understand intellectually. And perhaps they also remind us of what is lost when those tensions evaporate. Or, rather, when they are viewed as having been resolved.

Swann and a Chinese Odette

In his introduction to *My First Trip to China*, Orville Schell, a former CCASer, deploys religious and romantic metaphors to explain the attraction China's "exciting but elusive revolution" exercised over his generation. Young American students marooned in Hong Kong or Taiwan were like "Jews exiled from the promised land," and the few who got there resembled "Western pilgrims who made odysseys to China when it was still a world apart."[9] But perhaps Schell's most revealing and noteworthy analogy is a literary one. The attraction of China had nothing to do with the politics of "Mao's madcap experiment," but was due to China's own seclusion, its disinterests toward the ardent admirers. "We were, in a sense," Schell contends, "a group of forlorn Swanns in love. And, like Marcel Proust's anti-hero's unrequited passion for Odette, our infatuation with China was only made more ardent by the hopelessness of any possibility of attention, much less consummation."[10]

I will go back to the Proustian (and gendered) reference invoked by Schell later, but—while I obviously don't agree with him that Maoism was irrelevant—it is indeed difficult to ignore the tones of religious conversion, of sudden enlightenment, or even of love betrayed that permeate some of the accounts by former CCAsers. Perry Link describes his first trip as a voyage of discovery, in which the reality of conformity, brainwashing, and inequality was quickly revealed.[11] Jonathan Mirsky's story echoes Bernstein's "Paul on the way to Damascus" parable, one in which the blindness of the leftist visitor was miraculously lifted by a chance meeting with a Canton resident—"the bravest man in China"—who had the courage to tell the author that he was being shown only a facade and that theft and poverty were still present in Mao's socialist paradise.[12] Mirsky's reaction took the form of an immediate reversal of judgment. Allegedly, he went so far as to plead with his fellow travelers to let him leave China a week earlier than planned,[13] a reaction that is somewhat difficult to understand from somebody who had devoted all his life to the study of that very place, but one that gives the measure of the enormity of the perceived betrayal and disillusionment, as well as of the fragility of what can only be described as an idealized passion.

Mark Selden was part of the same 1972 CCAS delegation, but his assessment of that experience and of the value of those visits has been very distant from Mirsky's and has earned the latter's unabashed scorn.[14] In his recollection, Selden tries to detach himself from the game of sanitized memory and narrative neatness that other accounts indulge in, and he attempts instead to recover a different aspect of those experiences, one as crucial at the time as it is today: the position of "China" within the global experience of the sixties. Realizing that China was poor and that, as Bernstein plainly stated, "we were better" was not a great discovery, particularly in light of the efforts that CCAS had made in the previous years precisely "to understand other countries in light not only of their own history and culture, but also of the workings of global power."[15] "Reading these accounts," Selden continues, "which rightly remind us of the need to exercise independent judgment when visiting another country, I discern little of the kind of critical thinking that animated some of our work at that time that was preoccupied with the American exercise of global power that impinged on China and others and that led to ways of *thinking not only about China but equally about ourselves*, that is, about the U.S.-China relationship."[16] In his approach, Selden is probably closer to what participants to the 1971 trip stated at the time: "The questions we carried with us into China reflected our American concerns."[17] It was not just simply a question of visiting the Promised Land—and finding it sorely lacking of pleasurable amenities—rather "China," even when seen with one's own eyes and traveled upon on one's own feet, was part of the larger political framework and the larger set of issues (U.S. foreign policy, the war, but also the self-definition of the intellectual, and the connection between activism and politics, to name a few) that had been fundamental in shaping the gaze of the concerned visitors and that should remain central, according to Selden, in their assessment.

The sharp—and still acutely felt—differences between Mirsky and Selden point at different ways of making sense of the massive shift in political perspective that came by the middle and late 1970s, when both Maoist China and the global movements of the sixties disappeared as inspiration and framework for action. In relation to that truly global shift, it is convenient if one can pinpoint a moment of personal enlightenment that predates the collapse or if one can build for oneself a coherent political evolution in a more nuanced way. But these diverging accounts also, and perhaps more significantly, highlight a question that was central at the time and that, at least to me, still remains fundamental: how do we know a revolutionary society, and, specifically, how do we know Maoist China?

"Comment connaissons-nous la Chine?" was the title of a roundtable organized in 1972 by the French magazine *Esprit*. Five China scholars—"sinologues" was the term used—gathered to discuss precisely what kind of knowledge of China was available to the French public but also how China could be known by the experts themselves, through texts, contacts, and visits. The French did not suffer from the same heavy restrictions that the Cold War imposed on the U.S. scholars. Like other Europeans, they could spend longer periods in China and study in Chinese universities. Trips to the PRC, while complicated, were not such a rare event.[18] Yet these French sinologists were arguing about the same problem that plagued the U.S. scholars: the extent and the very possibility of any knowledge of contemporary China. And the divisions were as severe as on the other side of the Atlantic. Lucien Bianco, who also contributed his account of a recent trip to China, aptly titled "Voyage in a Glass," vented his frustration on the uselessness of any visit to the PRC: "In China, one does not glean anything but impressions, which are by nature subjective and debatable. One does not learn anything, one does not add anything to what was already known and catalogued: we all see more or less the same things and we repeat them *ad nauseam*."[19] There was nothing new to learn in China about China, because everything was staged, rehearsed, and repeated, Bianco contended. Marianne Bastid, on the other side of the issue, replied that there was indeed much to learn, for example, by looking at the Chinese press within its own logic of production, trying to understand that it was addressing a Chinese audience who could read between the lines and knew the context. It was in order to understand something of that unspoken context that Bastid also stressed the value of visits to China: "I believe however that a sojourn in China — especially if one speaks Chinese and they are allowed to stay for a while — allows us to appreciate, to feel the reality of which the newspapers speak often in an arbitrary or elliptic fashion, just because the Chinese are well aware and understand immediately."[20]

To be sure, Bianco and Bastid were separated not simply by their respective epistemological approaches but also by their varying degree of sympathy toward the Maoist revolutionary experiments. Politics influenced and framed the debate, which took place at a moment in which knowledge of and discourse on China had been appropriated by actors with no sinological background, including all the Maoist sympathizers who had visited the PRC and written about it. The volume in which the French Sinologists' debate was later published in 1976 was framed precisely as an "expert" reaction to the "ravings" of French intellectuals, and the China scholars singled out in their disapproval the Italian Communist Maria-Antonietta Macciocchi and the *Tel Quel* group.[21] In this sense, too, the French discussion signals that the issues concerned in understanding Maoist China were not so much or not primarily scholarly, they were political. And political in very specific ways.

It is not my intention to discount here the relevance of the subjective experience of revelation, of discovery, or of the first encounter with "really existing" China, but precisely because it was so personal, the psychology of that experience seems largely unrecoverable to me. Rather I would like to point at more general and shared issues that underpin the shifting understanding of what was knowable and true about China. Yes, China was, for the Concerned Asian Scholar and other travelers, an object of desire, elusive and repeatedly denied — an almost hopelessly unrequited love. And, like all objects of our affection, it was misconstrued and misinterpreted, maybe more so and more willfully than in other cases, in part because China presented itself as providing an alternative to the existent. The Chinese hosts, for their part, encouraged some of the misconstructions, and the visits prominently featured Potemkin villages, whose suspiciously utopian character was often glossed over by the enamored visitors. All of this is by now well known and almost banal. Yet the claim to a suddenly revealed new truth is as suspicious as the enraptured gaze that preceded it. What seems more important to me is what actually determines or frames the shift, and that is something that does not happen only or primarily at the personal level.

Even Paul Hollander, who has devoted years and tons of ink to debunking the illusions of leftist "fellow travelers," has argued that the dramatic political turn in the immediate post-Mao era was not due to "a wealth of new information," but to a switch in the political posture that allowed for the already available information to be seen in a new light.[22] In the same way, the long and complicated evolution of the historiography of Maoism and the Cultural Revolution from the 1960s to today is only partially connected to the discovery of new archives and of more "truthful" sources of information.[23]

In this sense, the kind of memory production displayed in *My First Trip to China* conveys only a partial reality, because it juxtaposes the "I" of today with the subject of forty years earlier. What can be achieved there is either a strident contrast or a massive flattening of differences, and, in both cases, the loss of the historical contingencies and context. Lucien Bianco, in one of his contributions to the 1972 debate, maintained that any statement about China should be assessed on the basis of its relevance to the problems of China and the Chinese, and not to "our problems," not even under the pretense of universality. Bianco dismissed any connection, for example, between May 1968 and the Cultural Revolution, which were, in his opinion, coeval events of a completely different nature. Works that looked at China for inspiration on how to solve "our" (or global) contradictions, Bianco went on, should simply be ignored.[24] Macciocchi, who was asked by *Esprit* to respond to the criticism of the French professors, provided a trenchant rejoinder that highlights the limitation of this scholarly view. First, she hurled a nice jab at the orientalism of the French scholars (remarkable because it comes before Said): "In the particular case of French sinologists, I am surprised to find out that they haven't yet taken the trouble to analyze and understand the end of their old role, which was, traditionally, to exert from the West a kind of cultural hegemony over China, modeled on those vaguely 'ideological' forms of neo-colonialism, through which the imperialist conquest of undeveloped market is achieved."[25]

To this kind of *savoir*, imbricated within a specific form of power, Macciocchi opposed, perhaps naively, a form of knowledge that is "concretely revolutionary," capable of combining theory and practice. And she cited another China historian, Jean Chesneaux, political militant as well as a scholar, who had praised her book precisely because it was not done in a scholarly way (no bibliography, no archives, etc.). "This book," Chesneaux had written, "is a contribution to the movement, which the author was able to write because she is herself already involved in the action. . . . Her practical experience of militancy was a precondition to know China."[26] The political connection, the shared global militancy—that is, the very a priori that Bianco assumed was obscuring the actual understanding of true "facts"—was instead essential for understanding China in those specific historical circumstances. What gets lost in many personal recollections as well as in the strictly scholarly debate is that, in the specific conditions in which the CCAS and other trips to the PRC took place, knowledge of revolutionary China was framed and perceived as a different enterprise, one that could and should not be restricted to an assessment of concrete, factual truths (largely unachievable even in the best of circumstances). Rather it was based on the idea of a shared project, a potential consonance of intents, if not of results. "What could we learn about China during an officially sponsored and organized trip?" Mark Selden asked. "Not surprisingly, we learned a good deal about the issues that preoccupied the Chinese party-state, our hosts, both directly and indirectly."[27] Even a Potemkin village, in this sense, could display the aspirations of the Chinese leaders, the dream of a possible society; in that dream, the visitors could recognize a mirror of their own political preoccupations, which might have to do with global U.S. power, the life of intellectuals, eradication of poverty, or student rebellion. There was no understanding of a revolution—and there never is, past or present—without the acknowledgment of one's subjective position vis-à-vis its potential meanings.

In this, yes, Schell is right—the approach of the young Concerned

Scholars to the revolution was very much like the misrecognition of the object of love, and one that does not seem possible once love is past. We should take Schell's gendered simile seriously. Odette, in the beginning of Proust's novel, becomes truly attractive to Swann only when he identifies her with a figure in a beloved Botticelli painting, that is, when the very active and flawed real woman can be idealized as the passive representation of a mythical feminine beauty. And while, as I have shown so far, the CAS strove to construe the Chinese as active political subjects, they were nonetheless the inheritors of a long history of American orientalism, in which "China" had been constantly figured in terms of passivity and inscrutability: China had been, in the end, America's to "lose." It is difficult not to see in the very abrupt about-face of *some* concerned scholars—exemplified by Mirsky's realization that he had been wrong on everything based on the testimony of a single "native informant"—the lingering traces of an orientalist perspective: China could be loved from a distance as an idealized but ultimately inscrutable whole, just to be abandoned when a closer look showed "her" imperfections, like an elegantly clad foot-bound woman whose deformity, once nakedly revealed, could provoke only absolute disgust. The complete—and literally overnight—shift from all-absorbing passion to absolute disillusion can be explained only once the relationship at stake is not the confrontation with a multitude of complex autonomous political subjects but is reduced again to a gendered object of desire. This tension between orientalist lingering and shared political subjectivity will resurface in the debates I describe in the following pages.

However, we should also push Schell's Proustian reference to its narrative end: Swann did marry Odette. He married her even though he did not love her anymore, and she continued to betray him (and others after him). And, in the last volume of *In Search of Lost Time*, it is the surprisingly youthful appearance of Odette among the spectacle of all the aging characters convened at a party and the remembrance of Swann's love for her that shock the narrator and force him into a reflection on memory and time. The shock is produced by memory, because memory by itself, "when it introduces the past, unmodified, into the present—the past just as it was at the moment when it was itself the present—suppresses the mighty dimension of Time which is the dimension in which life is lived."[28] Here lies the task Proust poses for himself, to reconquer Time through the power of memory, by placing the past of our feelings, of our relations, as it were, into the present. And not, one is tempted to add, by placing the present of our circumstances into the past. Proust writes, "At every moment of our lives we are surrounded by things and people which once were endowed with a rich emotional significance that they no longer possess. But let us cease to make use of them in an unconscious way, let us try to recall what they once were in our eyes, and how often do we not find that a thing later transformed into, as it were, mere raw material for our industrial use was once alive, and alive for us with a personal life of its own."[29]

Proust, in the novel, decides to recount Swann's love for Odette as it was at the time—no matter how undeserving he will find her later as a wife, a mother, a woman. I propose similarly—although with absolutely no literary aspiration—to try to see how young scholar-activists viewed, lived, and made sense of their opportunity to visit China at the time, in their specific political, historical, and intellectual circumstances. That is, as Sigrid Schmalzer has argued, to see their writings and their actions as speaking to different kinds of political truths, "the political truths of the Mao era in China and the Vietnam War in the United States."[30] This gives us a partial but significant perspective on some of the global connections that framed the long sixties, on the history of our understanding of China, and even on what China wanted to be understood of its own revolutionary experiments. More broadly, this poses crucial questions about the always unresolved connections between seeing and understanding, personal experience and scholarly authority, politics and knowledge production. By looking at how we knew and spoke about China at the time, this chapter asks indirectly how we can know and speak about China (or any other place) in general.

From China, with Issues

News of an upcoming CCAS trip to China reached the national representatives in early 1971; it was a surprise, an exciting yet shocking development. Committee members who were studying in Hong Kong had organized the trip without any support and any consultation with the national coordinators. In a letter dated June 9, they described the planning, which had taken shape since February through contacts with the "patriotic left" in Hong Kong, leading to proposals for a trip, informal acceptance, and a final formal invitation on June 7. The trip was to last a month, from June 23 to July 23.[31]

FIGURE 3.1 1971 CCAS delegation (CCAS Archives, Wisconsin Historical Society). The Chinese reads "Long live the friendship of the Chinese and American people." Back row, L to R: Paul Pickowicz, Judy Woodward, Uldis Kruze, Ken Levin. Middle row, L to R: Jean Garavente, Tony Garavente, Rhea Whitehead, Kim Woodward. Front row, L to R: Ray Whitehead, Paul Levine, Ann Kruze, Susan Shirk, Kay Johnson.

The CCAS trip had materialized through a fortuitous set of coincidences. Paul Pickowicz, then a graduate student at the University of Wisconsin working on his doctoral research at the Universities Service Center in Hong Kong, had befriended Lee Tsung-ying, the editor of the English-language, pro-China magazine *Eastern Horizon*. When Pickowicz broached the idea of a group trip to China for the students at USC, Lee apparently suggested they send their application to a mass organization, the *Zhonghuo renmin duiwai youhao xiehui* (The Chinese People's Association for Friendship with Foreign Countries). Nothing happened for months, but the process seemed to speed up exponentially at the time when the U.S. ping-pong delegation was invited to China.[32] Then, one day, all of a sudden Lee Tsung-ying announced that the application was under serious consideration, and soon afterward that it had been approved.[33]

Because of the delicate nature of the discussion and of specific instructions from the Chinese contacts in Hong Kong, these preliminary stages were kept secret and the national CCAS was presented with a fait accompli. It was a very pleasant surprise, but one over which they had no control. The June 9 letter presents what is essentially a series of requests from the Hong Kong chapter to the national CCAS, and there seems to be no opening for any consultation on the character of the trip, its goals, and even the means by which it should be advertised. The Hong Kong CCAS asked the national coordinators for money, the loan of a camera, and CCAS literature to give to the Chinese hosts. They requested that a press release be issued only on the day of their formal entrance to China (June 23), and they stated their decision not to publish individually during or after the trip. When they would do it, collectively, they would privilege "progressive" journals and news services. Perhaps even more significantly, the thirteen participants in this long-awaited trip had not been selected on the basis of activism, history within CCAS, or specific qualities. Many of them do not appear to have been really active within the organization before the trip (nor to have become active afterward), and this became the source of a certain amount of acrimony, in the United States and in Hong Kong. On the day after their return to Hong Kong, John Berninghausen wrote to the coordinators and mentioned in passing how burnt-out (and a bit resentful) Gordon White, a CCAS member from Stanford then stationed in the British colony, was: "It's real commitment when you bust your ass for the people who did get to go when you yourself didn't (and there's always the nagging issue for the activists, proven activists, about the non-proven ones who went)."[34]

The Hong Kong chapter also unilaterally made a decision that would have surprisingly momentous consequences for the internal consistency of the entire organization. They suggested that CCAS should reciprocate the invitation from the PRC and be prepared to extend "invitations, resources, and hospitality to Chinese scholars/students/journalists/friends who desire to visit, travel, or study in the United States."[35] In the letter, this is presented as a topic for further discussion within CCAS, but the opportunity of extending such an invitation was never in doubt. And, in fact, this happened in the most formal of settings, when the CCAS delegation met with Chinese premier Zhou Enlai and offered to organize a "return trip" for Chinese scholars. This gesture from a group of loosely affiliated CCAS members would eventually spark a major debate within the Committee, which went quickly beyond the organizational details or even the very opportunity of a such a trip, and centered instead on the very nature of the organization as well as on the scope and forms of its political activism.

While the Hong Kong chapter tried to sound a cautious note on the significance of the trip, the enthusiasm for the possibilities it opened was palpable. "We think it could be one of the best things to happen for CCAS since its inception, if properly handled," they opined. To the HK scholars, this seemed a departure from "ping pong diplomacy"; rather it was "a precedent in which American students *friendly to China* are given a deeper and more meaningful picture of China to take back to the American people." They were the first CCAS group to visit China; the obvious implication was "that others would follow. WOW!"[36] The enthusiasm was echoed by Charles Cell (CCAS Michigan), who wrote to the thirteen privileged travelers suggesting outlets for the future news release but also offering complete (and largely unsubstantiated) support for future Chinese ventures: "THE POINT IS THAT FOR BOTH CONTINUED VISITS THERE AND CHINESE VISITS HERE WE ARE BASICALLY PREPARED TO OFFER THEM A BLANK CHECK."[37] As the first group to be invited to China, CCAS wished to become the "contact organization for Asian scholars in the U.S."[38] Others, slightly more realistically, hoped that CCAS's newly recognized status with China would at least make it a looked-after and respected source for the establishment media, so that they could influence U.S. coverage of things Chinese and mitigate the anti-PRC slant they perceived as dominant.[39]

The excitement was slightly but progressively dampened when the group returned to Hong Kong (and eventually to the United States) and had to communicate their experience to their comrades and to the world at large. The first press conference at the border crossing "with a room full of reporters plus CBS, NBC" was apparently quite bad. They gave contradicting messages concerning the release of their interview with Zhou Enlai, but, more problematically, "the group answered largely in China phraseology sounding to the press like apologists."[40] There was a certain uneasiness among some Concerned Scholars in witnessing the public performances of the China trippers, who did not "seem to be able to talk in terms that would make sense and be convincing to people who don't read *Peking Review*." The memory of another generation of travelers to a different incarnation of the Socialist dream provided a cautionary tale. "I fear," warned John Berninghausen, "we will wind up typecast as the kind of mushy headed utopianists that come back from the Soviet Union in the Twenties and early Thirties praising everything there to the skies. Few Americans will listen to the exuberant and grandiose pronouncements that pour forth from Americans who keep talking about 'what people told them' with much attention. (Could it be that some of us *are* mushy headed utopianists?)"[41]

In addition to a certain inability to communicate in front of the press, the thirteen were blamed for lack of organization and of collective discipline. Molly Coye, one of the CCAS national coordinators who found herself in the middle of this momentous yet disruptive event, complained early that the group had promised an article to Pacific News Services (a progressive news organization, founded by CCAS member Orville Schell and China scholar Franz Schurmann), but nothing had materialized.[42] And while the group as a whole lacked communication skills, other participants tried to present their experience through other venues. Susan Shirk wrote a piece for *Parade* magazine,[43] and on August 3, 1971, she appeared on the Dick Cavett show, on the ABC late-night slot. Shirk was officially recognized as a member of CCAS,[44] but, according to Molly Coye, she did not know much about the history of the Committee, and "exhibited absolutely no understanding of what CCAS has been and is. AT ALL!!!"[45] Shirk remembers that experience with a certain discomfort, noting that it was difficult to say anything substantial about the trip, and that it ended up being a series of jokes about acupuncture.[46]

The immediate aftermath of the first CCAS trip to China highlighted the issue of having a delegation that was at the same time representative of organizational politics *and* completely self-selected.[47] Therefore it is not surprising that the July–August 1971 *Newsletter* published a coordinators' report that, while praising the initiative of the Hong Kong members and highlighting the "chapter-based" nature of CCAS, asked (or rather required) that all individual, small group or chapter initiatives to visit China be suspended. "All efforts to secure invitations in the name of CCAS should be coordinated," they stated.[48] The next trip, while organized through the Hong Kong chapter, was going to be a national affair. And that raised the issue of selecting who should go, on the basis of what criteria, and under which conditions. The coordinators mused in the *Newsletter* on the possible length of future trips (extended stays or repeated shorter tours?), the composition of the groups (chapter-based or selected nationally?), and the kind of expertise required (should it be restricted to Chinese speakers?).[49] Already in the immediate aftermath of the trip, it was evident that such problems would take an enormous amount of attention and energy; the enthusiasm surrounding the China trips was proportional to the anguish the process of managing them produced.

These problems dominated the CCAS retreat in Chicago in the summer of 1971, when debate over the China tours seemingly displaced planning and discussion of projects related to the Vietnam War.[50] Mark Selden remarked that this was the first gathering since 1968 "in which the war not only failed to dominate but actually seemed incidental."[51] "Overstatement to be sure," he commented, to revise his own assessment, highlighting hopefully that excitement over China was not incompatible with concerns over the war. "The war is and should continue to be the number one item on our agenda," he concluded. "We want the drive and excitement of new people turned on by their China experience to open new vistas for us but not undermine what has been our most important work in the past."[52] Members at the retreat established eight criteria for the selection process of the next CCAS delegation. They included representativeness of the various groups within CCAS (women, minorities, different regions), knowledge of Chinese, a history of activism, and willingness to meet before the trip and to speak/write after the trip. The selection process, they agreed, should be based on recommendations by local chapters, and it should "be designed to generate the minimum of competitiveness, hard feelings or divisiveness within chapters and CCAS as a whole."[53]

Divisiveness and strong (if not hard) feelings surfaced even before the selection process started. The debate centered not so much on the second delegation or technical procedures (even if there were indeed some complaints),[54] but on the fact that, despite all the cautionary advice to the contrary, chapters and members were devoting much time and energy to "one limited activity," and one place, China.[55] At the center of the often acrimonious discussion was the possibility for CCAS to organize a "return trip," that is, to arrange for a delegation of Chinese students or scholars to visit the United States.

The promise (or menace) of a "return trip" continued to be a problem for CCAS, resurfacing periodically in ebbs and flows over the following three years. I describe that development later in the chapter, but right now I want to show that the reactions to this project were conflictual since its inception and how these reactions identify specific political and organizational differences within the Committee. The idea of having been selected by the Chinese premier as a conduit for such a historic visit naturally elicited passionate responses among some members, and people started belaboring excitedly over organizational details. John Berninghausen, writing at the reentry of the first CCAS delegation, argued that the real possibility a "return trip" posed was "one of providing the American people with a chance to see Chinese from revolutionary 'real' China as living breathing people and to let them see lots of different kinds of 'Americas' and Americans." Berninghausen went on to discuss possible concession that CCAS might have to make to the U.S. government (out of practical necessity). "In terms of PR, it might be a mistake to try to prevent them from meeting with Nixon or other high official if such is desired in Washington. We can insist on a CCAS presence in the meeting and should be easily able to arrange for meetings with non-establishment political leaders (ie Chavez, Alinsky, Newton, Abernathy, McGovern?—gee, how come I can't think of any better leaders for them to meet? . . . maybe Hayden and Dellinger? . . . well, maybe they don't need to meet with leaders anyway)."[56] In the immediate aftermath of the encounter with Zhou Enlai, and at a specific moment in which U.S.-China relationships were being reframed, it was evidently possible to imagine a role for CCAS in which members would escort guests in meetings with high government officers and act as interlocutors in what would have been a diplomatic exchange of historical proportions.

This very optimistic outlook was not universally shared. Richard Kagan argued that CCAS had a "special responsibility" to the Chinese but was also "uniquely qualified" to play host and plan the content of the trip. But, he added, many CCAS members had serious reservations about sponsoring and organizing such a tour, which he labeled humorously the "Paper Tiger Trip." "The reasons range from not turning us into a travel agency, to the problem of cost and the tremendous problems of the managerial operations."[57]

With the publication of the November 1971 issue of the CCAS Newsletter, it became evident that the differences were not just over the opportunity of stretching the limited financial and organizational abilities of the Committee. The Newsletter published a statement by the Stanford chapter (one of the most active and vocal) that summed up their debate over the issue since the previous August. The chapter, they described, had originally focused on the "practical necessities" involved in the tour, the amount of organizational work required, and the fact that such an enterprise would likely "bring all other CCAS work to a standstill." At that point, however, the discussion shifted from assessing the organizational limitations to defining the political priorities of CCAS. "Our gradually growing uneasiness about the general drift in our chapter, and the directions evidenced in the national retreat, toward an emphasis on China at the expenses of continued work on the Indochina War," the Stanford members lamented, "has brought us to the point of concluding that the general Nixon thaw in U.S.-China relations has in effect defused the antiwar movement in the United States." They complained about the time spent on the next CCAS trip to China and argued that the attention devoted to "large, splashy ventures" had distracted them from antiwar and consciousness-raising activity at the local level. "In short," they concluded, "we find we have been failing, due to the euphoric climate surrounding US-China relations at this point, to continue to bring the war and US imperialism home. We have largely abandoned the Indochinese to American bombers because the issue is no longer appealing, flashy, and easy to get across."

The statement touched on the shifting international situation only obliquely (the Nixon thaw, whose implications for the global positioning of China was not clear at all at the time), but they argued that the commitment made by the first CCAS delegation had been de facto voided by changes in political necessities and political priorities, and that the prior commitment to fight U.S. imperialism had precedence over everything else. "China will be there for a long time," they concluded; "it is up to us to see that the US is not in Indochina much longer." On the strength of that priority, the chapter attached a proposal to modify the second CCAS trip to the PRC so that it could include a visit to the Democratic Republic of Vietnam. The list of reasons behind such a proposal illustrates how the shifts in global diplomacy affected the existing political tensions within the group:

> 1) To reaffirm our priorities and prevent us from going too far in what conceivably could become a 'China trip' mentality. 2) To express to the Chinese our continuing concern for the effects of American imperialism in Indochina as the grossest offense to people's freedom in the world. 3) To express to the Vietnamese that we have not been

coopted by what they rightfully consider to be Nixon's attempted manipulation of big-power chauvinism to create dissension among the socialist countries of the world. 4) To create an effective forum in which to refocus concern of the American people in our education when the CCAS delegation returns by emphasizing American imperialism's effect vis-à-vis both China and the three countries of Indochina.[58]

The Stanford memo explicitly pointed at the possible (and increasingly evident) contradictions within CCAS's major foci of interest and action: China, Vietnam, anti-imperialist and antiwar activism, as well as the state of the field and the role of the intellectual/scholar. As such, these contradictions were impossible to ignore, and this apparently prompted the national coordinators to slow down the process and temporarily halt the submission of a formal invitation to the Chinese. In turn, that generated further reactions from Hong Kong chapter members, who met on November 29 to discuss the issue and expressed their utter dismay over the delay in sending the invitation. At the meeting, "the question of the Stanford chapter usurping authority given by the national retreat to the invitation committee was raised. Some people took great exception to the assumptions in the Stanford memo that the trip would harm the antiwar movement and that it would overwhelm CCAS in a harmful way.... Everyone is wondering about how representative Stanford's thinking is of other chapters and CCAS members at large."[59] The Hong Kong chapter expressed opposition about carrying out a debate, or worse, a referendum, on whether to invite the Chinese. "*CCAS has already invited the Chinese,*" they stated emphatically. They worried that this breach in "symbolic reciprocity" (a Chinese trip for a CCAS trip) might seriously damage the "good relations that have been established between our organization and the People's Republic of China." And while it was not their intention to attack the Stanford position (praised for its "right-on political priorities and sensitivities"), the Hong Kong members argued their case on the basis of their clearer perspective on things Chinese: "We hope people in the States will recognize our superior vantage point in terms of judging the issues we are raising in this letter, just as we recognize the superior vantage point of people at home, like Stanford, to assess political/organizational pros and cons."[60] The letter ended with a veiled threat of taking unspecified "chapter-based" initiatives with regard to the Chinese if a referendum were to be held.

But even such chapter-based statements were not unanimous. Elaine Cell hastened to write to express her disagreement with her fellow Hong Kong chapter's members. While she approved of the major thrust of the letter, she objected to the tone, which resembled a "veiled ultimatum." But, and more importantly, she stressed that the fractured nature of CCAS could create the conditions for such positions. When it looked like Stanford acted unilaterally in setting national policies, that impression indirectly authorized the Hong Kong group to think of independent initiatives. Much of the antagonism and misunderstanding, she concluded, was due to lack of communication, within the U.S. chapters and even more between the United States and Hong Kong.[61]

However, while communication was indeed an issue within CCAS (as the heaps of carbon-copied letters in the archives show), the disagreement over China and priorities was not something to be addressed by a better organizational technique; it was political. It had been all the active CCAS chapters in the Bay Area (not only Stanford) that had questioned not so much the feasibility of the trip but its political desirability within that particular set of contingencies. In 1972, with a presidential election looming, and a president who was intensifying the shelling of Vietnam and Laos at the same time he was breaking the diplomatic impasse with the PRC, any decision of that kind required a political analysis. As Molly Coye argued in her reply, because of the diplomatic shift, the situation had changed a fair amount domestically: "The papers . . . are full of interesting stories—most of them good—about China, and *nothing about Indochina*."[62] That shift coincided with a shared feeling among CCAS West Coast members that most of their time had been devoted to China (including the instant book based on the first trip) and that the situation was not much different in other chapters.[63] If that was the direction in which CCAS was headed, they felt the need to correct it or at least address the issue in the open. "Our stand that a chinese [sic] delegation not come before the election (and of some people, before the war is over)," Coye concluded, "is not based on a rejection of china [sic], although probably some of the people involved do also have severe criticism of china [sic]."[64] For some within CCAS, the reconciliation between the United States and the PRC made China less politically acceptable, thus creating a rift with those in the Committee for whom contact with China was a suddenly possible realization of intellectual, scholarly, and political dreams.

Another letter in response to the Hong Kong chapter's criticism brought back the question of the political in much harsher tones. The letter, argued the author, stood as evidence of the kind of things that could "most easily corrupt and politically desensitize CCAS." "That alone," they continued, "should be reason enough to call a temporary halt to the current China frenzy and allow us to consider and critically evaluate what we have gotten ourselves into . . . we should all be suspicious of political movements that become so obsessed with their own importance that they can't take the time to face some serious criticism, self-criticism."[65] Hong Kong's reaction to the delay in the invitation was dismissive of the concerns expressed by Stanford and did not propose any opening for a discussion: it showed a "growing insensitivity for political dialogue and criticism-struggle-criticism which should be growing in CCAS and is instead diminishing." It was impossible, the author argued, to consider the China issue by itself, because it was so revelatory of tendencies developing within the organization, including careerism, which was evident in the seemingly single-minded desire by the people in Hong Kong to get themselves back to China; a conservative slant favoring bureaucratic procedures over central political questions; and an increasing passion for "limelight politics," for being "in the center of the stage." But the most worrisome element revealed by the whole debate was the lack of solidarity, the fracturing of a shared commitment, the lack of feeling as to the "political benefits to the Mvoement [sic], to the disadvantages, to a rel [sic] consideration of the political significance." In the fight over this decision, the author continued, in the refusal to allow for any discussion over the role of China in the larger scope of CCAS activism, "we have written off your solidarity in favor of some overwhelming commitment to a country which in the long run can not fight our revolution for us."[66]

In the following months, the issue of the return trip was dealt with through a long-argued negotiation. A six-member research committee was formed to study the issue and present a report at the New York national conference in 1972. They highlighted practical issues of funding, translation, timing, and security, but, in the end, the crucial questions remained the same, as summarized in Sandy Sturdevant's outline: "We should consider very carefully the questions of what is to be gained from

FIGURE 3.2 Badge for the 1972 CCAS delegation (courtesy of William Joseph). It reads: "Long live the friendship of the Chinese and American people," and "Down with US imperialism."

such a trip . . . on CCAS's part and on our Chinese friends' part. Could this trip be just as well handled by other groups. What is our contribution. What are our priorities. Has CCAS become too focused on China . . . to the detriment of work on the war, Bangladesh, Japan, Korea, US's South Asian/East Asian policies, etc."[67] In the end, CCAS members at the national conference voted (43 yes, 10 no, 8 abstain) on a compromise resolution, crafted specifically to avoid a showdown that was "certain to leave a scar." According to this text, a small, voluntary committee of CCAS was going to approach the American Friends Service Committee (AFSC) to organize a "small informal visit" of Chinese students. Collaboration from CCAS members was to be on a strictly voluntary basis.

I have argued previously that the China of the Cultural Revolution offered a positive grounding for CCAS political activism and intellectual commitment, but that this was not based on an imitation of a prefab model, on the veneration for a place of truly achieved success. Rather China named a series of shared political issues and identified subjects with which these political concerns were shared. With the China trips—and the coeval shift in the diplomatic posture of the PRC—China became a much more problematic location. First of all, it did become a "place," one that could be visited, that had a concrete, if elusive, existence, and one to which access was limited but no longer completely precluded. Then, this happened at the same time that China's political position on other crucial issues (decolonization, anti-imperialism, the war in Vietnam) seemed to significantly and surprisingly shift. The Nixon visit struck at the heart of those international connections that had been framed in the name of China's support for national liberation movements.[68] Then, at the same time that the "China-is-Mecca-business" was engulfing CCAS, the value of China as a referent was rightfully being questioned within the larger scope of activities of the organization.[69] Given the price paid by the Committee over this China focus, it is worth asking what kind of knowledge, or what kind of intellectual production and political sharing, the act of "going to China" (having close contact with mainland Chinese) granted the Concerned Asian Scholars.

China! China?

"It is today perhaps obvious that people interested in the culture of a certain part of the world should go there. But that idea depends on a certain theorization of the relation between culture and geography, aesthetics and politics." Eric Hayot, in his discussion of the Maoist phase of the editorial group of the French journal *Tel quel*, argues that their recognition of China as a "geopolitical entity" (and as such a place that needed to be seen) was consequential to their acceptance that Maoist China had a "reality-effect" in Europe, that its politics and culture were speaking to the West and had the potential of producing actual transformation in the West and globally. It was only after this realization had been achieved that it became necessary for these French radical intellectuals to go to China.[70]

"Why are we going?" and "What do we hope to accomplish?" were the first two questions set for discussion among members of the second CCAS delegation before their departure for China, in the spring of 1972. The thirty delegates,[71] selected nationally, met for a four-day retreat in Lantau Island, Hong Kong, to hammer out details and prepare for the trip. That a group of Asia scholars, which had invested years of work and activism on China and had just gone through a long and divisive debate over the specific issue of going to China, had to ponder first and foremost over those very questions might sound quite surprising. But clearly, the issue of what could be gained from an organized tour of China, of what kind of knowledge or political awareness this could produce, remained (and, in a sense, still remains) very much open. This was clearly true at the level of the individual scholar, but the issue was even more complex when such trips were viewed in the context of the entire organization, of what benefitted the concern(s) of the entire Committee. The agenda for the retreat listed several items that had to do precisely with the question of group solidarity, with the need of visiting *as an organization*, with common goals and positions; these questions hint at both the power and the problematic character of China as a signifier of radical politics in the 1970s. For example, they set out to discuss how they could present a shared agreement (within certain limits) on crucial and urgent political issues (Nixon's visit, Indochina, Sudan, China's foreign policy); they invited people to suppress "personal research obsession," and they planned for press conferences and communications (who talks, what is said); they also wondered how to frame an approach somewhere in between "China worship vs. radical freakout against China."[72]

The retreat clearly did not (and could not) provide a response for these sweeping questions about the nature, reasons, and goals of the trips, and for many months afterward CCAS was occupied by another series of exchanges on precisely these issues and, more importantly, on how they affected the group. In the immediate aftermath of the second trip, the assessment was ambivalent but still largely positive in tone. Stephen MacKinnon, himself a member of the second delegation, criticized the value of such "short junkets" and called instead for "extended stays" in one place. But the more worrisome doubts were explicitly political, starting once again from the relation between China's foreign policy ("Vietnam sell-out?") and the CCAS priorities concerning the Indochina war: "Judging from the content of the Bulletin and Newsletters, I don't see that this has changed," MacKinnon continued. "But in the long run—and the long-run view must be considered—the Indochina war vs. China dichotomy is false. If CCAS is to remain dynamic as a radical political force in community work as well as professionally in the Asian studies field it needs to further, not sever, the relationship with the PRC." MacKinnon, however, justified this positive assessment with a view of CCAS that foresaw for the organization (and for the American left) a future in which they "would have to be concerned with the meaning of socialism in the contemporary world and acting politically as socialists. Obviously, Chinese socialism is to be taken seriously and relate to it we must."[73] Not only was this view probably not universally shared within CCAS, but a shift toward fully embraced socialism would have also required a major rebuilding of the group on completely different theoretical and practical grounds.

Concerned scholars at the 1972 summer retreat hashed out their divisions over China, but eventually ended up entrusting an ad hoc committee (the China Exchange Committee, CEC) with the task of evaluating the first two trips and, on the basis of that evaluation, of advising on future tours.[74] The Exchange Committee responded in January 1973 with a long and thorough report, largely based on a survey of members.[75] The appraisal was generally positive in tone and content: the trips were considered successful and had benefited both individual participants and the organization. At the individual level, visiting China had been inspirational and energizing; it had renewed the "commitment to anti-war, anti-imperialist work" and provided "some increased understanding of China's support for the DRV and its foreign policy. Finally, the trips had made many people more articulate and confident about speaking and writing and increased their personal credibility in talking about both China and the war."[76] At the organizational level, while there was still doubt about the possible distraction from the antiwar efforts, many members seemed to agree that the trips "had increased the life expectancy of the organization" by helping it move "from simply an anti-war position to a broader anti-imperialist one." Yet the CEC (and the members surveyed) avoided clarifying the specific role of China within this anti-imperialist scope and, more importantly, what such a turn in the orientation of the group could imply. Finally, the report concluded, there was an inherent professional value in maintaining access to China in order to safeguard CCAS's role within the field, and that access should be protected, several members had argued, independently of Chinese foreign policy.[77] Yet one wonders what that access could mean politically for a group of declared scholars/activists once China's significance within the anti-imperial scene had waned.

The CEC then moved on to the negative aspects and the objective failures of the two delegations. The first friendship delegation was not representative of CCAS chapters, and, more crucially, they failed "to maintain a critical and objective perspective about their knowledge of China."[78] Therefore "many CCAS members and others interested in China were unhappy with their glowing, uncritical and therefore sometimes incredible reports."[79] The second delegation tried to remedy both these problems, but representativeness was achieved only through "an unfair and time-consuming process which caused severe divisiveness in the national organization."[80] And while they strove to maintain a more critical attitude, they too ultimately failed to reach a deep and realistic understanding of China and socialism. This was due to the careful Chinese planning of the tour, but the blame also lay with the choices and the very composition of the CCAS delegation—"insufficient language, relatively little representation of Asian-Americans, lack of preparedness and skill in interviewing, insistence on visiting some places (prisons, mental hospitals) where delegation members had insufficient expertise and where our hosts were unaccustomed to dealing with foreigners and answering their questions."[81] If the first delegation was too fawning and rosy eyed, members of the second delegation had occasionally showed lack of tact and political sensibility, for example, in making "irreverent allusions" to the Mao cult, which were not appreciated. Molly Coye recounted one specific incident that took place during a banquet. At the end of the dinner, after a lot of food and a lot of alcohol, the pièce de résistance came in the form of a whole fish whose eyeballs had been replaced with red light bulbs, shining brightly. One of the members of the delegation, probably Gene Cooper, stood up to give a toast. He thanked the Chinese hosts for their hospitality and for that beautiful fish with eyes "powered by chairman Mao's thought." The joke fell flat, and the Chinese reaction was stony silence. According to Coye, the CCAS members were later visited by their not-so-pleased hosts and had to undergo their own "criticism and self-criticism" session.[82]

In the end, the CEC admitted, there was very little that could be gained by sending another "friendship delegation" like the previous ones. They proposed instead an extended work-study research trip, with a clear mandate for critical investigation of Chinese socialism and the Chinese revolution, and they laid out precise selection criteria—ranging from language ability to knowledge of China and/or socialism, from a history of activism to commitment to extensive preparation before the trip. Yet, while this strategy possibly addressed some of the organizational and scholarly concerns, the CEC had nothing to say—and it is difficult to imagine how they could have—about what they identified as another source of division within CCAS in relationship to the trips, namely, the "diversity of priorities and levels of consciousness." The truth was that CCAS was not ideologically or politically unified, and every major decision the group had to make could only reveal it. "Therefore," the committee concluded, "much of the dissension surrounding the China trips should not be attributed to the China trips themselves, but rather to the fact that they were simply a major decision which the organization made."[83]

This quite candid yet shocking admission of a major political impasse was largely ignored in the rest of the report, which focused on selection criteria and practical fixes. This crucial omission was immediately singled out in the responses from members after the publication of the report in the January *Newsletter*. The opposition—"intense, but not widespread"—forced the CEC to postpone any actions until the following national meeting. Critics held the national discussion on the China trips to be crucial precisely because it touched "the heart of internal political schisms and the CEC report 'glossed over' these differences. Helen Chauncey wrote that she found the entire report lacking in general overall political direction, and for this reason it failed to resolve the basic problems at hand."[84]

The criticism focused on the proposed selection criteria in large part because they tried—and failed—to strike a balance between "sinological" competency and political proximity (suggested by an awkward reference to "expertise in socialism"). This in turn pointed to one of the main unresolved contradictions within CCAS—between academic scholarship and political activism—and one that, in the case of the China trips, expressed itself as "the basically antagonistic relationship between friendship delegations and investigatory junkets."[85] Members of CCAS seemed to agree that it was naive "to expect significant quantitative additions to knowledge of China" for future trips. So, the question still loomed, why go to China, and especially, *why go to China as China scholars?* And the only reason given was extremely vague: "Most people felt that these initial trips should still be aimed at getting a 'feel' for Chinese society and socialism, rather than enlarging a body of scholarly knowledge."[86] It was, then, almost a symbolic voyage, one that could nonetheless provide an aura of authoritativeness, increasing the stature of the returned scholar, who was finally able to speak of a place that he or she had actually seen (or, rather, "felt"). Even "friendship tours," many CCAS members agreed, "did accomplish minimal goals of initial contact with *Chinese people as people rather than objects of study*, and awakening to the dynamics of socialism in practice."[87]

At the CCAS national meeting in Chicago (March 29–31, 1973), a new China Exchange Committee was selected and new selection procedures/criteria for the third delegation were approved.[88] The request to the PRC was for a three-month-long visit, but, the CEC hastened to clarify, "the purpose of the extended stay is *not* for academic research. It is to obtain a deeper understanding of how socialism works in China. As such, friendship and understanding are not seen as mutually exclusive; indeed they are seen as compatible and necessarily intertwined."[89] It was, however, quite strange for a group of scholars to suggest that "understanding" and "research" were not intimately correlated. It almost implied that going to China under those conditions was primarily a political experience, and that "activists," rather than scholars, could understand that reality better on the basis of shared practices and commitments. Yet such an attitude simplified and minimized the real significance of the CCAS enterprise, which was not just a group of radicals, but rather "an organization essentially composed of people who find some usefulness in scholarship and try to be both scholars/educators and radicals in coherent and conscious way [sic]."[90] Yet the new guidelines implicitly denied the possibility of a "deeper understanding" of China that was at the same time both scholarly and political. Accordingly, the selection criteria deemphasized scholarly benchmarks—neither knowledge of Mandarin, background in the study of China and/or socialism and socialist societies, nor experience in living and interacting with Chinese people was highlighted as specifically required—and singled out "activism" as the sole characteristic "to be universally possessed by each applicant." "How much shit work have you done in CCAS?" seemed to be the only deciding factor for the selection committee. Similarly, the most important skill to be considered was the ability to communicate with popular audiences.[91] These criteria implicitly defined going to China as almost an emotional voyage of "understanding" by sympathetic activists who will then convey that poignant experience to the American people.

John Berninghausen, a witness to the return of the first delegation in Hong Kong and himself a member of the second delegation, took up the task of unveiling the implications of these guidelines in a detailed letter to the CEC. One of the crucial problems of the second delegation, he argued, was precisely that they did not have a clear mandate from the organization; they basically did not know why they were going to China "*other* than to do China-related public education work afterwards." The proposal for the third delegation, he continued, did not really address this issue. Yet sponsorship of a delegation requires "at least a vague understanding of what the purposes of that trip should be and some consensus of how those purposes fit into the overall political-educational-scholarly goals of the organization." The CEC guidelines spoke of achieving a "deeper understanding" of Chinese reality and Chinese socialism, but they never really clarified why this was needed and how it would be achieved. Clearly, the demand for a deeper understanding had to be based on an implicit judgment on the state of the existing information and perspectives on that place, be it from mass media, from government propaganda, or from the general opinion of the field itself. "Otherwise, why bother to go?"

The Committee of Concerned Asian Scholars, Berninghausen added, was a "peculiar organization," and the goals and tactics of sending a delegation to China should reflect its opposition to "establishment" groups of Asian scholars (who were gaining access after the Nixon trip) as well as its difference from generic "antiwar/movement groups." If, in the very framing of the trip, the prospect of actual research, of scholarly knowledge and, as such, of any significant intervention in the field was denied (in the name of "friendship"), then CCAS was largely reduced to acting as a "PR agency" or a "booster" for a "foreign nation-state or ideology/worldview-prescribed-by-a-foreign-nation-state." That's the reason why "there was, in actual practice, a contradiction between being a good 'friendship delegation' and being a better 'fact-finding reality-probing no-nonsense truth-seeker.'" Understanding and friendship, Berninghausen was saying, might indeed be closely intertwined, yet friendship was not sufficient for understanding, or at least not for the understanding to which concerned scholars should aspire. And that's why, for CCAS, as an organization of scholars *and* activists, it was self-defeating to adopt "the tone of 'anti-scholarism,'" that is, to underplay the usefulness of linguistic and historical knowledge. "When the information and interpretation of past and present realities,"

Berninghausen concluded, "is so closely watched over and structured as we (or just me if no one else agrees with me) found it to be, it is silly to ignore the extra disadvantage that people who must depend on guides/interpreters completely have to face."[92]

In the contrast between friendship and understanding, we can see at play two different sets of issues that animated CCAS. First, their criticism of the Asian studies establishment had been based on an idea of scholarship that embraced a political position, in part because recognizing new Chinese realities required a political shift in the scholar's perspective. Going to China tested the limits and the boundaries of that conception; it probed the extent by which political sympathy could unveil knowledge, and knowledge was necessary for shared militancy. Second, behind the adoption of the "friendship" attitude lies always the lingering possibility of an approach that took Maoist China as an unquestioned and unquestionable object of love, to be felt, touched, and accepted, rather than a set of subjects with whom to engage theoretically and politically.

Here the case of CCAS, because of their particular double concern for scholarship *and* activism, reflects and reframes in an even more trenchant way the tensions that seem to inform most accounts of (politically sympathetic) Western visitors to Maoist China. French travelers, for example, often stated their desire not to write a scholarly account of their experience, one judged to be dull, even unreadable, but also, to a certain extent, unfit to the reality described. Even Michelle Loi, a China specialist by training, wrote that she was not going to compile a "sinological work" but rather "a work of popularization in the most noble sense of the word."[93] Through this declaration of ignorance, the traveler, according to Francois Hourmant, erases the difference between him- or herself and the reader but also claims a different form of authority than that of bookish learning. Rather than being justified by an intellectual "system" (which supposedly denies the reality of the place visited), the traveler is endowed with the authority of his or her own naked, unobstructed, and unveiled eyes.[94] As Sigrid Schmalzer notes, speaking about China to the larger public becomes "a privilege of those who had been there, not of professional China scholars."[95] It is precisely the very separation from the intellectual/scholarly/institutional system (the sinological world) that allows the unveiling of the true reality of China, a reality that is then visible in the same way to the readers, because of the presupposition of a shared "zero degree of knowledge." The travel account, then, according to Hourmant, "constitutes itself also as a tool in the fight against 'the monopoly of university specialists.'"[96]

This characterization was probably best summarized by Maria-Antonietta Macciocchi, who wrote a travelogue of huge influence in the French intellectual Left. "My purpose," she stated, "is not to write an erudite treatise on China, in the manner of Byzantine Sinologists, but to 'tell the story' of China after the Cultural Revolution." Because, she continued, citing the French economist Charles Bettelheim, "what is needed at present is the *story of China*, told simply and movingly, just as the country would be seen by millions of European activists."[97] The detachment from erudition is, in this perspective, what supposedly lets Macciocchi see China through the eyes of an activist and to describe it in a way that would be immediately comprehensible to activists in Europe. Political understanding stood in diametrical opposition to scholarly knowledge.[98]

Here lay, however, the central conundrum for CCAS in relationship to the intellectual and the political goals of the China trips. As scholars, concerned or not, they could not realistically claim ignorance, yet, in their need to access China, they found themselves cornered into the "friendship" format and into a de facto devaluation of their own scholarly expertise. This contradiction is in full display in the instant book CCAS published with Bantam in the aftermath of the first trip in 1971. A truly collective production,[99] the volume is usually dismissed as yet another rosy-eyed view of Maoist China, full of all the excessively positive stereotypes of the genre and populated with descriptions of happiness, abundance, and Potemkin villages.[100] Yet here I propose to look at that publication precisely for what it can reveal of the tensions hidden behind the need to see and understand Maoist China.

The book starts with the declaration of a subjective position. The writers present themselves as members of CCAS, representing "a new generation of China scholars." And it is their identity as scholars that allows them to speak with a special authority, different from that of other visitors in similar tours. "What had we seen? Even now, we are not quite sure. And not all of us agree with each other. Like most visitors, we were taken to certain cities, certain factories, certain communes, and there was a great deal we did not see. But we speak Chinese, we read Chinese, and we have studied China for many years."[101]

They were scholars *and* American: they brought with them American concerns but also their desire to change the minds of their fellow countrymen, minds shaped by the mythology of the McCarthy era, "compounded by twenty-two years of ignorance and reinforced by sensationalist 'China watchers' in Hong Kong." They had tried to do it as scholars, working from books alone, but "book learning," they went on, "was never quite convincing enough." Now, finally, they could see for themselves. But, they asked, "Where would the line be drawn between the myths we had fought and the 'reality' we had studied?"[102] American-ness brought with it the burden of the layered history of U.S. perceptions of China, but it also identified a connection, a perceived political nearness, which made it possible to see in the present reality of China those "new things" that spoke directly to issues concerning "the mind of America." Closeness in terms of politics was, in this sense, an antidote to the blinders crafted by years of China watching. Macciocchi made a similar case in her (programmatically nonscholarly) account of visiting China. She contemplated the objective inability of writing about China from the West, due, in her opinion, to "mental habits and unconscious reflexes rooted in the conviction that our world represents, in the words of Candide, 'the best of all possible worlds.'"[103] To those habits, detached pedantry was no remedy. Rather what is needed, Macciocchi hinted, was an emotional connection, based precisely on the realization of a shared political horizon, the awareness that "our struggle is both directly and indirectly linked to the struggle of the Chinese Communists."[104]

By embracing their political emotions, the visitors clearly opened themselves to huge lapses in judgment, and *China!* is scattered with glaring examples of voluntary myopia. The description of the history of the Cultural Revolution is surprisingly accurate (for the time), and it includes mentions of student infighting and a reference to the Wuhan incident. But there is nothing on the Red Guards' excesses and military repression. In *China!*, famines and harvest failures belong exclusively to the "old society," because "in the years since Liberation sweeping changes have transformed the countryside. Now, even in hard years, everyone eats."[105]

Yet, despite its pitfalls, *China!* offers glimpses of those aspects of a different Chinese "reality" (beyond the factual evidence, one is tempted to say) that became visible and appeared crucially important only because of that perceived political closeness. These aspects mark, in a sense, the space of political connections that "China" indicated, a space that could be possibly investigated scholarly but that could be individuated only politically. In that it offers an example not only of a different understanding, "but also a different understanding of *how* to understand."[106]

For example, CCAS highlighted the influence of the "Yan'an spirit" in Chinese society in terms of an extension—and multiplication—of the political. They wrote: "There is no division into things 'political' and 'nonpolitical.' Leadership structures are essentially the same for factories, hospitals, communes, schools, government offices, and agencies; everyone is a politician and no one is *only* a politician."[107] While this assessment made light of the differences between party and people, leaders and led, it also correctly identified one of the main impetuses of the Cultural Revolution, that of displacing politics from its privileged and sanctioned spaces (parties, elections, politicians), which was in turn one of the moves that defined the global sixties everywhere.[108]

Similarly, the CCAS delegation devoted particular attention to issues that concerned education and the positions of intellectuals. They saw the educational policies introduced after the high tide of the Cultural Revolution, such as the worker-peasant-soldier universities (*gong nong bing daxue*) and rural education, as potentially egalitarian measures, because they promised to reduce the role of school in the reproduction of class differentiation.[109] Like other well-educated visitors, they expressed support and admiration for the May Seventh schools—where cadres and intellectuals were reeducated through participation in labor—an "exciting experiment in attacking the universal problem of bureaucratic stagnation," which blurred the lines between manual and intellectual work, rural and urban.[110] Paul Hollander, in his disdainful critique of pro-China intellectuals, makes an inadvertently acute observation on the enthusiasm the May Seventh schools elicited. Those intellectuals, he argues, were disenchanted with their own historical role and therefore ready to abdicate it. They were ready to give up those characteristics that had historically defined them, "such as detachment, critical thinking, sense of autonomy, etc." because they "welcomed a society in which their occupational identities could in effect be dissolved, where they no longer stood apart from the rest of society by virtue of their intellectual status."[111] For many "fellow travelers" who visited China, including many in CCAS, what Hollander sees as a renunciation of autonomous thinking meant instead the possible liberation from a passive role behind a desk or inside a classroom, the mirage of a fuller participation, the opportunity of living an integrated life, combining the political, the intellectual, and the everyday.

There was, however, one particular issue in which the perceived political closeness between Chinese and American concerns allowed the visitors to take a much more critical position, even if with an ironic twist: that of gender. The overall tone of the chapter on women in *China!* was more somber and less celebratory than any other part of the book—with the possible exception of foreign policy, another sour note. Delegates from CCAS could not but point out the still existing gender disparities in Chinese society, but, more importantly, they noticed with dismay how these seemed to be largely invisible to their hosts. The CCAS delegation highlighted continuing inequalities in wages, education, and access to leadership roles. When, during a visit to Peking University, they asked how many women were members of the revolutionary committee, the answer was a blank stare. "Since women and men are completely equal in China now, who would think to ask that question?" their hosts asked.[112] Similarly, they noted that the old patriarchal division of labor within the household had not been much modified in the PRC. Unlike other lingering problems of Maoist China (bureaucracy, oppression, mismanagement, poverty, etc.), the issues of gender inequality were glaringly visible to these visitors precisely because "women's liberation" was part and parcel of that shared political horizon. It named, for both the Chinese and the Americans, a supposedly coincident set of concerns. Yet, the visitors realized, it was not so much that the Chinese reality did not yet fully manifest the promised change, it was that, for many of their interlocutors, the supposedly shared concerns were actually incomprehensible. The discrepancy was visible politically. It is somewhat ironic that in its last years, CCAS, like most New Left organizations, would be torn by the rightful criticism of many of its female members who protested the subaltern role they still held within the group and within academia.[113] Similarly, the following generation of radical Asia scholars will articulate their critique on the basis of a renewed theoretical engagement with gender, identified as one of their predecessors' most glaring blind spots. One could see a forewarning of those debates in the fact that only the female members in the first delegation went to meet with eight Shanghai "liberated" women.[114]

The act of going to and organizing trips to China involved some of the crucial tensions that shaped CCAS since its inception, and much of the debate, the angst, the contradictions within the group was generated not so much by a simple opposition between believers and skeptics, between dreamy travelers and savvy scholars, but by the very problem of finding the "right way" to look at China. How could these radical intellectuals produce knowledge of a place that defined itself by practical distance and inaccessibility as well as by its political closeness to their concerns? How could they be at the same time friends and investigators, comrades, and scholars? And what difference in terms of understanding could the emphasis on one of the two poles make? In a note jotted down during his 1974 trip to China, Roland Barthes remarked cryptically that the right gaze toward China could come neither from the inside, nor from the outside (the West). "The right gaze is *a sideways gaze*,"[115] he concluded. "*Le bon regard est un regard qui louche*,"[116] in the French original, where "loucher" means to look askance, to squint. The Committee tried desperately to find the right gaze, and much came out of their squinting. One only wishes Barthes had been clearer.

On Not Going to China

The Committee's relations with China remained a divisive topic even when the actual practice of sending delegations to the PRC (or inviting people from there) practically ceased. It was therefore in part around "China" that the Committee framed an internal debate leading to a spiral of organizational involution and fragmentation. Specifically, two major lingering issues continued to agitate the group and reveal hidden fissures and contradictions after 1972: the "return trip" and the aftermath of the selection of the third delegation.[117]

The debate over hosting a delegation of students/scholars from China (as verbally promised to Zhou Enlai) had been solved solomonically by entrusting the management of the trip to the American Friends Service Committee, a Quaker organization,[118] and limiting the CCAS participation to a monetary contribution—revenues from the first delegation's speaking tour—and the voluntary effort of individual members.[119] The debate at the 1972 national conference, as I mentioned, had been harsh, splitting the group between those who considered that proximity to China to be crucial and those who viewed with suspicion the overemphasis on the PRC, especially in the light of Beijing's shifting policies toward the DRV,

Pakistan, and the United States. News of the debate filtered outside, however, when Stanley Karnow published an article in the *Washington Post* reporting on the disillusionment of the American radical Left regarding Chinese foreign policy. Karnow quoted a CCAS member on the "big row" at the convention and on how it had left a "big split" within the group. He also cited Jim Peck's gloomy assessment of Beijing foreign policy, marking "the end of any meaningful commitment to an internationalist ideology."[120] A few months later, John Gittings wrote a similar, and even more caustic, article in the *Guardian*, reporting on how Nixon's (and Beijing's) diplomacy had turned the table on radical scholars in the United States. The media reporting on China had changed massively at the time of the Nixon visit, and there seemed to be no need to defend the PRC "against all comers." "Perhaps the Chinese," concluded Gittings, citing an unnamed CCAS member, "can now look after themselves."[121]

The Committee's reactions were immediate, but they took the form mostly of internal, panicked letters. There was, for many, a fear that the Chinese would start viewing the Committee as an unreliable, divided, and incapable organization, and that they would therefore rescind invitations and cease a direct relationship. They asked Larry Lifschultz and Carl Riskin—who were visiting China with a delegation of radical political economists—to intercede with the China International Travel Services. Lifschultz apparently tried to explain that, while "questions existed in US radical circles and in CCAS too about China's foreign policy," the notion of a "deep split in the organization consisting of pro and anti China factions was a fabrication."[122] There were calls for unity, such as from Ray Whitehead in Hong Kong, who declared CCAS to be under attack and mentioned an "academic stooge" who had followed Henry Kissinger to Beijing with the task of discrediting CCAS, depicting it as an "amorphous and disorganized association that is incapable of carrying through exchange visits." In a draft message for the national coordinators, Whitehead reiterated once again that CCAS's work was instead coherent and focused on their struggle against imperialism, the same imperialism that was wreaking havoc in Indochina, controlling the academic world, and damaging relationships between Americans and other people. "Our struggle agains [sic] imperialist war and our struggle against academic and cultural manipulation is one struggle," he concluded.[123] Frank Kehl, another member who was very active in planning the "return trip," echoed the same point, stressing how facilitating the relationship between the United States and socialist countries dovetailed "with one thrust of CCAS's anti-imperialist work: breaking down anti-communist stereotypes and myths among the American people."[124]

Yet, affirmations of coherence and unity aside, there was a sense among many in CCAS that the descriptions provided by Karnow and Gittings, while sensationalistic in tone, were not that far off the mark. As Jean Doyle commented, opposition to the return trip continued unabated (especially in the Bay Area), and at least one group within CCAS viewed the division around this issue as a crucial ideological split, while others saw it as a difference over procedures, not substance. It was therefore not surprising that the coordinators did not even try to write a collective response to Karnow's claim: there was not even agreement on the nature of the division, let alone on its possible solution.[125]

This division, which indeed concerned the very nature of the Committee, resurfaced a year later, after the selection of a third China delegation. The CEC selected thirty-three delegates, but, immediately after announcing the list, they removed Marilyn Young and John Israel from it for violation of CCAS national policy.[126] Young and Israel were found to be in violation of the CCAS boycott of the SSRC and ACLS, which had been adopted and voted as a "national initiative" in 1972.[127] There was an immediate and fairly widespread outrage at the removal of the two (especially Marilyn Young, a founding member of CCAS), and the debate was waged in the open, with much of the correspondence published in the *Newsletter*. Young and Israel wrote in defense of their positions, and received support, mostly from people who argued against the advisability of the boycott and for the need to conduct good research even if with tainted money.[128] Jonathan Mirsky went so far as to resign from CCAS over the incident.[129]

And while the outrage over the ouster of Young and Israel was not universal, most members viewed it as a crucial turning point in the history of the group. For Angus McDonald, it posed "the most important CCAS crisis of the last four or five years, and the way it is handled will determine the *nature* of CCAS for the foreseeable future."[130] The act of sending people to China led indirectly—and, in a different sense, directly—to probe the nature of the group and the extent of its political mission. It stretched the limits of required conformity, questioning what the Committee had a right to demand from its membership and what they had a reasonable right to expect. Once again, it led to asking, "What is the nature of our organization?"[131] If CCAS was a disciplined political organization, then it had the right to demand solidarity from its members; it could expect that they would follow in practice principles to which they had agreed by identifying as Concerned Asian Scholars.[132] Yet the very issue of whether CCAS was indeed a political organization remained open. For some people, CCAS was only a "'community in spirit,' a sort of club within the 'profession,'" and, as such, incapable of "becoming a vehicle for really major political commitments."[133]

In a very practical sense, the China trips had created the mirage of a "reward" just for being associated with CCAS—John Israel was very bluntly called an "opportunist"[134]—and that had made it more pressing and more urgent to discern who really belonged, who really could be representative of the Committee, and, in turn, what and whom the Committee represented. The question of policies and goals was essential to the group's survival, and, as Judy Perrolle remarked, being "vaguely against the war or against imperialism" was not enough anymore.[135] Yes, CCAS had its origins in the antiwar movement, but with the 1973 ceasefire in Vietnam and the problems of China's foreign policies, being antiwar was clearly not a cogent or binding position anymore, and Jon Livingston found himself wondering what the political raison d'être of CCAS was and whether, without some larger unified purpose, they could continue their struggle within the profession.[136] The political crisis that the China trips had opened directly affected CCAS's stance within the field.

This was both an existential fear—what is CCAS, what do we represent—but also a very practical one, given the changes produced in the China field by the new diplomatic situation. By late 1972, the National Committee on U.S.-China Relations and the Committee on Scholarly Communications with the PRC were busy providing access to China to an increasingly large number of organizations.[137] The mirage of an exclusive, or even privileged, connection to Beijing was quickly being revealed as such. The Committee reacted by stressing their difference from the rest of the field, by marking the history of "unfriendliness" to China of all those famed and powerful scholars now vying to get to Beijing. Already in 1972, the coordinators had sent a letter to the China International Travel Services, tracing the connections between the official organizations tasked with relationships with Beijing, the funding of the field, and its history in relations to China. "The leaders of these organizations," they argued, "are the same persons who through their Cold War rhetoric and anti-China bias have contributed to the frigid atmosphere of the fifties and sixties which has silenced until recently those like John Stuart Service, the late John Vincent Carter, Owen Lattimore, and John Davies purged by the attacks of McCarthy."[138] The coordinators here were staking their fundamental difference from the profession and reacting to the bad publicity concerning divisiveness within the group, specifically in relation to China. Yet it was difficult to maintain that CCAS had a closer political connection to the PRC when the very nature of CCAS politics—concerning war, imperialism, and China itself—was, at that stage, completely obscure.

Not surprisingly, the third CCAS delegation never went to China, and there was never a "return trip." This had to do with the changes in the diplomatic relationships and the establishment of official academic contacts between the United States and China. In that new situation, CCAS was not a player. But the idea of a CCAS-sponsored visit persisted, periodically resurfacing—and constantly frustrated—in the following years. The justifications for such trips, however, changed over time. It was not so much a question of "understanding," or connecting to socialist realities; it was a fight for the possibility of alternative views within the field, "struggling against the Establishment monopoly of scholarship and analysis of the People's Republic of China." And having visited China boosted the legitimacy of radical scholarship.[139] It was also a very mundane question of individual survival within academia. As Angus McDonald remarked in 1975, in a tight job market, traveling to China might mean a PR advantage and legitimacy, but also, very plainly, it "might make the difference between getting a job and not getting one."[140]

If, by 1975, "going to China" had been largely reduced to a frustrating question of career and power struggle within Asian studies, I have shown in this chapter that it had a much different and much more fundamental character in the previous years. Investing time, energy, and political capital into the China trips of 1971–72 had practical and organizational relevance for CCAS. It brought forth a discussion of priorities, the definition of a political line of sorts, and, eventually, a debate over the enforcement of that line. This happened in the midst of a massive reassessment of the international scene—low ebb and end of the Vietnam War, waning of the New Left movement in the United States, the Lin Biao affair in China,[141] and the major turn of Beijing's foreign policy—and the case of CCAS allows an insight into how macro-political events are reflected in the untidy world of micro-politics and everyday organizational practices.

Much more significantly, the China trips also brought to the fore, even more vividly, one of the issues at the very core of CCAS's existence and mission, that of the production of alternative knowledge and of knowledge of alternative politics. The Committee had framed its role within academia (and within the larger movement) in opposition to any form of "neutral" and "objective" scholarship, because that scholarship—their teachers'—was not only politically tainted but also incapable of producing any coherent and true understanding of the new things in Asia. New political realities required a radical political perspective not just to be studied and understood but to be acknowledged, seen as such. When the first CCAS delegation was invited to China, that understanding gaze was returned and recognized, and that recognition in turn was perceived as solidifying CCAS's position within the field. Many in CCAS viewed the China trips as confirmation of political closeness as well as of the correctness of their analysis. And that, in turn, they perceived as boosting their legitimacy as China scholars, in contrast to an "establishment" who could not understand and, very literally, could not see that China. Much of the self-importance that CCAS showed after the China trips—their aspiration to be the gatekeepers to China, to be a part in framing international relationship—was in part connected to the idea that radical truth tellers had a better understanding of China (precisely as "radicals") and as such should be empowered.

However, while shared political concerns might help identify what was new and different in China, they were not guarantees of knowledge, let alone understanding. And the Concerned Scholars, once in China, were faced with a different kind of *doxa*, produced by a different kind of establishment—the relentless propaganda of the Chinese hosts—one that required the visitors to behave like "friends" rather than scholars.[142] The harsh and consuming debate within CCAS is, in this perspective, a reminder of the difficulties that Maoist China posed to sympathetic observers globally. It would be much easier to dismiss the whole "China-tripping" experience as a naive dream, the fulfillment (or crushing) of an Orientalized romantic desire—and in some cases, it looked precisely like that. But CCAS's own internal debate invites us to take the questions it raised seriously. Looking back at the tortuous history of knowledge production about Maoism and the Cultural Revolution, these issues seem still very much relevant today. These were questions of how we see, how we write, how we study politics, how we produce knowledge about political events, and how all of this shapes our own roles as scholars, political beings, and intellectuals within specific historical circumstances. We have since gained new critical understandings about our own projections and new empirical data about China's recent history, but we might have constructed a new "limitation on seeing"; specifically, we cannot see as travelers and prospective travelers tried to see Communist China, politically and scholarly.[143] And maybe there is something to be recovered in that gaze. As Dora Zhang writes at the end of her review of Barthes's Chinese notebooks, "alors la Chine?" remains very much an open question.[144]

CHAPTER FOUR

FACING THERMIDOR

Global Maoism at Its End

It's all in vain. We've tried in various ways to change the world; the point is now to interpret it.
—Jacques Rancière, *Althusser's Lesson*

Le Maoïsme n'existe pas. Il n'a jamais existé. C'est sans doute ce qui explique son succès.
—Christophe Bourseiller, *Les Maoïstes*

On January 10, 1981, Bryant Avery, then editor-in-chief of the *Bulletin of Concerned Asian Scholars*, wrote almost in despair to his coeditors: "In my 5 years at this, I've never had so many little and big troubles putting something together as has been the case with these China mss. [manuscripts]."[1] Avery's frustration was understandable: the idea of a special issue on "Post-Mao China" had been proposed to the BCAS editorial board in 1978, and a call for papers had formally gone out in early 1979. Three years later, the editors were still struggling with incomplete essays, poor quality of submissions, conflicting ideas about revisions, and general dissatisfaction about the whole project. This tortuous process was the manifestation of a political and intellectual malaise, one specifically centered on the meaning of "China" in the post-Mao era.

With Deng Xiaoping's formal ascent to power in 1978 and the official sanctioning of his reform program by the Third

Plenum in 1979, China presented a starkly different image from the one that had so fascinated CCAS. Immediately after the death of Mao, the PRC had initiated massive imports of technology from the West, and now it seemingly stepped firmly into the world of capitalist trade by adopting the "open door policy," which allowed foreign investments in specific areas under exceptionally favorable conditions. Even more significant were the internal reforms: the official approval of market methods allowed for an explosion of entrepreneurship in both the cities and the countryside, mostly in the form of petty private enterprise. Increasing wage differences and factory discipline were promoted, in a clear departure from the Maoist-declared search for equality. The economic and social models of the high Maoist era (such as Dazhai) were summarily discredited and abandoned at the same time as old cadres were being rehabilitated and revolutionary rebels jailed.[2] All the political experiments and debates of the Cultural Revolution were not only interrupted but declared meaningless, a pernicious diversion from rational economic pragmatism. The process of dismantling the People's Communes, one of the hallmarks of Maoist life in the countryside, started in earnest, and by 1980 the adoption of the Household Responsibility System sanctioned their fragmentation in private plots. Economic differences increased rapidly. "Somebody will get rich first," Deng had indeed forecasted.[3]

Alessandro Russo has identified the "thorough negation" (*chedi fouding*) of the Cultural Revolution as the defining character of the Deng reforms and the basic subjective condition for the solidity of the Chinese state over the last thirty years.[4] This does not simply imply a reversal of verdicts (people almost literally exchanging positions in and out of jail) but a complete denial of the political subjectivities that animated the previous era. This is a position that has made the Cultural Revolution programmatically nonunderstandable—or rather not even worthy of understanding—if not, in terms of psychology, "ten years of madness." In this sense, we can consider the massive political shift of the late 1970s in China (which was part and parcel of a global transformation) precisely as a form of Thermidorean reaction, a subjectivity at the end of a political sequence that makes the political sequence unthinkable.[5] Thermidor, in Sophie Wahnich's analysis, marks also denial of the ability of the citizens, the people, to think politically; with Thermidor, politics is once again restricted to its proper places (the Party, the State) and subsumed under a discourse of law and order.[6] Thermidor represents, then, the ultimate negation and the complete reversal of what I have described earlier as one of the defining characteristics of the long sixties: the declaration of the ability to think and speak by people who had been always denied that ability.

In this chapter, I illustrate the forms the Thermidorean reaction took outside China and the consequences it had for those who had taken Maoism seriously in the United States and France. I describe and analyze the intellectual and political debates among the BCAS editors, writers, and "fellow travelers" related to the publication of two special China issues in 1981 precisely as they embody a reflection by a few scholars/activists on the seeming end of the conditions of their scholarship and activism.[7] The Committee of Concerned Asian Scholars, the organization behind the *Bulletin*, had already disbanded in 1979, and the discussion around the "China issue" was possibly the last attempt to retrieve meaning for an intellectual and political experience that had been so crucially marked by the existence of "new things" in Asia. I draw on this case study to analyze what political and intellectual possibilities disappeared when reference to "Maoist China" suddenly became politically dangerous and intellectually problematic for scholars working in a particular post-Mao context. Two concepts are crucial and suggest important connections to the wider crisis of the late 1970s, marked by the waning of the political subjectivities that had animated the long sixties and the contemporary rise of neoliberalism worldwide.[8] First, with the end of Maoism, the category of "class" became extremely problematic. The Cultural Revolution—as well as contemporary movements such as May '68 in Europe—had challenged the understanding of class as a political and economic signifier.[9] The debates in the last decade of Maoism centered on the permanence of class difference, on the very existence of class struggle under socialism, and on the nature of class itself. The Deng-era reforms, however, were instead predicated on the absolute insignificance of these issues, which were reductively posited as little more than empty ideology. The China scholars at BCAS found themselves in a difficult position as the new Chinese regime dismantled and denied much of the experiments CCASers had supported while simultaneously dismissing the concepts (such as class) that scholars could employ to analyze these shifts, either by flattening them into a new economicism or by pronouncing them irrelevant to the new situation.

The second concept that animated the post-Mao crisis was a particular understanding of "culture," which, in this case, pointed to a profound change in the relationships between production and production of knowledge, intellectual and manual labor, and politics and scholarship that the Cultural Revolution had promoted and that the Concerned Scholars found so inspiring. The "culture" of Maoism, which was clearly not separable from "class," extended way beyond the sphere of "cultural production" narrowly understood; rather, it embodied a rethinking of the possibility of the intelligence of the people. That culture was one of the first casualties of the post-Mao era.

The political and intellectual collapse was reflected in and reinforced by objective conditions in U.S. universities. If at the time of the CCAS founding there were plenty of opportunities for budding Asia scholars, the job market presented a much bleaker picture by the late 1970s and early 1980s. By then, many CCASers (often the most active and radical) were living at the borders of academia, as a new form of precariat. Data on Asian studies are difficult to come by (AAS does not have easily accessible records), but we can extrapolate from both anecdotal evidence and hard data from related disciplines. In the case of history—many unemployed CAS were trained as historians—the 1970s witnessed a massive disproportion between available jobs and new PhD holders (the disparity between new jobs and new PhDs rose close to 50 percent).[10] Several former CAS I interviewed confirmed a similar situation for employment in other Asia-related disciplines.[11]

Subjectively, the dire situation in terms of jobs, the perception of an ongoing persecution of radical academics, the rifts within the former Concerned, and the massive changes happening in Asian and global politics were often combined to paint a picture of crisis and at times even betrayal. At the time, this was often framed as a split between careerists and purists; to some, it seemed logical that it was the true radicals who were left out (or kicked out) of the disciplinary boundaries, while the more compromising colleagues proceeded to professional success. Without neglecting the obvious practical conditions of employment, I propose instead to take the crisis and the splits within the CAS as a sign of the reduction in the possibilities for rethinking the role of intellectuals and the production of knowledge under Thermidor.

As described in chapters 1 and 2, the Concerned Asian Scholars were not especially theoretical in their analysis, and their institutional and personal archives are often concerned with seemingly mundane and practical matters. In an effort to extrapolate some more abstract reflections from these sources, here too I have found it illuminating to employ concepts and analysis from French Maoism to highlight what was at stake, theoretically, in this specific historical conjuncture.

French Maoism was articulated precisely on the issues of "class" and "culture," especially after 1968, which abetted the temporary collapse of the barrier separating students from workers and a major attempt to rethink the meaning and role of ideology and the daily practice of knowledge production. Maoist groups such as the Gauche Prolétarienne called specifically for the integration of the intellectuals with the working class, the dissolution of the distinction of manual and intellectual labor through the practice of *etablissement*, and a workerist policy.[12] Richard Wolin has recently suggested we view French Maoism as a necessary step toward a more "modern" understanding of politics in terms of human rights and/or of identity (gender, sexuality, etc.). This also implies a crucial shift for intellectuals, with the disappearance of the "prophetic intellectual," vanguard of the masses, and the emergence of the "universal intellectual who morally shames the powers-that-be by confronting them with higher ideals of justice and truth."[13] I argue here instead that if Maoism was necessary for this shift, it was because, through the refracted example of the past several decades in China, it had made unthinkable "traditional" class politics—defined in socioeconomic terms and represented by a party—but it had also exhausted the possibilities of a production of knowledge under conditions of equality. Again I use here the work of Jacques Rancière to articulate an understanding of the crisis of class and of the intellectual in connection with the Cultural Revolution, French Maoism, and their aftermath. Finally, I examine some of the documents of the Union des Communistes de France Marxistes-Léninistes (UCF-ML), which remained "Maoist" through part of the 1980s, and I show the limits and the possibilities of surviving the Thermidorean reaction of the late 1970s.

China, Disappeared

By 1977, members of CCAS as well as the editors of the *Bulletin* were well aware that, in the almost ten years of existence of the organization, the political situation had fundamentally changed. With the collapse of a wider New Left movement, it was evident that progressive intellectuals were now much more likely to succumb to the pressure of "backsliding into 'apolitical academicism' or selfish individualism."[14] Marjorie King, in her final address as CCAS coordinator, stated, quite bleakly, that the Committee existed only as a bureaucratic organization, connecting "progressive" teachers by informing them of different activities. Any effort to revive it as a political organization had failed due "to the changing political situation nationally and world-wide."[15] Bryant Avery looked at the same shift from the point of view of the *Bulletin*: the change between 1968–69 and 1978–79 had also been a geographical one, with more—and more interesting—articles on India, Thailand, and Korea, and on the almost complete disappearance of China (and Vietnam). "China appears increasingly to be a problem," he concluded; "one doesn't have to live in a college community to recognize how many persons are going thru the 'god that failed' syndrome . . . around us there is doubt, frustration, and anger."[16] Frustration was palpable, for example, in a letter from Gail Omvedt (India specialist and member of CCAS almost since inception), who commiserated: "I find China right now depressing. . . . Is there any way to believe that the cultural revolution or all the 'maoist' things we appreciated so much still survive—or were correct—except now as a tradition being repressed?"[17] The depression was quite understandable in the case of Omvedt, who had forcefully argued that what India needed was a radical revolution, Chinese-style.[18] But even Helen Chauncey, who had never been, by her own admission, terribly sympathetic toward China, remarked on the grim experience of visiting the PRC. "Part of that can simply be dismissed as the price of facing up to the rather ugly reality of Mao's China," Chauncey contended, "but a good part of the problem is having come face to face with post-Maoist China, at least as it looks in the short run. It will be very hard to say the things most of us would like to say about China, because we will sound like raving rightists. (Believe me; we've practiced on each other!) But it may be equally unacceptable not to say them, in the interests of some kind of political honesty."[19]

After the death of Mao in 1976, China had largely disappeared from the pages of *BCAS*, and that disappearance did not go unnoticed, especially because of the history of the journal and the composition of its subscribers.[20] The *Bulletin* had begun as a publication with primary interests in two fields: the war in Vietnam and the Cultural Revolution.[21] Both events were now over, yet the readership remained heavily skewed: one-half to one-third of the subscribers were still in the China field, and they were apparently complaining vocally about the lack of "good, meaty articles" on China. The editors also assumed that the hemorrhaging of subscribers from BCAS was in large part due to people's perception that the publication offered nothing of interest for China specialists.[22]

The perception was, alas, correct, but it was not for lack of effort on the part of the *Bulletin*'s editors. Despite the shoestring nature of BCAS operations,[23] the editors had actively solicited essays on China, for more than two years, with almost no result. In 1980, Bryant Avery was compelled to complain vociferously (in capital letters) to the members of the editorial board—many were China specialists themselves—of the "stoney, [sic] silly silence on China in the pages of the Bulletin." The problem was not only the paucity of submissions related to China; it was also their quality. The reviewing process at BCAS was complex and seemingly redundant: at least two or three of the editors plus members of the editorial board (or outside readers) read and commented on each manuscript. This was another way in which the *Bulletin* strove to present a different mode of scholarly production, one that functioned on the basis of a collective—I am tempted to say "mass-line"—form of decision making. This process produced an incredible amount of paperwork and criticism, which documents the increasing editorial dissatisfaction with China manuscripts after 1977, a dissatisfaction that was never based solely on "scholarly" premises. For example, in 1980, editor Robert Marks reviewed three manuscripts on China, including one by a member of the BCAS editorial board, and rejected all of them. They lacked analysis, he argued, did not have any new information, or, more generally, seemed completely irrelevant to the current situation.[24] Bryant Avery was more charitable in his comments on one of the same manuscripts: he found the piece a "trifle boring," yet, he confessed, he found 99.5 percent of the stuff written about China "a trifle boring."[25] That these submissions were so lackluster and dull, however, had little to do with the actual situation in post-Mao China, which was going through a massive, possibly devastating, but definitively interesting, systemic and political earthquake.

In an attempt to find reasons for this disappearance of China from the pages, the *Bulletin*'s editors also pointed to the competition posed by other, more traditionally "scholarly" journals, such as *Modern China* or *China Quarterly*. Many former CCASers published regularly in such venues in the late 1970s, yet, according to the editors, never submitted anything to the *Bulletin*, or passed along rethreads and reprints.[26] This was, according to early CCAS member Helen Chauncey, a realistic choice, one connected to the needs of a scholarly career: people need jobs, then people need to publish—in "respectable" places, one could add. And "the *Bulletin* was not that respectable," Saundra Sturdevant remarked. It was not something that looked good on a CV; it was a red flag, potentially damaging for those whose main goal was an academic career.[27]

Yet, while there were indeed issues that were very practically related to the academic careers of China specialists (access to archives and to the "field," decline in the number of jobs, the pressure of tenure), I argue later in this chapter that "career" was also the name for a specific shift in the politics of knowledge production and the role of the scholar/intellectual, one intimately connected with the crisis of the late 1970s. As Chauncey was also keen to point out, one true political conundrum related to the new global position of China: "The China folks, who were on the outs (along with China) during the 1960's debates, are now backing a power very much in the thick of international (and often anti-socialist) rivalries."[28] At the most fundamental level, the choice to publish on China in a "scholarly" journal while refusing to do so in a venue like the *Bulletin*—which had been, declaredly and always, politically committed, especially to the experience of the Cultural Revolution—reflected a profoundly political decision. In the tectonic reassessment of the early Deng era, any analysis of China that remained in some way faithful to the "concern" of the *Bulletin* required a political self-reflection and new intellectual tools. To remain "concerned" meant to examine not only what was changing in China in terms of policies and economic decisions, but also how that change related to the subjective political concern that Maoism had such a huge role in framing. Scholarly, uncommitted, objective (and "a trifle boring") analysis was a much easier path. As Bryant Avery bleakly concluded, the choice not to publish in the *Bulletin* at that specific time was "a political choice ... or perhaps a careerist choice with political implications."[29]

What We Talk about When We Talk about Post-Mao China

The process leading to the publication of two special issues on China in 1981 was painful, long, and deliberated down to the smallest details. Yet, despite all the discussions, the questions that the end of Maoism posed seemed to remain slippery and ungraspable to the authors, the reviewers, and the editors. In retrospect, this lack of clarity seems to have been the major reason for the slow and difficult nature of the publication process.

The scarcity and (allegedly) poor quality of submissions was only part of the problem. The silence of the BCAS in the previous years had been too evident a sign of embarrassment, too loud an affirmation of intellectual distress; to finally decide to publish extensively about China could not but have powerful implications for the entire enterprise. Despite all the statements to the contrary, a "China issue" could only be understood as a reassessment of the positions that CCAS and the *Bulletin* had held in the previous decade, and, as such, it was a crucial and eventful step. One year after the call for papers, editorial board member Mark Selden was still urging caution, asking for a slower pace: "We are no longer sitting on top of the volcano on the China question. What is needed at this moment is more mature long range reflection and rethinking of basic assumptions. And some careful martialing of evidence. You will not achieve that quickly. Of course it is true that it would be a 'hot issue' to peddle at AAS [the annual meeting of the Association for Asian Studies]. But we want one that will sizzle for a good period of time not pop like a firecracker . . . poof. Right?"[30] While it took two more years for the China issues to finally be published, that delay did not actually help in producing long-range reflection or (intellectual and political) sizzling.

Editors wrangled not only over the contents and the quality of the essays, but also on who should be tasked with writing them. Edward Friedman and Bruce Cumings initially suggested that it was the CCAS founding generation—including those who had already left the field—who should hold a symposium with some prominent non-BCAS people and "excoriate each other over how far deMaoization has gone."[31] These were the people who had become involved with China and CCAS in part because of Maoism and who had been politicized by the Vietnam War and the Cultural Revolution; personally and politically, a rethinking and a reassessment was due on their part. But others among the editors objected to this insistence on the "old guard." Could these people say anything new about China? What about a younger generation, whose experience of China was shaped after the Nixon trip in 1972 or even later?[32] In the end, the two published issues would see essays from the old guard, from European contributors, and from a few relatively new names.

Much more crucial was the question of why and how to write about China. Clearly there was a need, a need embodied in the stony silence of the previous years. But, given that other venues had fewer problems in publishing about the post-Mao era, the need was not simply an academic one. It was also obviously and urgently political. The editors singled out repeatedly the fact that, for example, the "Gang of Four" and the Hua Guofeng inter-reign had never been addressed in the *Bulletin*. This was clearly not just a product of scholarly laziness.[33]

The editors suggested wide-ranging topics for investigation. In a draft proposal in 1978, Saundra Sturdevant produced a list that was both comprehensive and exemplary of the kind of massive change going on in China. She asked for contributions on 1) substantive theoretical changes or modifications (bourgeois right, dictatorship of the proletariat, party, base-superstructure, productive forces, class struggle, etc.); 2) practical matters (workplace, wages, education, four modernizations, democratic centralism, *xiafang*, revolutionary committees, etc.); and 3) Chinese foreign policy. In the end, she concluded, the obvious central question was the fate of Maoism after 1976.[34] In another call for papers, the editors proposed areas such as "agriculture, heavy industry, accumulation and investment, education, art and literature, women, and foreign policy."[35] Richard Pfeffer (one of the founding members of CCAS) joined in with his own suggestions, asking for new "facts" but also for a revision and a rethinking of Marxian theory in the post-Mao era. But, more interestingly, he highlighted that any such rethinking and revision also required "some self-conscious consideration of our own position as analysts." The Maoist emphasis on transforming the relations of production was central in the CCAS's perception of their own position as intellectuals and activists. Pfeffer then indirectly inquired about what the consequences of the end of that emphasis, the closure of that opening, would be. And, he wondered, "how does our living as academics in a liberal, capitalist, leading imperialist nation affect our perception of China?"[36]

Clearly there was no lack of important things to write about, yet the editors seemed to have been repeatedly discouraged by the inability of authors to ask "good questions" about the current China situation. In 1981, Saundra Sturdevant wrote to John Gittings,[37] urging him to submit a revised paper: "Your 'dilemma' of being able to ask questions better than to answer them is a methodology that we could use more of. I find that a good number of the ms. [manuscripts] we have so far are not as good at asking questions as providing answers. I intend to correct that somewhat by my introduction to the issue. It would be good to have some ms. that do the same."[38] The editors and reviewers complained repeatedly about the lack of precision in the submissions, the vagueness of the focus, the inability to stake a position, or even (and worse) to identify the crucial problems. Even people who eventually embraced a radically Thermidorean position, such as Edward Friedman, had no specific argument and no real assessment of the theoretical and political consequences of the post-Mao shift. Some authors were more cautious, others more blunt, choosing to side with the new regime, but the intellectual paralysis was similar and shared.

Class and Depoliticization

Mark Selden had been right in predicting that the long-awaited special issue on China might pop like a firecracker. With the exception of three contributions (which were, in opposite ways, politically straightforward), all the essays published in 1981 straddled a middle ground, either assessing in very cautious and declaredly "pragmatic" ways the new policies, or underestimating their differences from the previous period, despite evidence to the contrary. They often skipped over issues that had been central in the Maoist era (and in the *Bulletin*'s analysis); this did not go unnoticed by the editors, who were very keen at identifying the signs of conscious or subconscious avoidance. Robert Marks commented on the grammatical choices in Victor Lippit's essay on the communes: "Might it be that not specifically addressing the issue of equity and stratification leads to the use of passive voice to obscure the issue?"[39] Even with the publication of the 1981 issues, the *Bulletin*'s silence over the end of Maoism continued, albeit in different forms.

However, while these cautious and pragmatic essays did not add much to the evaluation of post-Mao China, they did offer a perspective on what the end of Maoism meant for the activists/intellectuals of the BCAS. First and foremost, in their form and content, they testified of the disappearance of the political, which was particularly striking for a publication like the *Bulletin*. The various authors showed enthusiasm for the new opportunities to do fieldwork and study change as it was happening,[40] but they largely refrained from any political evaluation of that process of change. Their assessment was almost universally based on the very code words of the new post-Mao policies: cash income, productivity, modernization, and, above all, the separation of politics and economics that was, explicitly, at the center of Deng's project.

One of the crucial elements of Maoism since the Great Leap Forward had been to challenge the economic assumption of technocratic modernization precisely in the name of politics, by making the reduction of inequalities—the political issue par excellence—the fulcrum of any perspective on economic development. Both the Great Leap Forward and the Cultural Revolution were predicated, in different ways, on that assumption. "Class," in the Maoist perspective, had moved away from a strict socioeconomic connotation—although the class labeling system maintained a certain amount of almost biological determinism, often with disastrous effects—and the elimination of class differences had become a problem that could not be reduced to the simple restructuring of private ownership or to the equalization of income. Rather, it had to do with overcoming divides—manual/intellectual, urban/rural, leader/led—with the subjectivity of the workers and the peasants, and eventually with the very existence of the party-state.[41] The history of the last decade of the Maoist period is, in this sense, an attempt to invent practices that could reduce those divides and that were grounded in the autonomous self-consciousness of the people.[42] As Jacques Rancière summarized: "Proletarian ideology is neither a summary of working-class representations of virtues, nor the body of 'proletarian' doctrines; it is a stopped assembly-line, a flouted authority, a cancelled system of divisions between jobs, a mass response to the 'scientific' innovations of exploitation; it is also barefoot doctors and the entrance of the working class into Chinese universities."[43]

However, the experiments of the Cultural Revolution decade, no matter how innovative, were still predicated on a system of reference that preceded their inception and that was shared with those who opposed them. "The working class must lead in everything" was a slogan the "Maoists" deployed in defense of their experiments, but, as Alessandro Russo highlights, "the working class was the same historico-political category to which their adversaries also referred, with the aggravating factor that the Maoists were committed to defending political dynamics rooted in turbulent, mass-scale indecision on what working class really meant as a political category."[44] The categories of class, class struggle, worker, proletarian dictatorship, and, ultimately, party and party-state were at the same time fundamentally challenged and continuously deployed during the Cultural Revolution, leading to a series of theoretical and practical contradictions: What is a worker (or an intellectual) in a socialist society? How can opposition within the same class be justified? How can new "classes" emerge under a party-state?[45] In this, according to Alain Badiou, the failure of the Cultural Revolution configured an experience of "saturation" of these categories, marking the impossibility of defining new forms of struggles within the articulation of class and the party-state.[46] The post-Mao reaction was to not only deny the debates and practices of the Cultural Revolution any political worth, but also to label them as dangerous for society and the state.[47] Deng's "pragmatism" meant a refusal to engage in any way in the political issues raised in the previous decades while accepting the demise of the categories that had framed those issues. It was a massive process of depoliticization shaped as a separation of the political (dangerous, ideological, empty, and abstract) from the economical (pragmatic, practical, real). "It does not matter whether a cat is black or white; as long as it catches mice, it is a good cat,"[48] Deng famously quipped. This was not the folksy expression of a matter-of-fact embrace of pragmatism, but a declaration of the independence of economic efficiency from any political consideration, and as such a complete reversal of the Maoist perspective.

The authors writing in the 1981 *Bulletin* accepted—directly or indirectly—this post-Mao separation of politics from economics. And, once they did, all the issues concerning class, equality, the state, and subjectivity of the people became immediately obscure. "Class," in particular, which had been already dismantled of its strict socioeconomic value in the previous years, could not be recovered in any sense. In this perspective, it is less surprising that the assessment of the new Dengist policies in the *Bulletin* often lacked even the most basic attention to what sectors of the population those polices benefited; it lacked even a rudimentary class analysis. Almost all essays (with two exceptions) dealt with the rural areas and agricultural production, which had been the focus of the early years of reform. Yet all the essays refused to engage in conversations about the kinds of inequalities the new system produced, who benefited from them, and, more importantly, what political consequences and motivations accompanied such choices. Most essays refused to discuss how the new agricultural policies (NAP) differed from those of the proceeding years in principle—and not just in pragmatic terms.

Peter Nolan and Gordon White, for example, stressed the continuity of the new policies with those of the Maoist period and argued that, despite the introduction of market economy, the weakening of the collectives, and the encouragement of inequalities, "the basic commitment to collectivized agriculture appears to be unimpaired."[49] They justified such a baffling statement by a distinction between "Maoist goals" (which remained valid) and "Maoist methods" (which were being supplanted). After ten years, during which the entire country (and sympathetic foreign observers) had obsessed about revolutionary practice as both a goal and a method, this distinction is particularly perplexing. Similarly, in his contribution, Victor Lippit on the one hand affirmed that the communes were going to be strengthened and that they remained the core of the "Chinese model"; on the other, he painstakingly described all the ways in which the reforms were actually damaging the very existence of this institutional form (incentives, mechanization, increased division of labor, etc.). Lippit argued that the new development strategy was both practical and necessary, in part because of the failures of the Cultural Revolution policies, "expressed most notably in the failure of incomes to rise, the perpetuation of social hierarchy, the rigid censorship, the failure of educational reform in the critical area of the substantive content of education, and the inability of the direct producers to control their own workplaces or participate meaningfully in higher levels of social decision-making."[50] Yet, except for the first issue, that of income, all the other ones had been central in the Maoist discourse and practice—even if that practice had been unsuccessful—but they were programmatically not part of the Dengist discourse of modernization.

The editors and reviewers often challenged the assumptions, silences, and contradictions in the manuscripts; their comments give proof of another entire layer of intellectual production about these problems and show that there were indeed people in BCAS asking crucial questions. Their comments allow us the rare chance to follow closely a political and intellectual debate centered on a publication, at a time when that publication was (politically) a life-and-death issue. The editors took the authors to task for not stating a clear position and for ignoring the conflict between their present argument and what they had written in the past. Saundra Sturdevant, in a dense and thorough review of Lippit's manuscript (over five pages, typewritten, single-spaced), challenged him on almost every front. She contested his equation of "livelihood" with "income"—an obvious form of economic reductionism; she brought forth evidence on the actual disruption of communal work produced by the new policies; she pointed at the contradiction in what "practical" meant now and during the Cultural Revolution;[51] and she singled out Lippit's refusal to see the class (i.e., political) reasons for the NAP. "Surely Victor is correct is [sic] stating the current policies will have the advantage of increasing 'the maximum earning capacity of the most productive workers.'" Yet, she challenged, "he says NOTHING at all about those who aren't in this category. NOR does he deal with WHY this 'category' [class] is being singled out for rewards. THIS QUESTION MUST BE ADDRESSED."[52] And, she concluded, "What does pragmatism mean to the Chinese in 1981? . . . We're seeing how the solution evolved, what classes it serves and how it fits into the international order of things. But WHY take this route?"[53]

Sturdevant was equally thorough in her comments on another manuscript, by Marc Blecher and Mitch Meisner, and, once again, she highlighted the silence obscuring the political questions behind their otherwise very precise analysis. Sturdevant sounded rightfully exasperated: "There is no attempt to analyze WHY each policy, the contradictions of each policy."[54] Blecher and Meisner examined the dismissal of the Dazhai model—the "Chinese contribution" to developmental literature with respect to agricultural development in the Third World[55]—but they did so only by focusing on the changing administrative relationship between the country and the commune. Moving away from Dazhai and toward marketization and personal incentives was, for Blecher and Meisner, a move toward a different "redistributive policy," one not centered on the commune but on a larger, macro level. It was, if anything, an administrative shift, not a political one.[56] From this starting point, the authors could easily dismiss as irrelevant the elimination of class distinctions in the countryside, despite the fact that, as Sturdevant reminded them, the NAP favored "middle-rich peasants" ("but they don't discuss the ramifications of this").[57] Interestingly, the authors recognized the stalemate behind the issue of class after the Cultural Revolution: "What we may see, then, in the flight from 'politics' to 'pragmatism' is the continuing inability to find a socio-economic or class analysis that is appropriate to the present Chinese situation while at the same time adequate for economic development programs and socialist political leadership."[58] Yet they confronted neither this inability nor the intellectual and political distance from the previous period, when such an analysis—even if it was not successfully achieved—remained nonetheless one of the crucial goals.

While the BCAS contributors were not alone in their intellectual paralysis regarding post-Mao China, the frustration of Sturdevant and the other editors becomes even more understandable if we take into consideration that instances of much more trenchant analysis of the Chinese reforms and their relationship with the previous period were available before 1981. Possibly the most glaring example was that of the French Marxist Charles Bettelheim, who submitted his resignation as president of the Franco-Chinese Friendship Association in the form of a public letter in *Le Monde* on May 11, 1977. In the letter, Bettelheim argued that a "revisionist line" was triumphing in China, and that, despite the lip service paid to the Cultural Revolution, its gains were being practically liquidated.[59] When the Canadian activist and scholar Neil Burton urged him to be cautious and less definitive in his assessment, Bettelheim answered with a long essay, published by *Monthly Review*, in which he made his case in detail, providing quotes from Chinese newspapers and radio broadcasts. He described the "withering" of the practices associated with the Cultural Revolution, the return to a "one-man management," the praise of the "obedience" of the working class, and the reemergence of "factory despotism."[60] Bettelheim pointed at the return to a strictly economistic and productivistic logic, in which, for example, the "*development of agriculture is seen mainly from the standpoint of his contribution to the accumulation of capital*" and workers are submitted to the demand of profit. The failure to understand and answer to these developments was due, Bettelheim argued, precisely to "*the absence of a class analysis of present-day China.*"[61] That somebody with no knowledge of the language and who relied only on translated sources could produce such an assessment—which is, of course, questionable—shows that the problem was in the political and intellectual posture, not in the availability of documentation and information.[62] One of the more far-reaching effects of Thermidor is that it makes it (almost) impossible to think in the terms of the previous political sequence.

On the whole, the essays published in the BCAS special issues configured a surrender to economic reductionism, and, to anybody familiar with the history of the *Bulletin* and of the CCAS, the China issues also marked a 180-degree shift from the work of the previous decade. The Chinese experience had been interesting to these American scholars because, as the lonely voice of Phyllis Andors reminded the readers of the special issues, it "viewed social revolution as an integral part of the process of economic modernization."[63] As I have shown in the previous chapters, the CAS had persistently analyzed Maoist China in those terms, and they had viewed the Maoist experiments as a challenge to the fixed meanings of modernization, to the technocratic and bureaucratic character of modern life, and to the univocal acceptance of the inequalities of development. China was interesting not because it had achieved a perfect balance, but because, especially during the Great Leap Forward and the Cultural Revolution, it seemed to be invested in a stubborn, if inconclusive, search for development *and* equality. Maoist China addressed questions of "individual attitudes toward authority, responsibility, and purpose" and questioned "the political and organizational consequences of technology and industry,"[64] but it also directly challenged any assumed meaning of "modernity." The CAS had supported for a decade the assumption that China had promised and, at least in part, was realizing a model of development, both economic and social, that was not only based on local realities and on the people, but one that was also declaredly "human" and egalitarian and therefore completely different both from capitalist markets and Soviet dirigisme.ABandoning that perspective clearly implied a political and intellectual loss of major consequence.

Thermidor and Its Contradictions

To analyze the extent of this loss in more theoretical terms, I propose to shift here to the cases of other intellectuals who saw Maoism as an inspiration, but whose reactions to the post-Mao era were different, although, in some cases, not less doomed. L'Union des Communistes de France Marxistes-Léninistes (UCF-ML) was a latecomer in terms of French Maoism, but it outlasted all the other organizations by stretching its existence into the eighties, "precisely as a result of the self-imposed task to continue interrogating the events of May and June 1968 in terms of both their backlash and their belated consequences for the political situation in France and abroad."[65] Because of that, and because of the intense intellectual production of the group (Alain Badiou, Sylvain Lazarus, and Natacha Michel were among its leaders), it provides an interesting counterpoint to the CCAS case. In 1976, precisely at the moment when the Chinese "new things" were being denied and demolished, the UCF-ML reclaimed the legacy of both the Cultural Revolution and May '68, specifically in terms of class. The French group argued that the Cultural Revolution had fundamentally changed the concept of class away from the strict ownership of means of production.[66] It had revealed the continual existence of the bourgeoisie within the party and the state, unmasking therefore how class difference could be reproduced precisely by the very existence of the state bureaucracy—while being hidden by "pseudo-Marxist ideology."[67] In a later pamphlet, Natacha Michel wrote that one of the contributions of Maoism and May '68 was the challenge and disruption (*la mise en crise*) of traditional Marxist categories, including, obviously, "class."[68]

With this new understanding of "class," the leaders of the UCF-ML argued, the Cultural Revolution and May '68 had demolished the distinction between economic struggle and political struggle at the base of trade unionist grievances, the fixation on improving the fate of workers expressed in strictly economic terms: "What is born with '68 is a different distinction, a decisive confrontation, between two realities and two concepts of the mass struggle themselves: on the one hand, the reactionary conception, of the purely vindicating type, of the workerist type, with its robust syndicalist and bourgeois parliamentary framework. On the other, and meeting syndicalism head-on with its political conception, there is the novelty of a political and autonomous mass struggle."[69]

The novelty was precisely that of a politics of autonomy, meaning the absolute autonomy of the proletariat from any bourgeoisie, including the bourgeoisie that was reproducing itself within the party and party-state. The "working class," in the words of these French Maoists, could become a leading class (*classe dirigeante*) only if it constituted itself as political class.[70] That meant, first of all, the rejection of strict socioeconomic claims—but also of socioeconomic definitions for class belonging and class consciousness—and, more importantly, a rethinking of the entire relationship between the subjectivity of the workers/peasants and the very horizon of political liberation. "It is not a question of giving back to the proletariat forms of consciousness and activity of which the bourgeoisie has deprived them," they wrote; "it is on the contrary that by which the working class exceeds its elementary being as social class to become a political class, a leading class. It is that by which the working class substitutes, in the horizon marked out but its own immediacy as class, the space, not only of its specific interests and grievances, but rather that of the political and social interests of the people as a whole. The liberation of the working class requires that of the people, and therefore that of the working peasants."[71]

For these French activists, one of the basic teachings of the Maoism of the Cultural Revolution was precisely that it suggested a new relationship between "proletarian dictatorship" and "class struggle": the autonomous movement of the people could not be limited to the seizing of power, the improvement of the economic conditions, and the wielding of the state apparatuses. In this perspective, what is lost with the denial of the Cultural Revolution (and of May 1968, which happened more or less simultaneously) is the very possibility of an autonomous subjectivity in the countryside or in the factory, or the possibility that "class" in this sense names a political project that overcomes the barrier of the socioeconomically defined "class" and the need for its representation through a party (or a party-state).

In 1981, the same year in which the BCAS published the two issues on post-Mao China, the UCF-ML assessed its own trajectory with a special issue of *Le Marxiste-Léniniste* titled "Ten Years of Maoism." They recognized that their points of reference, May '68 and the Cultural Revolution, had dissipated; they had failed. "These referents," they wrote, "are today without a power of their own. We carry their questions rather than their outcomes." It was that failure that left the questions open; and it was the stubborn fidelity to those questions and the realization that "the working class as political reality is a task rather than a given" that allowed the UCF-ML to survive—in some fashion—the post-Mao reaction,[72] and to do it in the name of a Maoism that was not framed as nostalgia for the past but as critical thought and experience for the future, embodied in a new, if unfinished, understanding of "class."

The lesson of the Cultural Revolution, according to Jacques Rancière, another former Maoist, could be summarized precisely in the affirmation of the autonomous subjectivity of the masses, "the capacity of the dominated": it was this capacity that challenged the need for the "dominated" to be represented, to be spoken for, and, eventually, to be made

Facing Thermidor / 161

conscious of their own status and of the patterns of their domination. It was the affirmation of this capacity that made the Chinese case new and truly "revolutionary," and that framed the Cultural Revolution as "an anti-authoritarian movement which confronted the power of the state and of the Party with the capacity of the masses."[73] And while, as Rancière recognized, much in this view of China was imagined or misperceived, this perspective on the Cultural Revolution allowed the French Maoists (and others) to thoroughly shift their understanding of what was possible but also of where the struggle was located. If the masses had an intelligence that went beyond "what it takes to get a pay raise" (i.e., strictly economic grievances),[74] then class struggle had to be located somewhere else, specifically in the "various forms of bourgeois ideology—be they traditional ideologies of individualism or obedience, or 'modern' ideologies of skills and technicities—which continue to sprout even after the takeover of political power."[75] These were the forms in which class division continued even in a socialist society, and therefore, argued Rancière, "the 'duty' of workers is no longer to exceed productivity norms; it is, instead, to invent a new world through their barely perceptible gestures."[76] Maoism therefore required, for those who took it seriously, a rethinking not only of what "class" meant but also of the subjective ability of the workers and peasants to wage class struggle as well as of the forms this struggle would take.

This perspective had been largely shared—if not clearly theoretically formulated—by CCAS. Since their founding in 1968, they had advocated for an understanding of the Chinese "new things" in their own terms, as examples of a drastically different approach to development, one that could not and should not be reduced to economic modernization, but rather that attempted to achieve the fundamental reduction of all inequalities—including those inscribed in the "barely perceptible gestures"— precisely by summoning the equal intelligence of the masses. They had understood that change had to be located in the daily practices, where ideological differences were inscribed into social and intellectual divisions (see chapter 2). The return to economicism in the 1981 issues is then even more striking. It was also quite sudden.

In 1978, Edward Friedman published in BCAS a long and vitriolic critique of Simon Leys's famous exposé of the evils of Maoist China—*Chinese Shadows*[77]—and of the American fascination with his account. Friedman pointedly and rightfully criticized Leys for missing the crucial issues behind the struggles of the Cultural Revolution, thus ignoring the principles that were discussed in debates ostensibly centered on practices and tactics. Friedman also argued that Leys's portrait of a uniquely inhuman China had the political advantage of dismissing any significance of the Chinese experience for the rest of the world: "What is the relevance to other agrarian, developing nations of the Chinese way of handling population control, rural administration or intermediate technology? If China is the bleak world discovered by Leys, there is no point in seeking answers to such questions as these in the Chinese experience."[78] Friedman was very keen to point out how Leys—the "lover-turned-hater"—was forced to represent the "cretinized villagers" as lacking any autonomous ability to understand or act politically in order to make the entire country appear to be a puppet game for Mao and those at the top. Once one fails to recognize the political subjectivity of the people, one automatically reduces them to victims.

Less than three years later, the very same Edward Friedman contributed two essays to the China special issues that represented the most inflammatory and most unabashedly revisionist texts in the whole publication, similar in tone and partly in argument to the writings by Leys that he had so adamantly criticized. It is understandable that Friedman—like all the other scholars—would rejoice at the new possibilities of knowing "the real China," one "no longer so hidden by gaudy, phony technicolor."[79] Less easily explained was Friedman's total embrace of the new policies and the new leadership, which took the form precisely of a celebration of material advantages and economics over "ideology." In an attempt to deny that the new policies were in any way "revisionist" or "counterrevolutionary," Friedman insisted on calling the Deng group "Marxist materialists" and their adversaries (the Maoists of the Cultural Revolution) "Marxist ideologues." Only the former, he argued, truly had the interests of the peasants in mind, and their policies were aimed solely at improving their livelihood. In Friedman's perspective, there was no Thermidorean reaction taking place in China: "What occurs in a France or Soviet Union or China or Kampuchea is that, if a new ruling fraction tries to force society beyond what society desires or will bear, the new state must resort to terror. It is the use of terror that indicates that the revolution has passed what is progressively possible, that the revolution is over."[80] The terrorists had to be thrown out of power for the gains of the revolution to be consolidated. While there was obviously an argument to be made on the failure of Maoist policies to dramatically change the life of peasants (something recognized by many CAS at the time and by Mao himself),[81] Friedman clearly erased the meanings of the policies of the Cultural Revolution, which he simply reduced to their economic successes or failures—understood, as they were, only through largely anecdotal evidence.

Even more striking is that once Friedman embraced that perspective, the peasants (and the workers) disappeared as subjects in his account, or rather they disappeared as the subjects of politics. Friedman described seeing people in the foothills of Jiangxi spending money on Japanese color televisions and wondering about the wisdom of that investment. Yet, he concluded, that was a mistake due to the bias of the Western observer, because watching TV was actually "liberating" for the poor and rooted Chinese.[82] This view was clearly far removed from "liberation" understood as the attempt of peasants and workers to affirm the equality of their own intelligence—as Rancière would put it. Rather, in Friedman's revised account, peasants and workers existed only as victims of the terror of the Cultural Revolution and economic experimentation, or, at best, as consumers of foreign technology.

And this is precisely one of the signs of Thermidor. "With Thermidor," argues Sophie Wahnich, "citizens had to renounce the expression of their point of view; they no longer had access to the political logos." In short, with Thermidor, the political subjectivity of the masses had to be thoroughly denied. "Rejection of the revolutionary democratic model in which, in the face of governments that were always assumed to be fallible, each citizen was responsible for maintaining the rights of man and the citizen, was the Thermidorian characteristic."[83] Thermidor also marked the inception of the age of emotional victimhood,[84] when the victim (usually of some form of terror) takes the place of the citizen, the martyr, and the hero. The political statement of the revolutionary mass is substituted by the powerless wailing of those always and already condemned to be oppressed.

What Are We Doing Here?

Christopher Connery has argued that Maoism in the 1960s and 1970s was globalized as a "specific, situated practice."[85] Maoism, that is, was globalized as a specific, located experience—the practice of the Chinese revolution—which was perceived as a global event, having world significance, yet one whose truth could only be revealed in the experience of other localized activities. If that is the case, then the crisis that I described earlier in reference to the issue of "class" was not simply a crisis of intellectual understanding; it was a crisis of situated political practices. As Rancière's quote at the beginning of this chapter ironically illustrates, this crisis resulted in a political declaration of impotence. And that declaration could not but have major effects in the organizational structure and in the daily lives of the Concerned Asian Scholars. The Cultural Revolution had identified "culture" precisely as the realm in which inequalities were reproduced through systemic structures, claims to expertise, and power relationships deployed in quotidian acts; the Concerned Asian Scholars had resituated the Maoist praxis in their search for alternative roles for intellectuals and scholars who wanted to be, at the same time and in the same positions, political activists. The denial of the Cultural Revolution in the post-Mao era was reflected and refracted in the organizational crisis of CCAS/BCAS but also in the starkly divergent paths that opened to (or were chosen by) the former Concerned Scholars. This divergence was framed, at the time and afterward, as one between career and commitment, but the issues at stake were more complicated and more profoundly political. It was ultimately a crisis—and a choice—over the political confines of the militancy of intellectuals and scholars.

At the same time they were struggling to put together a "China issue"— and the timing is obviously not coincidental—the editors and some readers of the *Bulletin* were also engaged in an attempt to rethink what their journal and the group behind it meant in a postrevolutionary world. The Committee of Concerned Asian Scholars, the organization behind the founding of BCAS, disbanded unceremoniously in 1979, thus marking the end of the "movement" side of this enterprise. Already in 1976, Jon Livingston had commented somberly on how most CCAS people, "mainly being China people," had "slid quietly back into their own research" or "slipped comfortably into China Friendship work."[86] The Committee embodied the organizational effort of a generation of Asia specialists to be at the same time scholars and activists, to join research with political practice. The fragmentation of the antiwar and New Left movements restricted the avenues for outward activism, and many perceived that there was thus no need or utility left for the Committee; most of the Concerned retreated into their scholarly identities, reducing politics to a function of intellectual production.

Yet, to the editors, the *Bulletin* remained stubbornly political, even after the dissolution of the Committee. In 1979, Bryant Avery wrote to a publisher interested in purchasing the journal that the editors had always "perceived of the journal as part of a low-key 'movement' within the Asian studies field. We have not worked so hard at this solely because we like having a journal around; rather the journal has a political purpose." "Political" here, added Avery, was broadly defined: "As per IRS stipulation we do not 'lobby' for particular legislation etc., but within Asian studies itself there are cliques and power brokers whom we have spent ten years criticizing."[87] However, that specific political posture—which had been closely related to the Vietnam War, U.S. imperialism, and revolution in Asia—was clearly not so self-evident to a new cohort of budding scholars. Avery recognized that they had failed to incorporate a different generation of Asia specialists, who often asked what the *Bulletin* was all about, where it came from, what "concerned" meant.[88] From an organization of brash—and not always polite—grad students, the *Bulletin* had seemingly become one managed by and catering to "reputable scholars."[89] An organization that was, at the time of its major expansion, posited to take over the field "in a peaceful Kuhnian intellectual revolution" found itself to have instead largely been swallowed up by the field, "its ideas being chewed and spit out when they have proven to be indigestible."[90] CCAS and BCAS had become, in some form, part of the "establishment." This was clearly not an unusual path for a ten-year-old organization, and there was an understandable fear of obsolescence among the editors. But this was compounded and exacerbated by the profound change in the global and national situation around the Concerned Asian Scholars, something that made the political purpose of the *Bulletin* and the "concern" of these scholars even more obscure and contradictory.

Communications among the editors and the editorial board reflected uneasiness and a sense of aimlessness, and there were proposals to formally redefine the goals and principles of the *Bulletin*'s enterprise. Already in 1975, Angus McDonald sent his draft of a possible new statement of purpose for the Concerned Asian Scholars; and in 1980, Bryant Avery submitted a much longer and more elaborate (six-page) proposal for the *Bulletin*. Both revisions, despite the five years between them, tried to reestablish a firm footing for the CAS to address an "Asia" that was obviously shifting. In McDonald's prose, CCAS aimed at promoting "sympathetic understanding of the aspirations of the common people of Asia," and it worked as a conduit to transmit their demands "to American and other citizens of the economically advanced world."[91] Avery discussed how the global movement of which the *Bulletin* was part was now exhausted and the future was uncertain, but he hastened to add that the journal still aspired to "keep the overall Asia-centered movement alive on a steady but quieter note by performing an educational role well."[92] It is difficult to imagine what "Asia-centered movement" was viable in the 1980s and what political commitment informed the educational role the *Bulletin* claimed. But even McDonald's "sympathetic understanding" was a far cry from the actual inspiration CCAS had drawn from China and Vietnam in the previous years. Even if we are not yet at the level of the generic victimhood of Friedman's and Leys's descriptions, "Asia" here could only stand for a set of concerns that require understanding and maybe tolerance, but it was clearly no longer a source of autonomous and alternative political practice.

The proposals were also very vague in terms of political positioning of the group. Both McDonald and Avery envisioned "a broad united front-type organization, with many rooms and many roles," or an "umbrella-type organization," open to a variety of views. Yet there was clearly a contradiction between the continuous assertion of the political character of the *Bulletin* and the vagueness of these guidelines, a contradiction that could not be solved by a largely empty reference to anti-imperialism.

> These general guidelines have their costs, most notably a lack of a clear political line of particularly heated issues such as the intention of the Soviet Union in Asia, the nature of the Pol Pot regime, or the direction of China under Deng Xiaoping. But such "fuzziness" is not to be confused with overall lack of purpose. And it will not be so confused if the editors and the readers of the *Bulletin* remain committed to the other important goal, to maintain as large a united front of progressives as is possible while still remaining consistent with the *traditional anti-imperialist base*.[93]

"Anti-imperialism" recurred as a mantra in the discussion among the editors on the destinies of the group. The *Bulletin* looked for articles that were "critical and anti-imperialist, but non-sectarian";[94] it was "anti-imperialist and in a continuing struggle against the conservative traditions that pervade each of the area studies";[95] its foci were "imperialism, revolution, social change."[96] However, especially in the light of the complete intellectual and political paralysis that I described earlier, it is difficult to see what "anti-imperialism" meant, and this uncertainty was highlighted in the comments to Avery's draft by many BCAS editors and former CCAS members. Bryant's statement "is giving me fits," wrote Joe Moore. There was very little to disagree with, but there was also very little that answered the questions about what the *Bulletin* stood for.[97] Joseph Tharamangalam also pointed to the lack of a clear political and theoretical direction for the journal. Yes, everybody shared an anti-imperialist perspective, and the *Bulletin* would not publish anything that actually supported imperialism. But that was a low bar indeed. Avery had used the terms "progressive" and "collective humanism" as positive attributes for the *Bulletin*, but they too remained undefined, Tharamangalam commented. "Do they include a critique of capitalism, of class society, of social systems that alienate human beings? And what about human welfare, the welfare of the masses of the people? In particular, do they include any commitment to human rights, human rights not in the bourgeois sense or in Jimmy Carter's sense, but the rights of human beings to live lives free of oppression, torture, etc. from a basic humanistic standpoint?"[98] The very terms of the debate seemed inadequate to the enormity of the change that was happening, politically and theoretically, in Asia and the United States.

It was true that the *Bulletin* had "sought to find alternatives and to disclose the stake that the established scholarship has in the status quo here and in Asia,"[99] but those alternatives were no longer available. Two of the major inspirations for social change and revolution in Asia—China and Vietnam—had fought a short yet brutal war, were currently engaged in forms of occupation and expansionism, and were going through a massive restructuring along lines that looked suspiciously "capitalist." Without these alternatives, without a clear—if misperceived—political grounding, there was no hope of being the "watchdogs of the profession,"[100] precisely because it was only a political stance that marked their distance from the profession. Without that political stance, as the China issues displayed in full evidence, the formerly Concerned scholars could only oscillate between acceptance of the new status quo and commiseration for things lost, or readily embrace the role of spokesperson for the newly victimized Asians.

Career and the Academic Precariat

The difficulties in putting together the China issue highlighted some crucial and very stark divisions within the CAS. Many of those who had published on post-Mao China in other journals, but not in the *Bulletin*, were people with somewhat established careers, often tenured, or who envisioned for themselves a path strictly within academia. On the other side, there were scholars, often the most politically outspoken ones, who had just lost their jobs, who were in the process of being denied tenure,[101] or who never got a permanent teaching position. Bryant Avery, the editor in chief, survived on a small salary from the *Bulletin*, his wife's income as a physical therapist, and working at the family store a couple of days per week.[102] Saundra Sturdevant, after a few stints in temporary teaching positions, lived for a while in Berkeley managing a food cart in the morning (selling soup) and working at the Center for Chinese Studies in the afternoon.[103] It is not coincidental that it was these editors who were pushing for more far-reaching questions concerning China, and that it was the established scholars who were loath to answer them.

At times this conflict took the form of a sweeping indictment of the careerism of the most successful colleagues, as in this scathing assessment by Saundra Sturdevant, well worth citing in full:

> The contradiction is a political/careerist one. China controls access to archives, people to interview, trips very carefully. It's a whole new ball game in terms of careers, with even this limited access. Scholars and a good number of journalists are not writing anything which takes into account what was received wisdom before the fall of the Gang of Four in 1976. And it's difficult to deal with for, as you know, many of the people who wrote for us, worked with us in the past are those who did dissertations and built reputations on pre-1976 materials. A good number have spent a year or more doing research/work in China and are sitting on materials they won't publish . . . and in some cases, won't even acknowledge the existence of publically. Some say that if they did, they'd never get to go back to China. Others are fro-

zen: they have not been able to put down on paper what they saw and learned and make an analysis of why and how . . . their findings don't fit with what they wrote on earlier occasions. Still others, defending a socialist position usually, follow B. Holiday's wisdom: 'If you can't say something real nice, then don't talk at all . . . that's my advice.' And then there's the other side of the coin: those who send us ms. which take into account ONLY the CURRENT received wisdom. It's all quite disgusting.[104]

Sturdevant might have been a bit unfair toward the political conundrum of former "comrades," but her concern was generally shared by other editors. The China issues were supposed to be preceded by a short editorial introduction (never written), which was going to highlight the connection between the politics of the profession and the post-Mao situation in China, underscoring the caution with which people were approaching China and their careers. "Even someone like Ed Friedman, who is brash and wordy," Bryant Avery wrote, "has chosen a path of analysis which stands his career in good stead: he has just recently (Feb. 1) become Assoc. Staff Director of the Subcommittee on Asia, US Rep. Commi. On Foreign Affairs in Washington DC."[105]

There were certainly very practical reasons to choose less contentious paths of analysis, given how some members of CCAS had lost or were in the process of losing academic positions: there had been "purges." Richard Pfeffer, who was not granted tenure at Johns Hopkins, somberly pointed out that "studying a socialist country like China is related to the politics of living in a capitalist country like America. 'Purges' are only the tip of that relationship."[106] Pfeffer, Angus McDonald, and Herbert Bix (who was denied tenure at UMass) seemed to be examples of how certain political positions had become largely untenable within academia. Stephen Andors, who did not get tenure at SUNY Oswego despite an excellent research record, was suspicious about his firing and about "a 2yr. difficulty in getting work." While he had no proof of an actual purge, he had "heard rumors that there were people in academia who were anxious to 'settle accounts' with the anti-war individuals," and he pointed at the "*staying power* of the right and the apologists for imperialism, capitalist society, etc." within the field: "Look at the major institutions and graduate centers—no left, and awfully few Marxist people (fewer on tenure). I don't think that's a sign of anything more (or less) than the political realities of academia. They could have left me at Oswego with no sweat. But Columbia, Johns Hopkins, Harvard, Berkeley, etc.?? Not 'the Positions' to be held by the Left-Marxist group. To the countryside for them if lucky. Otherwise, into some other way of earning a living."[107]

The *Bulletin*'s editors tried to call attention to this issue and asked for contributions that would shed some light on "the institutional and ideological roots of the efforts by the various colleges to cleanse themselves of 'troublemakers' and of the field of Asian studies to reinforce the mainstream(s) of American bourgeois scholarship."[108] But no such analysis was published in BCAS, and, in general, the support among CAS for the fallen comrades was probably expressed more at the personal than at the professional level.[109]

The evidence of actual purges is flimsy, and there were other, very practical factors that made it increasingly more difficult to obtain academic positions in the 1980s, first and foremost a shrinking job market. It is not my intention here to pile moral outrage on those who made specific career choices. Rather, I want instead to highlight the coincidence between this fracturing within the group and the collapse of a certain set of possibilities grounded in large part on a particular understanding of Maoism. To a certain extent, we witness here a separation of politics and scholarship, or rather a redefinition of what is permissible within the politics of academic production and academic life. In its early years, CCAS had argued for the need to reduce the distance between living and studying, between the scholars and the actors. "Only after the scholars are driven from their libraries into the streets and political life of the nation, will politics reflect sanity," Orville Schell had written. "For the reality of a revolution is not always to be found in a library or a reprinted journal article. It is more often than not found in the experience of involvement."[110] Without that experience, the division between learning and activism could not be obliterated, and the scholar was destined to analyze impotently what other people were creating. In this perspective, the debates over the China issue, viewed in connection with the practical and political shifts in the profession, signal precisely the end of that search for an integrated life, and a redefinition of the intellectual and academic practice in more canonic terms. Here again, Jacques Rancière's analysis of Maoism and post-Maoism is particularly insightful and useful.

Rancière, whose first contact with Maoism was mostly through the Althusserian circle in Rue de l'Ulm, diverged from his teacher during May '68 on the question of the role of the intellectual. He accused Althusser of waging "class struggle in theory," that is, of introducing Maoism simply as another theory, one that was the exclusive privilege of Marxist intellectuals to explain and interpret. In that, Rancière argued, Althusser's Maoism combined "the discourse of impotence and the discourse of power—the impotence to change the world, the power to reproduce the power of specialists."[111] To this, Rancière opposed the lesson of the Cultural Revolution, which was precisely to challenge the privileged position and access to knowledge of intellectuals, one that obliged every "Marxist philosopher" to reconsider his place in the distribution of spaces of power and knowledge that reproduces bourgeois domination."[112] Rancière then joined the Gauche Prolétarienne, which was on the forefront in the project to abolish the division that separated intellectual from manual labor, scholars from workers. The members of the GP became *établis*, they joined factories and remade themselves into proletarians, transforming themselves into manual laborers. If CAS tried to alter academia by making political activism inseparable from scholarship, French Maoists declared the futility of fighting within bourgeois ideology and moved intellectuals in the workers' space, the factory. However, this project failed as well, and it failed also because it did not ultimately reform intellectual practice. "Intellectual *établis* who took on a proletarian identity 'represented' proletarian to other intellectuals, and used the authority their dual identity conferred on them to reestablish the authority of proletarian ideology (for which they were the interpreters) over the supposed petty bourgeois deviations of their non-*établi* peers."[113] The militant (intellectual) leader thus continued to speak in the name of the people.

In France, the end of gauchism coincided with the emergence of the New Philosophers, who criticized the master narratives of Marxism and confronted them with the Foucauldian multiplicity of power and the omnipresence of resistance. Yet even this shift did not alter, at least in Jacques Rancière's view, the role of the intellectual. While fighting against the "Marxist master-thinkers" in the names of the suffering, the powerless, and the rebellious, the New Philosophers were once again enthroning intellectuals, the only ones who could act as a mouthpiece for the oppressed.[114] The "universal intellectual" still claimed the duty and the right to speak for the dominated, not unlike his militant predecessor. What was seemingly lost at the end of Maoism was rather the possibility that the dominated could speak for themselves, under conditions of equality—or change the conditions of their oppression.

From Rancière's perspective, then, the trajectory of global Maoism is one that challenged yet ultimately reaffirmed the role of intellectuals, a productive if failed rethinking of how class struggle is waged in culture (ideology), and that ended in the almost complete unavailability of class as an analytical category. The case of BCAS in the late 1970s and early 1980s shows a very similar trajectory: with the dissolution of "China" as a referent and the global political shift of the 1980s, not only was intellectual analysis paralyzed, but also any attempt to rethink the political praxis of scholars was abandoned. However, Asia scholars were not left "to sit in their offices studying the second hand shadows of revolutions that others make."[115] They could now consider themselves entrusted once again with the task of speaking for the victimized of revolutions and with interpreting the reasons for inequalities, without any hope of resolving them.

EPILOGUE

AREA REDUX

The Destinies of "China" in the 1980s and 1990s

The global forces that are reconfiguring our world continue to sustain formulations of nation, gender, class, and ethnicity. We propose to call into question these still-pressing yet unstable categories by crossing academic boundaries and rethinking the terms of our analyses. These efforts, we hope, will contribute toward informed discussion both in and outside the academy.
—"*positions* Statement of Purpose"

Hostility to theory usually means an opposition to other people's theories and an oblivion of one's own.
—Terry Eagleton, *Literary Theory: An Introduction*

During a recent meeting of a search committee for a job in the department of East Asian studies, I quietly voiced my displeasure about my colleagues' enthusiasm for one candidate and their neglect of another one, in my opinion much more interesting. I was then amiably chastised by one senior colleague who half-jokingly reminded me of the reality of the field. Yes, the latter candidate was more ambitious, broader in the perspective adopted, and the research touched on several different themes, but that was risky. The preferred candidate instead showed the ability to mine the archive of choice and minutely dissect the unearthed material within a definite scholarly tradition. It was boring, but boring is good. "Boring is what we do," concluded my colleague.

Now, I don't want to make too much of an exchange that was certainly meant to be tongue-in-cheek, but—probably because almost everything we encounter in our quotidian feels like it has a connection to our current research—that sentence hit a scholarly and political nerve. Expanding on my colleague's witty explanation, "boring" and "safe" can be made to describe a relationship to Asia and China as an archival preserve, where the sinologically armed scholar ventures only to retrieve some material— whose form does not matter—and subject it to their analysis. The process is safe because the relative positions of the subject and the object are never questioned and the process itself is never open to challenge, provided that the methodology is accurate and solid. It is a boring and definitively not risky relationship.

My colleague's remark brought to mind (BCAS editor) Bryant Avery's disparaging assessment of what was being written on China in 1980: it was all "a trifle boring."[1] Avery's dejected evaluation was particularly unsettling because it came from a place that, for about a decade, had existed in a relationship with China and Asia that was definitively unstable, potentially quite risky, and certainly not boring.[2] As I have described, in the long sixties, "China," possibly for the first time, was viewed as inhabiting a coeval chronology—even while it remained spatially distant and inaccessible—and that coevalness rested on the perceived contemporaneity of revolutionary politics.

Yet by the end of the 1970s, many radical scholars, for whom Maoist China had been both an inspiration and an unreachable dreamland, realized that their political and intellectual grounding had been shattered while their area of study had become suddenly accessible. With the opening of China and the repudiation of Maoism in the 1980s, China became spatially reachable yet moved backward in the developmental timeline, back to the position of a "not yet."[3] China and the Chinese, that is, moved from the position of subjects back to that of objects. And specifically, China shifted into the position of an empirically knowledgeable object that could be mined for information and scrutinized from the safe position of the knowledgeable observer. China became—or rather became again—an area, a field.

In the following few pages, I briefly evaluate the evolution (or rather "devolution") of "China" in the 1980s, paying particular attention to how this was reflected in the *Bulletin*, but expanding the gaze to the larger field of Asian studies. Then I concisely address the changes that took place with the introduction of more theoretical approaches in the 1990s and the debates that this generated, in particular around another journal, *positions*. These debates often saw older radicals of the CCAS cohort clashing with younger scholars, who considered themselves the intellectual heirs of that generation. Once again, my goal here is not to indict individual political and intellectual paths. Rather, I look at these moments in search of possibilities for recovering a meaning of "China" today, one that, as in the long sixties, would allow for political and intellectual connections across borders.

Down with Imperialism!

As described in chapter 4, China had made only sporadic appearances on the pages of the *Bulletin* since the late 1970s, and the trend continued between 1981 and 1990. And that's already noteworthy, given the space it had occupied in the collective brain of CCAS throughout the previous years and given the epochal changes that were taking place in the PRC. But what is even more significant is *how* China appeared. With a few notable exceptions, the contributions that touched on the PRC can be grouped under three main themes: the continuing debate on the role of imperialism, the evaluation of the economic reforms, and the analysis of intellectual/political trends, in particular with reference to the democratic movements of 1986 and 1989. Each of these themes and the way they were approached is indicative of the larger epistemic transformation that, by the 1980s, had caused China to be reinserted into a specific field of scholarly discourse, to be remade into an "area," in the narrowest possible terms.

Imperialism had been central for the identity of the Concerned Asian Scholars, who framed themselves in opposition to the imperialist venture of Vietnam and to U.S. policy in Asia in general, but who also eviscerated the field of Asia studies specifically for promoting views that explicitly or implicitly supported these policies. As mentioned earlier, one of the most famous and widely read issues of the *Bulletin* hosted a debate on "China and Imperialism" between Joseph Esherick and Andrew Nathan, in which the former criticized the dominant approach to Modern Chinese history (the so-called Harvard School) for underplaying the role of Western colonialism.[4] By the end of the 1970s, editors of the *Bulletin* claimed "anti-imperialism" as one of the defining traits of the publication, and one of the very few tenets—possibly the only one—that could be deployed to give a minimally unified background to the now divided concerns of writers and readers. As late as 1989, the editors, Bill and Nancy Doub, listed "imperialism" as one of the main concerns of the *Bulletin*, but they qualified it as "both domestic and international, capitalist and socialist/communist, including the suppression of minorities."[5]

In the 1980s, the *Bulletin* published two major contributions on China and imperialism. In the first, Elizabeth Lasek argued for a broader perspective that would go beyond analyzing the economic and financial impact of colonialism and focus instead on the interactions between imperialist penetration and regional state/class formation. Compared to previous contributions, Lasek's article lacked a direct political perspective but the stakes of her proposal are clear behind the analytical prose.[6]

Significantly, the possibilities for such an integrated view were denied in another article published three years later, penned by Tim Wright. The essay echoed some of the Chinese scholarship of the time, which had started to celebrate (for obvious reasons) the positive role of foreign capital in breaking down the "feudal system" of Qing China and move the country onto its "normal" evolutionary path toward capitalism and modernity. Even more striking is that Wright also argued forcefully for an idea of imperialism restricted specifically to the evaluation of its economic impact. If there had been one constant characteristic of the *Bulletin* since its inception, it was the adamant admission of the unbreakable connection between scholarship and politics, the call for an intellectual exploration that refused to separate itself from the political concerns of the time. Wright's reductionist view of imperialism as a strictly historical phenomenon and one whose impact should be assessed mainly in the economic sphere marks then a further shift in orientation for the *Bulletin*. It is also a shift that configures an emptying out of the very political meaning of the concept of imperialism itself.[7]

Tani Barlow has convincingly argued that the structure of Cold War China studies was predicated on the erasure of the category of colonialism, which, if dealt with, would have revealed the essence of area studies as part of a geopolitical project. This erasure, however, had to be occluded through a series of analogies and elaborations that placed China—as the "never really colonized"—outside the natural path of cultural and economic evolution.[8] It was the expurgation of colonialism that allowed for Cold War China studies to proclaim the persistence of China's difference. In this sense, CCAS's forceful recovery of imperialism and colonialism as central political and scholarly categories was an indispensable element in their attack on the dominating framework of Asia studies.

Placing colonialism back at the center of the scholarly enquiry on China's past and thus reinserting China within the global history of capitalist expansion was the necessary counterpart of CCAS's indictment of contemporary U.S. imperialism and of their recognition of Maoist politics as potentially viable. However, while CCAS demonstrated "the prevalence of diplomatic, military and economic imperialist relations in East Asia,"[9] they never produced a theoretical analysis of the various forms of colonial domination, and often the Concerned seemed content with distinguishing victims and victimizers or parsing the extent of victimization. By the end of the 1970s, gone were the larger connections with the Vietnam War and with Maoism. Without theoretical engagement, even the *Bulletin* could not but revert to an analysis of an empire devoid of any larger significance and one in which China was once again condemned to a history of minutely detailed differences. What was left was a hollow notion of imperialism that had little to say about the homogenizing power of global capitalism and its ability to produce long-lasting cultural, structural, and political effects.

I will return to imperialism soon, but first I want to stress how a similar mechanism was also at work in the second set of BCAS essays on China, those devoted to the post-Mao economic reforms. With the notable exception of an article by Phyllis Andors on women and labor and one by Jonathan Unger and Jean Xiong on the decline of standards of living in the countryside,[10] the *Bulletin* presented a quite positive, or at least forcefully anodyne, view of the reforms. Even more importantly, as in the case of imperialism, the economic evaluation of the reforms was emptied out of any kind of political consideration, of any assessment of what the dismantling of the Maoist structure and the embrace of the market meant politically, and not only for China. Most of the analyses printed in the *Bulletin* were also very narrow, with an exclusive focus on internal change, and with no larger theoretical opening onto the global significance of the Dengist shift. It was a Chinese problem, a Chinese experiment. Now this was very similar to what was going on in other scholarly publications, and if anything the *Bulletin* was slightly less gung ho about the reforms than the majority of U.S. scholarship, but in this case the contrast with previous positions was much sharper.

In the 1960s and 1970s, the *Bulletin* produced (or at least tried to produce) scholarship that looked at China as a subject of its own history and politics but also—and because of that—as a crucial participant in the development of global historical trends and in the solution of global political problems. China was near, but more than that, by looking at China, historically and coevally, the Concerned argued that they were also dealing with issues that were relevant to different realities and different temporalities, including their own present. By the 1980s, instead, we see at play a strategy of separation: separation of the economic from the political, of China's experience of colonialism from the global expansion of capitalism, and of the experience of Maoism from the history of China itself. And the final effect of this strategy of separation was to reconstitute China as the place of difference, one that must be examined in isolation, within its own distinct but also largely incommunicable subtleties.

In this specific aspect, BCAS also seemed to reflect a sharp turn within the larger field of China studies in the 1980s, one perhaps best exemplified by Paul Cohen's proposal of a "China-centered approach" (CCA). Published in 1984, Cohen's *Discovering History in China* is a cautious and well-intentioned analysis of American history writing on China, and one that tries very carefully to move out of the Cold War mentality by striking a middle ground (or maybe a completely different ground) between modernization theory and anti-imperialist approaches. Cohen contended that both approaches had been informed—and therefore distorted—by an almost exclusive emphasis on the West-China binary, an emphasis that deprived Chinese people of any actual agency and overvalued issues that were solely of Western derivation and concern. To amend these defects, Cohen called for a "China-centered approach," in which what is important is not the comparison between China and the West but "between earlier and later points in time within a single culture."[11] Yet while Cohen was adamant in rejecting the culturalistic assumption of previous scholarship as well as in staking the ground for specifically Chinese historical patterns of analysis, it is difficult not to see in action here a new way of separating China, by which everything can be explained within its own evolution. Then, the massive rifts produced by capitalist expansion can be addressed as an afterthought, secondary to the long-term development of endogenous forces. While the CCA was meant to return agency to the Chinese, it did so by forcefully extrapolating China from the actual transformations of modern history, thus indirectly remaking China into a field of exceptionality whose contribution to the world lies in its own separated progression.

Interestingly, Robert Marks, member of the BCAS editorial board in the late 1970s and early 1980s, provided a trenchant and punctual critique of Cohen's work. In a 1985 review essay, Marks pointed at another, perhaps more crucial, weakness of the CCA. Cohen had identified commercialization and, in part, demography as the forces primarily responsible for shaping Chinese history. Yet, Marks argued, this was a choice that happily confirmed and coincided with the preconceived assumptions of American scholars about the naturalness of the practices and beliefs of market society. These were the same unspoken yet shared assumptions that had shaped John K. Fairbank's impact-response model and modernization theory, and all the scholarly work aimed at disproving any imperialist-based critique. Therefore, Marks concluded, the China-centered approach did not challenge in any serious way, but rather continued and extended the Cold War paradigm of China studies, as it remained based on the presupposition of "the force and primacy of market forces."[12]

Marks's review was not published on the pages of the *Bulletin*. Yet it is significant that this critique came from somebody who had shared part of the experience of the BCAS. The Concerned had fought many battles to unveil the rhetorical lens and the political biases that shaped the academic field of China studies during the Cold War. But even more significantly, they had argued that scholarship could not exist in separation from politics, even if the political position was disguised under the pretense of objectivity; rather, good scholarship could only exist together with the right politics. It was only by taking a political position that specific aspects of the history and the present of China could become visible and that China could finally be viewed as a subject participant in global history. Thus, Cohen's idea that disenchanted observers could objectively identify forces and trends specific to China—thereby overcoming their West-based biases—appeared as a retreat from CCAS's criticism of the previous decade and as a way of isolating "China" once again as an object that could be observed only within itself.

The dismissal of any integrated perspective on imperialism and the separation of politics and economics concurred with the reopening of China to the gaze of U.S. scholars. If, following Tani Barlow, the erasure of colonialism was the unspoken premise of Cold War area studies, the marginalization of imperialism-based analysis in the 1980s accompanied the transformation of China into an area open to different forms of penetration. The possibility of fieldwork and the disclosing of historical archives paralleled the opening of China itself to foreign capital and the logic of the market. And while, as a historian, I deeply cherish the accessibility of archives, I find it difficult not to see an unspoken connection between the new erasure of imperialism and the potential "normalization" of China to market forces.

The third theme under which China appeared in the *Bulletin* through the 1980s also presented a particular kind of retreat, and another form of separation. In the previous decade, politics had been a central defining character of almost every BCAS essay that dealt with China—and declaredly so. Now politics, when it appeared, was confined to specific realms: the outward demonstrations of mass activism by students and the speculations of intellectuals. In the 1980s, the *Bulletin* published a special issue on Marxist intellectual Su Shaozhi and a few essays on the Xidan Democracy Wall, the 1986 protests, and the 1989 demonstrations. These were obviously very important events that attracted the attention of China watchers and Western audiences in general. Yet for formerly radical scholars who had championed the emergence of Chinese subjectivities in the factories and the countryside during the Mao years, the reduction of politics to the outward activities of a relatively small group of intellectuals was a definitive turnaround, and one that mirrored the political shift taking place both in China and within U.S. academia. As Harry Harding poignantly pointed out, "the ordinary peasant, who constitutes some 80% of China's population, plays little role in the recent reassessment of China."[13] And in that, there was not much difference between BCAS and somebody on the other side of the spectrum like Simon Leys, whose *Chinese Shadows* contained only one passing reference to "peasants."[14] With the end of Maoism, the large majority of the Chinese people lost their status as political subjects and could be accounted for only as victims, or, at best, beneficiaries of market reforms. At the same time, the scope of politics itself was reduced to ill-defined calls for democracy and human rights. "China" then moved from being the name of experiments that, while specifically located, proposed alternatives to global problems, to being a place of historical difference now trapped in the unending process of becoming "like us," of becoming *sameness*, as Daniel Vukovich has articulated.[15]

This is obviously a phenomenon that goes beyond CCAS and even beyond Asian studies. In a recent piece on the Taiwan sunflower movement, Wang Hui has remarked how "China," which used to be a political category during the Cold War, is now reduced to being simply the sign of a geographical location. The source of this transformation, he argues, "can be found in the failure of socialist practice and in the failure of the efforts to solve the problem of political identity through the socialist movement." Socialist liberation was predicated on the categories of the "leadership of the working class" and "the workers-peasants alliance," and it was on the basis of these categories that transnational connections, such as the relationship between the Second and Third World, the alliance of formerly colonized people—and, I would add, the very recognition of political subjects across continents—was possible. With the disappearance of these categories, "China," concludes Wang Hui, has no political meaning at all.[16] In this sense, the academic emptying out of "China" as a political category, which I just traced through the 1980s, reflects a more global collapse, be it the failure of the "Communist Hypothesis," the disappearance of a revolutionary horizon, or the fracturing of class-based political identities. "China" in the 1980s stands as an example of this shift, which both feeds into and is provoked by a massive process of depoliticization, one that also affects academia—and especially those sectors of academia that had more strongly identified with China as a category of politics.

This shift was probably unavoidable, precisely because of the extent of the failure and the collapse, and I don't mean to single out personal intellectual choices. My goal here is rather to highlight the shift but also to point out its consequences for China studies, in particular to show what possibilities were foreclosed by the "normalization" of the field in the 1980s.

As I have argued, with the separation of politics from scholarship, "China" could only be once again the name of a location, a place of difference—or at best a place of "becoming sameness." After a decade that had challenged, from a political standpoint, the field's assumption about the production of knowledge, the depoliticization of the 1980s led to a new empiricism of sorts, a blind faith in the transparent nature of the archives, archives that could be finally raided for nuggets of unquestioned facticity. For Chinese (and Asian people in general), this configured a probably more significant transformation, one from subjects of politics to objects of inquiry, from actors to victims, from political protagonists to (yet immature) capitalist consumers. Up until 1989, both within and without China, political apathy and frenzied consumerism were the catchwords to describe China's national mood. For China scholars, this set once again their boring, safe relationship with China as one between observer and observed. There was nothing anymore to think *with* China, only *about* China. China was reframed as an area of exclusion, a geographical and intellectual location of separation.[17]

Before I move to the different possibilities that opened up in the 1990s, I need to at least hint at the parable of the *Bulletin* up to the present. In March 2001, the journal changed its name to *Critical Asian Studies* and produced a new statement of purpose that highlighted both continuities with and distance from the enterprise of BCAS. The statement reaffirmed the "continued commitment as activists and scholars" but also marked the massive shift of global perspectives due to the end of the Cold War, globalization, the rise of East Asia, and the collapse of socialism.[18] The journal, now published by Routledge, has hosted quite a varied fare of essays, ranging from the quite scholarly—articles that could have appeared in any other academic publication—to the more politically engaged (on the CIA and 9/11 or contributions by Arundhati Roy and Vijay Prashad, for example). Perhaps the main continuity is that *Critical Asian Studies* follows in the footsteps of the *Bulletin* of the late 1970s and 1980s in devoting plenty of space to a variety of Asian locations (Thailand, Burma, Okinawa, etc.) and to the voices of Asian intellectuals.

Yet, since the first time I looked at that shift in nomenclature, I was struck by the change it presented and represented: the political and intellectual subjects (the scholars) have disappeared to leave their place to the object (Asian studies). Also gone, rightfully, is that awkward "concern" that could exist only when inscribed in a particular relationship with a global situation and localized political experiments. Yet, without that, the commitment "to human rights, democracy, social justice, self-determination, and equality" reaffirmed in the *Critical Asian Studies* statement, while absolutely sincere, cannot but sound a bit hollow.[19]

China, in Theory

In the early 1990s, (some) scholars of Asia started to think of ways to move away from the separation I just highlighted, and strove to reframe (in a completely different global political context) the possibility of thinking *with* people across divides. Perhaps the clearest and most exemplary declaration of this new search is the statement of purpose of the journal *positions*, which appeared in 1993. The last paragraph is worth quoting in its entirety:

> *positions*' central premise is that criticism must always be self-critical. Critique of another social order must be as self-aware as commentary on our own. Likewise, we seek critical practices that reflect on the politics of knowing and that connect our scholarship to the struggles of those whom we study. All these endeavors require that we account for positions as places, contexts, power relations, and links between knowledge and knowers as actors in existing social institutions. In seeking to explore how theoretical practices are linked across national and ethnic divides, we hope to construct other positions from which to imagine political affinities across the many dimensions of our differences.[20]

There are obvious echoes of CCAS's own statement of purpose, dating twenty-four years earlier, and of the activities of the Committee and the *Bulletin*: the call for a self-critical scholarship, mindfulness of one's own position in relationship to others; the attention to power relationships in the production of knowledge; the declared linkage between scholarships and politics (and specifically the politics of knowledge production and the struggles of Asian people); and the recognition of the possibilities of connections across locations and boundaries.[21] Yet *positions*' statement (as well as the scholarly practices of the journal) was framed around a different foundational tenet, identifiable in the avowed and unabashed theoretical engagement, the conviction that it is specifically in "theoretical practices" that linkages and connections between political and intellectual subjects can be found and established.

In this last section, I offer a brief, lacunose, idiosyncratic, and very partial account of how "theory" entered the field of Asian studies in the 1990s, what that meant, and what reactions it elicited. Specifically, I describe how "theory" allowed for a renewed critique of the structure of area studies, how it helped shape a challenge to a resurgent empiricism, how it fostered a possible new connection between politics and scholarship, and, finally, how it reframed the possibility of thinking with Asian subjects. All these issues had been central to the CCAS enterprises, yet opposition to a theoretical engagement with "China" has come often from *some* of those who had fought for a different "China" in the 1960s and 1970s. *positions* was the target, direct or indirect, of many of these attacks, and that is in large part due to the centrality of the journal as the crucial location for the theoretical engagement within Asian studies. Yet it is also worth highlighting that in the 1990s, it was once again a journal—and one specifically founded by a group of declaredly political intellectuals—that reopened the discussion on the meanings of Asia. I specifically analyze examples of this opposition in order to highlight what was and is at stake politically and intellectually and what are the continuities and discontinuities with the project of the long sixties—as exemplified by my analysis of CCAS in the previous chapters.

First, however, I need to provide a disclaimer of my liberal use of the term "theory." Personally, I find the whole idea of a "theoretical shift" misleading, as it implicitly postulates that some scholars have "theories" while others don't—they simply go on with their business in blessed neutrality and objectivity. And even if we take "theory" as the shorthand to indicate the influence of philosophical and critical texts from Europe (but also Asia and Latin America) in U.S. academia, the term is generic and confusing. The complex works of thinkers as different as Foucault, Deleuze, Derrida, Said, Spivak, and Jameson cannot be easily distilled into one giant trend. It is not by chance that generic references to "postmodernism" or "postcolonialism" are usually deployed by people who resist explicit theoretical engagements. Yet, for reasons of brevity and simplicity, I am forced here to use the shorthand anyway. In the next pages, with "theory" I refer to a series of texts and contributions from thinkers such as Foucault, Derrida, and Gramsci, and from the postcolonial theorization of Subaltern studies—as well as to the scholarly contributions within Asian studies produced in conversation with these works.

The intervention of *positions*—and of other scholars—through theoretical engagement reflected a larger shift in academia but also embodied a specific reaction to the situation within area studies, which I have described previously. While other disciplines, notably literary studies, had been affected, at least since the late 1970s and early 1980s, by Said's critique of orientalism—just to make the most obvious example—area studies seemed to have reconstituted itself throughout the 1980s into a renewed form of Modernization Theory, cast as the analysis of the alternative paths pursued by other "civilizations." The staunch refusal to involve "theory" in area studies was necessary to maintain the separation between the West and the Rest, between subject and object, and to defend the modes and location of knowledge production.[22] In the reemboldened area studies of the 1980s, the relationship with Asia (or any other area) mirrors that of the ethnographer with the "field," that is, the study of an outside belonging not only to a different spatiality but also to different temporality. As Harry Harootunian remarked, in area studies, Euro-America remained "the privileged site of production, in every sense of the word, while the outside was simply the space for 'development' which originated elsewhere."[23]

Each and every one of these traits had been a target of harsh criticism by CCAS for a decade, and it is surprising to see Asian studies reestablish itself specifically along those very same uncritical lines. This was definitively related to a larger political and intellectual retrenchment (the end of revolution, the end of history, the triumph of capitalism in its neoliberal form), but I think we can also see in this reemergence a reflection of the incomplete nature of the CCAS project. The concerned were very critical but failed (and it was a tall order indeed) to rethink the patterns of knowledge production within disciplines and to shape alternative theoretical practices of understanding. And without that, it was relatively easy to return to Asia and China as "fields," especially once those fields were finally open for scholars to collect the "raw material of pure facticity."[24] And here lie both the continuity and the major difference between the "philosophical turn" of the 1990s and the critique of the 1970s: at its best, any theoretical engagement calls for both the criticism of established positions and the continuous creation of new (self-critical) ones. In that, in the case of Asian studies, "theory" does not simply name a critique of orientalism but also a search for post-orientalist scholarly practices.[25]

The engagement with theory also challenged another element that had returned (or had never ceased) to be constitutive of Asian studies. The faith in empirical neutrality, which had been at the center of CCAS's attacks on the field, was boldly resurgent throughout the 1980s, in part because there were finally plenty more empirical nuggets to unearth in newly opened China. The most clarifying statement of the empiricist position was perhaps the famous and often-cited essay on "the paradigmatic crisis in Chinese studies" by Philip Huang, who, as the founder of *Modern China*, had been himself a somewhat radically engaged scholar in the 1970s. Looking at the state of Chinese history in the previous decade, Huang set the tone with an indirect jab at the experience of CCAS. He celebrated the successes of Western scholars of the Ming-Qing period, who, through new "empirical findings," had contributed more toward undermining the old "unchanging China" scheme "than the earlier political criticisms of John Fairbank and others by radical scholars."[26] In broader terms, Huang described the recent evolution of Chinese studies as a shift from a paradigm based on "imperialism" to one based on the "market," the former condemning the devastation of colonialism, the latter tracing the beneficial impact of commercialization. Both paradigms, Huang concluded salomonically, had to be dismissed as codependent prefab explanations that could not apply to the complexities and diversities of the Chinese case. They had to be dismissed specifically because they were Western, because for too long, Chinese studies had "borrowed analytical concepts entirely from Western-derived schemes, attempting in one way or another to force Chinese history into the classical models of Smith and Marx." What was necessary instead, he continued, was to reestablish the "theoretical autonomy of Chinese studies . . . in creative ways that would relate the Chinese experience to the rest of the world."[27]

Besides the fact that grounding any "theoretical autonomy" on a geographical/cultural location is extremely problematic (at least not without the risk of embracing some form of national essence), what is even more striking is that Huang's practical suggestions for such "creative ways" all reverted to an unquestioned empiricism. In order to escape the "paradigmatic crisis" and the clutch of Western "theories," Huang found no better solution than to follow the Rankian dictum and "look at what actually happened."[28] In the end, his assessment of the theoretical crisis of Chinese studies resolved itself in a declared refusal of theoretical engagement and in the embrace of a supposedly antitheoretical (but China-centered?) empiricism. However, as Terry Eagleton aptly noted, "hostility to theory usually means an opposition to other people's theories and an oblivion of one's own,"[29] and Huang is no exception. One example will suffice. While discussing whether concepts such as civil society or public sphere were useful in analyzing China's development in the 1980s (his answer: they really were not), Huang suggested that "instead of starting from Western-derived assumptions, we would do better to begin with the empirical paradox of marketization and civil associations without democratic development."[30] Obviously, that is a paradox only if one *starts with* the (Western-derived? American? capitalist? ideological?) assumption that markets, civil associations, and democratic development are always and necessarily coincident and coeval.

Huang was part and parcel of the intellectual debate in the 1970s, and, as I showed in chapter 2, *Modern China* claimed (not without controversy) to follow on the path first traced by the *Bulletin*. For him to return to a blissful celebration of empiricism and neutrality might seem shocking, but it exemplifies both the regressive shift that took place at the end of the 1970s and an attitude still pervasive in the field. I described Huang's position in detail precisely because it points to some of the issues that the theoretical intervention within Asian studies addressed. To Huang's (and many others') claim that Western theory did not fit Asia and that any theoretical intervention was a (colonial) imposition of meaning, theoretically engaged scholars responded in two ways. First, they deployed theories that singled out and challenged the very position of the Western (male) theorist—without discarding their intellectual and political contributions. Any analysis could only start from self-criticism, as only that could prevent falling in the unmindful worship of one's own empirical objectivity. Second, this younger generation of scholars critically embraced the work of those "others" who, *from Asia*, had developed a global critique set in dialogue with Western and non-Western theories. Here, of course, the work of the Subaltern Studies Collective is of crucial importance, not only because it shows the continuing possibility of thinking theoretically with others but also because it connects, in its complex history, Mao to poststructuralism.[31] In its best expressions, then, the theoretical engagement of Asia scholars recovers the political force of CCAS's commitment to Asia as a subject—not one that speaks only of its own separated history but one whose thought and struggle have global relevance. In its self-critical approach and in its connection with the work of Subaltern studies, there is also an obvious echo of Maoist lessons, pushing forward the legacy of the long sixties.

There were manifest, and at times harsh, reactions to theoretical interventions within Asian studies, and these reactions generally took two forms, often overlapping: on the one hand, people came to the defense of the stability of the field and the archive, a stability that they saw challenged by the theoretical questioning of the conditions of disciplinary production; on the other hand, theoretically engaged scholars were attacked "from the Left" by those who viewed postmodern theory as an intellectual and defeatist escape from a truly political engagement with capitalism. Surprisingly, some of the most ferocious critiques came from people who had shared similar concerns in the past, ex-Maoists of sorts.

Perhaps the most glaring example of the first kind of reaction (but with many elements of the second) is the 1998 (in)famous debate between Joseph Esherick (a former CCAS member) and James Hevia, whose *Cherishing Men from Afar* had been awarded the Levenson Prize for the best book on pre-twentieth-century China in 1997.[32] The selection committee had praised Hevia's work on the Macartney Mission of 1793 for his combination of "post-modern interpretation and new archival resources," and while Esherick was eager to dispense with both praises, it is to postmodern theory that he devoted most of his ire. Hevia was also a founding member of *positions*' editorial board, and the journal was clearly another target of Esherick's criticism. Without going into too much detail, Esherick accused Hevia of indulging in a reimagination (and misreading) of the sources specifically in service of his theoretical bent. Hevia was wrong because his reading of sources was obscured and muddled by "theory." Two points are worth highlighting in Esherick's pieces, specifically because they exemplify the main elements of the antitheory backlash: his understanding of "theory" and his use of native knowledge. First, "theory" appears as an amorphous whole, a generic threat. Esherick did not mention any of the critical works deployed by Hevia except for Said's *Orientalism* ("the sacred text of 'postcolonial' scholarship").[33] As he admitted at the very end of his response to Hevia's rejoinder, he had no qualms about not being up to speed in his theoretical readings.[34] That disregard allowed Esherick to find refuge in a largely unquestioned faith in the transparency of language, the immediacy of hermeneutics, and the very unproblematic nature of archives, a faith that would have been untenable with even a minimal frequentation of translation and literary theory.

As for native knowledge, Esherick's first salvo ended with a reference to "Chinese scholars," which was meant to have a double effect.[35] First, native witnesses were called to testify to the mistakes in Hevia's interpretation, according to their translations of the archive into modern Chinese. Unlike Hevia, these scholars, in Esherick's recounting, were more than willing to chastise the Qing Empire for its illusions about itself and for its lack of interest in Western technological achievements. Thus, native scholars' disdain for late imperial obduracy and backwardness, and their embrace of the successes of a scientific-technological "modernity" were offered as proof that Hevia's readings of Chinese history did not represent the view of the (semi)colonized natives. Secondly, Chinese scholars were deployed as part of a more directly political attack on postcolonial approaches. The postcolonial criticism of the colonized adoption of the colonizer's framework of "science," Esherick concluded, denied Asians the right to adopt the values and practices of modernity, now strictly identified (by postcolonial theory, according to Esherick) with imperialism— rather than with the Enlightenment project of rationality, science, and democracy (as if the two could be easily separated). Esherick implicitly lionized Chinese historians' opposition to "theory" as evidence of their resistance to a new form of academic imperialism, which, in his view, would condemn the Chinese to be voiceless about their own history precisely because they refused to view it through the prism of Western postmodern jargon.

As for this last point, Esherick clearly missed or misrepresented the meaning of the theoretical practices he was attacking—and that, by his own admission, he did not know. The goal of these practices was to think with others through the self-critical assessment of *any* category or position, including that of "China." So, in the end, it is Esherick who reaffirmed the separation between the West and the Rest, according to which only Westerners can think theoretically while Asians are prevented from doing so by their civilizational difference. In other words, Esherick exempts Chinese intellectuals from being called upon to self-critically examine their own categories. From this perspective, it is then less surprising that, in his criticism of Hevia, Esherick indirectly reasserted the old "Harvard school" view of China (immobile, culturalistic, trapped in ritual, self-absorbed), one that CCAS (and Esherick himself) had confronted because it was functional to imperialistic pretensions and because it implicitly denied the possibility of a shared political horizon with Chinese people. In that light, it is difficult not to find in Esherick's enthusiasm for "modernity" (defined in its most liberal and technocratic terms) the hidden acknowledgment of a new, shared connection with China, this one framed under the acceptance of capitalist modernization.

In Esherick's critique of Hevia, we also catch a glimpse of the political reaction to "theory," not surprisingly coming from somebody who probably considered (or had considered) himself to be on the Left. Here the implication is that the theoretical challenge to the stability of truths and positions will lead to politically disastrous relativism and to the abandonment of the positive legacy of "Western civilization" (democracy, civil society, individual liberty, the Enlightenment) in the name of a fractured and valueless multiculturalism and indentitarian morass. Poststructuralist and postcolonial theoretical approaches have indeed been criticized (by scholars of the old and new Left) as directly anti-Marxist, anti-revolutionary, or, at best, "post-revolutionary," in that they are perceived to be displacing "capitalism" as the constitutive elements of modernity, thus shifting the scholar's gaze from economic realities to symbols, fostering cultural nationalism, and substituting politically engaged scholarship with the powerless repetition of a few French namesakes.[36]

While I don't subscribe to this critique, I am wary of the twin risks of relativism and academic impotence (awareness of the latter has been one of the impulses behind writing this book). Yet rather than seeing the instability of meanings and positions as a threat to political coherence or political effectiveness, we should strive to view (and deploy) a well-considered theoretical attack upon established positions, established texts, and established discourses precisely as an essential element of political struggle. This struggle, I would argue, does not betray but rather mirrors and continues that of the long sixties, specifically in its asserting of the capacity of thinking, acting, and speaking of those to whom this capacity had been historically denied. Any intellectual engagement involves the risk of abstraction, detachment, and separation. But it seems to me that theoretical practices that break fixed connections between texts and interpretations, between conventional discourses and power relationships, between authorship and authority, are precisely one of the conditions for the emergence and recognition of alternative political subjectivities. Because "where interpretation is obvious, where it is *not* a question, power reigns supreme; where it is wavering, flickering, opening its uncertainty to unpredictable uses, empowerment of the powerless may be finally possible."[37]

As for theory's alleged abandonment of an anticapitalist critique, while it might have taken place at times, it is not the necessary or even the more likely outcome, especially if we take "theory" seriously. It's true that the success of Foucault, Deleuze, and Derrida in American campuses was in part due to their perceived anti-Marxism. But, as François Cusset has illustrated, this was because their texts were extrapolated from the contexts of their production, which was indeed the revolutionary situation of the long sixties: these texts were "neither pro-Marx nor anti-Marx. They were, rather, an endless confrontation with, discussion on, reinterpretation of Marxism."[38] As for other sources of the theoretical engagement within Asian Studies, such as Subaltern Studies and postcolonialism, the dismantling of colonial discourse has often been based on and fed into a larger critique of capitalism, with Mao and Gramsci being crucial influences in that formulation.

So unless we want to flatten ourselves again onto an untheorized anti-imperialism of sorts, or separate Asia once again as a cultural object to be studied, then it seems to me that a theoretical engagement with "China" and "Asia" is the only possible political and intellectual way forward. And by "China" here I don't mean a separated, geographically defined area. Rather "China" names a category always open to be challenged, a location where certain processes that affect or have affected the globe can be rethought from a different perspective and, potentially, with subjects that share a similar intellectual and political horizon. "Theory" is the imperfect name we give to that horizon, a form of thinking completely opposite of any primacy of native knowledge, rather a knowledge that unsettles the very idea of belonging to a location. "China," in this sense, defines not an area, but a site of inclusion, opening, and possibilities.

That site of "China" is one of the crucial legacies that we can and should rescue from the struggles and the concerns of the long sixties.

NOTES

INTRODUCTION

"The fear of hope and the love for desperation. They are not the same feeling, nor do they exist in the same person. Not necessarily. But let's talk about them, because 'China' stirs up both." Franco Fortini, "Ancora in Cina" [In China once again], *Quaderni Piacentini* 48 (1973): 138.

"'Ah then,' said Truptin, 'you want to talk about the Cultural Revolution, *dageming* [the great revolution]? An invention, madame, miss, a journalistic invention, I have never seen such things in China. China is a French invention, or rather a Parisian invention; all those ignorants, who don't know the language, who don't know the writing and yet they speak, they speak because they can't read. . . . Let me tell you, madame, let me tell you that China does not exist.'" Natacha Michel, *La Chine européenne* (Paris: Gallimard 1975, 44–45). I am thankful to Alessandro Russo for pointing out this novel and this specific passage. Truptin is a not-so-veiled caricature of the sinologist Jacques Pimpaneau.

1. The *Bulletin* changed its name to *Critical Asian Studies* in 2001.
2. "Concerned" was a definition shared by several groups that were formed in the sixties, for example, the Union of Concerned Scientists (UCS) (1969) and the National Emergency Committee of Clergy and Laymen Concerned about Vietnam (CALCAV) (1965).
3. In interviews with the author, Tom Engelhardt, John Berninghausen, Moss Roberts, Sandy Sturdevant, and Mark Selden all stressed the role of the Vietnam War in eliciting their activism.
4. "Jon Livingston to the *Newsletter*" (May 26, 1976), CCAS Archives. In 1972, Mark Selden noted that the *Bulletin* editorship had been held "overwhelmingly by China specialists." "Mark Selden to Schurmann, Friedman, Peck, Riskin, McDonald, Lippit, Kehl, Pickowicz, Nee, Esherick, Oldfather" (November 17, 1972), Saundra Sturdevant's personal archive, hereafter SSPA.
5. Marilyn Young, interview with the author (June 27, 2011). Saundra Sturdevant

confirmed a similar politically motivated interest. "I wanted to do China," she stated unequivocally. Interview with the author (August 30, 2011).

6. Richard Pfeffer was refused tenure at Johns Hopkins and became a workers' safety advocate for the federal government. He passed away in 2002. Angus McDonald refused a position at Georgia State in 1979 but continued lecturing in different colleges. He died in 1995 of ALS. Stephen Andors was refused tenure at Oswego and left academia. Saundra Sturdevant, after receiving her PhD at Chicago, held temporary positions for a few years. She left academia in the early 1980s and became a renowned documentary photographer. Bryant Avery, while he was the main editor at BCAS, had no formal academic position. Others, like James Peck, Tom Engelhardt, and Jon Livingston, did not stay in academia but left to pursue careers in publishing and graphic design. I also want to remember here Phyllis Andors, who died in 1992 when she was only forty-nine.

7. Belden Fields pointed out a macro-similarity between the United States and France in the 1960s. These were the two Western countries with the largest student movements, and Fields argued that these movements developed precisely because both countries had been involved recently in colonial wars. Belden Fields, "French Maoism," in "The 60s without Apology," ed. Sohnya Sayres, special issue, *Social Text* 9/10 (spring–summer, 1984): 148–177.

8. Alain Badiou, "The Cultural Revolution: The Last Revolution?" *positions: east asia cultures critique* 13, no. 3 (2005): 481–514; Jacques Rancière, *Althusser's Lesson*, trans. Emiliano Battista (London: Continuum, 2011).

9. Arif Dirlik, "Chinese History and the Question of Orientalism," *History and Theory* 35 (December 1996): 96–118.

10. Recent works on the Cultural Revolution include Wu Yiching, *The Cultural Revolution at the Margins: Chinese Socialism in Crisis* (Cambridge, MA: Harvard University Press, 2014); Andrew Walder, *Fractured Rebellion: The Beijing Red Guard Movement* (Cambridge, MA: Harvard University Press, 2009); Paul Clark, *The Chinese Cultural Revolution: A History* (Cambridge: Cambridge University Press, 2008); Alessandro Russo, "How to Translate 'Cultural Revolution,'" *Inter-Asia Cultural Studies* 7, no. 4 (2006): 673–682.

11. Fredric Jameson, "Periodizing the 60s," in "The 60s without Apology," ed. Sohnya Sayres, special issue, *Social Text* 9/10 (spring–summer 1984): 178.

12. Rey Chow summarized these attitudes in the figure of "the Maoist," which she described as the sibling to "the Orientalist," who imagined the Mainland Chinese of the 1970s "in spite of their 'backwardness,' a puritanical alternative to the West in human form—a dream come true." Rey Chow, *Writing Diaspora: Tactics of Intervention in Contemporary Cultural Studies* (Bloomington: Indiana University Press, 1993), 12.

13. Arif Dirlik made a similar point in his response to Rey Chow. See his *Marxism in the Chinese Revolution* (Lanham, MD: Rowman and Littlefield, 2005), 270–272.

14. "E ora per me la Cina è vera, ha una sua realtà misurabile. Fa parte del mondo." Fortini, "Ancora in Cina," 128. Franco Fortini (1917–1994) was an Italian poet and leftist intellectual. He visited China in 1955 and in 1972. Emphasis in the original.
15. Quinn Slobodian, *Foreign Front: Third World Politics in Sixties West Germany* (Durham, NC: Duke University Press, 2012), 111.
16. Quinn Slobodian, "Maoism in the Global 1960s," presentation at NYU Shanghai (March 13, 2016), 2, www.academia.edu/26839510/Maoism_in_the _Global_1960s.
17. Richard Wolin, *The Wind from the East: French Intellectuals, the Cultural Revolution, and the Legacy of the 1960s* (Princeton, NJ: Princeton University Press, 2010); Julian Bourg, "The Red Guards of Paris: French Student Maoism of the 1960s," *History of European Ideas* 31, no. 4 (2005): 472–490; Julian Bourg, *From Revolution to Ethics: May 1968 and Contemporary French Thought* (Montreal: McGill-Queen's University Press, 2007); Cristophe Boursellier, *Les maoïstes: La folle histoire des gardes rouges Français* [The Maoists: The crazy story of the French red guards] (Paris: Points, 2008); François Hourmant, *Le désenchantement des clercs: Figures de l'intellectuel dans l'après-Mai 68* [The disenchantment of the clerks: Features of the intellectual after May '68] (Rennes, France: Presses Universitaires de Rennes, 1997).
18. Wolin, *The Wind from the East*, xii.
19. On this motto, see Camille Robcis, "China in Our Heads: Althusser, Maoism, and Structuralism," *Social Text* 110 (Spring 2012): 51–69.
20. For an example of this kind of narrative, see Richard Bernstein, "A Bridge to the Love of Democracy," *New York Times*, December 29, 2010.
21. Perry Link, "Dawn in China," in *My First Trip to China: Scholars, Diplomats and Journalists Reflect on their First Encounter with China*, ed. Liu Kin-ming (Hong Kong: East Slope, 2012), 51–52. Link's work has had two facets: an academic one focused on Chinese literature and language, and one aimed at the larger public, for which he is translator, observer, and critic of contemporary Chinese society, with specific attention to intellectual debates and human rights.
22. Fabio Lanza, *Behind the Gate: Inventing Students in Beijing* (New York: Columbia University Press, 2010); "Springtime and Morning Suns: 'Youth' as a Political Category in Twentieth-Century China," *Journal of the History of Childhood and Youth* 5, no. 1 (2012): 31–51; "Deng's Children: Chinese 'Youth' in the Beijing Spring, 1989," in *Transnational Histories of Youth in the Twentieth Century*, ed. David Pomfret and Richard Jobs (Houndmills: Palgrave Macmillan, 2015), 260–282.
23. An interesting analysis of youth in the postwar era is by Richard Ivan Jobs, *Riding the New Wave: Youth and the Rejuvenation of France after the Second World War* (Stanford, CA: Stanford University Press, 2007).
24. Slobodian, *Foreign Front*, 3.
25. There is a growing corpus of historical works on the global influence of Maoist

China, especially in the 1960s, ranging from black radicals in the United States to French intellectuals, from Peruvian rebels to Australian Communists. Robert J. Alexander, *International Maoism in the Developing World* (Westport, CT: Prager, 1999); Gordon H. Chang, *Fateful Ties: A History of America's Preoccupation with China* (Cambridge, MA: Harvard University Press, 2015); Robeson Taj Frazier, *The East Is Black: Cold War China in the Black Radical Imagination* (Durham, NC: Duke University Press, 2015); Alexander C. Cook, ed., *Mao's Little Red Book: A Global History* (Cambridge: Cambridge University Press, 2014); Alexander C. Cook, "Third World Maoism," in *A Critical Introduction to Mao* , ed. Timothy Cheek (Cambridge: Cambridge University Press, 2010); Matthew D. Johnson, "From Peace to the Panthers: PRC Engagement with African-American Transnational Networks, 1949–1979," *Past and Present* 218, supplement 8 (2013): 233–257; Jon Piccini, "'Light from the East': Travel to China and Australian Activism in the 'Long Sixties,'" *The Sixties: A Journal of History, Politics and Culture* 6, no. 1 (2013): 25–44; Sanjay Seth, "Indian Maoism: The Significance of Naxalbari," in *Critical Perspectives on Mao Zedong's Thought*, ed. Arif Dirlik, Paul Healy, and Nick Knight (Atlantic Highlands, NJ: Humanities Press, 1997), 289–312; Orin Starn, "Maoism in the Andes: The Communist Party in Peru—Shining Path and the Refusal of History," in Dirlik, Healy, and Knight, *Critical Perspectives*, 267–288.

26. For a vivid and personal account of how these questions played in a different location, see Luisa Passerini, *Autobiography of a Generation: Italy, 1968* (Hanover, NH: Wesleyan University Press, 1996).

27. Alessandro Russo, *Le rovine del mandato: La modernizzazione politica dell'educazione e della cultura cinesi* [The ruins of the mandate: The political modernization of Chinese education and culture] (Milan: Franco Angeli, 1985); Joel Andreas, *Rise of the Red Engineers: The Cultural Revolution and the Origins of China's New Class* (Stanford, CA: Stanford University Press, 2009); Cheng Jinkuan, *"Jiaoyu geming" de lishi kaocha, 1966–1976* [An investigation of the history of "the educational revolution," 1966–1976] (Fuzhou: Fujian jiaoyu chubanshe, 2001).

28. Sigrid Schmalzer, *Red Revolution, Green Revolution: Encounters with Scientific Farming in Socialist China* (Chicago: University of Chicago Press, 2016).

29. Beyond the Red Guard movement, sympathetic foreign observers showed particular interest in the experiments of the "worker-peasant-soldier universities" (*gong nong bing daxue*) and, in general, in attempts to integrate labor and education. On the worker-peasant-soldier universities, see Hai Tian and Xiao Wei, *Wo de daxue, 1970–1976: Gong nong bing daxuesheng* [My university, 1970–76: Students at the worker-peasant-soldier universities] (Beijing: Zhongguo youyi chuban gongsi, 2009); see also Cheng Jinkuan, *"Jiaoyu geming" de lishi kaocha*.

30. François Cusset, *French Theory: How Foucault, Derrida, Deleuze and Co. Trans-

formed the Intellectual Life of the United States (Minneapolis: University of Minnesota Press, 2008), 46.
31. I am thankful to one of my anonymous readers for formulating this point with extreme clarity.
32. Ellen W. Schrecker, *No Ivory Tower: McCarthyism and the Universities* (Oxford: Oxford University Press, 1986), 8. See also Robert P. Newman, *Owen Lattimore and the "Loss" of China* (Berkeley: University of California Press, 1992); and Owen Lattimore's own memoir, *Ordeal by Slander: The First Great Book of the McCarthy Era* (New York: Carroll and Graf, 2002).
33. See John K. Fairbank, *Chinabound: A Fifty-Year Memoir* (New York: Harper and Row, 1982): 338–339.
34. Schrecker, *No Ivory Tower*, 338.
35. David H. Price, *Threatening Anthropology: McCarthyism and the FBI's Surveillance of Activist Anthropologists* (Durham, NC: Duke University Press, 2004), 33.
36. Schrecker, *No Ivory Tower*, 341.
37. See Geoff Eley, *A Crooked Line: From Cultural History to the History of Society* (Ann Arbor: University of Michigan Press, 2005).
38. For evidence of trends in the "new PRC history," see the website prchistory.org and the H-Net channel H-PRC. For an interesting assessment of new historical approaches to the Maoist period (coming not from a historian but from a social scientist), see Vivienne Shue, "Epilogue: Mao's China—Putting Politics in Perspective," in *Maoism at the Grassroots: Everyday Life in China's Era of High Socialism*, ed. Jeremy Brown and Matthew D. Johnson (Cambridge, MA: Harvard University Press, 2015), 365–379.
39. "Human Nature: Justice versus Power. Noam Chomsky debates with Michel Foucault" (1971), accessed October 2015, www.chomsky.info/debates/1971xxxx.htm.
40. See, for example, Peniel E. Joseph, *Stokely: A Life* (New York: Basic Civitas Books, 2015); Joshua Bloom and Waldo Martin, *Black against Empire: The History and Politics of the Black Panther Party* (Berkeley: University of California Press, 2013); Kristin Ross, *May '68 and Its Afterlives* (Chicago: University of Chicago Press, 2004); and the aforementioned Wolin, *The Wind from the East*; Frazier, *The East Is Black*; and Slobodian, *Foreign Front*.
41. *The Sixties: A Journal of History, Politics, and Culture.*
42. Allison Landsberg argues for the existence of a "prosthetic memory" based on our interaction with the past through movies and museum exhibitions. One could extend her reasoning to "prosthetic nostalgia." Alison Landsberg, *Prosthetic Memory: The Transformation of American Remembrance in the Age of Mass Culture* (New York: Columbia University Press, 2004), 2.
43. I was astonished by the amount of material—typewritten or handwritten—that the Concerned Scholars produced, and some of the other groups I examine in France had similar outputs. I saw the same need to communicate and record

every single scrap of communication in my previous work on the May Fourth years, another period of comparable intellectual and political intensity.

1: AMERICA'S ASIA

Mao Zedong's "Talks at the Chengdu Conference," excerpted in the second epigraph, was quoted in BCAS 9 (January–March 1977). It is also available at www.marxists.org /reference/archive/mao/selected-works/volume-8/mswv8_06.htm. The quote was placed on the back cover of the issue. A famous picture of the young Mao Zedong appeared on the front cover.

1. Edward Friedman and Mark Selden, eds., *America's Asia: Dissenting Essays on Asian-American Relations* (New York: Pantheon, 1969).
2. Edward Friedman and Mark Selden, "Introduction," in *America's Asia*, vii.
3. On CCAS's view of the legacy of McCarthyism, see Richard Kagan, "McCarran's Legacy: The Association for Asian Studies," and O. Edmund Clubb, "McCarthyism and Our Asia Policy," both in BCAS 1 (May 1969): 18–26. For an example of one of the many debates with the founding fathers of the field, see John K. Fairbank and Jim Peck, "An Exchange," BCAS 2 (April–July 1970): 51–70. For a detailed CCAS analysis of the founding (and funding) of China studies in the United States, see the special supplement "Modern China Studies: How the Foundations Bought a Field," BCAS 3 (summer–fall 1971).
4. Leigh Kagan, "A Statement of Directions," *CCAS Newsletter* (May 1968): 1.
5. Stephen Andors, "Revolution and Modernization: Man and Machine in Industrializing Societies, the Chinese Case," in Friedman and Selden, *America's Asia*, 438.
6. Marc Frey and Nicola Spakowski, eds., *Asianisms: Regionalist Interactions and Asian Integration* (Singapore: NUS Press, 2015).
7. Christopher Leigh Connery, "Editorial Introduction. The Asian Sixties: An Unfinished Project," *Inter-Asia Cultural Studies* 7, no. 4 (2006): 545.
8. Quinn Slobodian, *Foreign Front: Third World Politics in Sixties West Germany* (Durham, NC: Duke University Press, 2012).
9. One of the working titles for *America's Asia* was "The Scrutable East and the Inscrutable Asian Scholar." "Letter from Ed Friedman and Mark Selden to the Contributors to the Volume" (August 28, 1968), CCAS Archives.
10. "Intellectuals and Power: A Conversation between Michel Foucault and Gilles Deleuze," in Michel Foucault, *Language, Counter-Memory, Practice: Selected Essays and Interviews*, ed. Donald F. Bouchard (Ithaca, NY: Cornell University Press, 1977), 205–17. Available at libcom.org/library/intellectuals-power-a -conversation-between-michel-foucault-and-gilles-deleuze.
11. Joyce Mao has shown how the preoccupation with China markedly influenced the rise and evolution of the American conservative movement. See her *Asia First: China and the Making of Modern American Conservatism* (Chicago: Chicago University Press, 2015).

12. Charles O. Hucker, *The Association for Asian Studies: An Interpretive History* (Seattle: University of Washington Press, 1973), 43–44.
13. In 1969, the NDEA Title VI "put $15 million dollars into university programs and their students." "The comparable figure for Asian studies is about $2.5 million for some 42 programs in 1969." Richard D. Lambert, "Patterns of Funding of Language and Area Studies," in Wm. Theodore De Bary, Richard D. Lambert, and Gerald D. Berreman, "The Funding of Asian Studies," *Journal of Asian Studies* 30 (February 1971): 401.
14. John Berninghausen, interview with the author (April 7, 2016). Marilyn Young mentioned that she switched from European history to U.S.-China relations following the advice of professor William Langer, who told her to speak with John K. Fairbank, who had "just come into a lot of fellowship money." Fairbank agreed to provide funding for however long it took her. The money came from the historian Dorothy Borg's bequest funding the development of U.S.–East Asian relations. No teaching requirements came with the fellowship. Marilyn Young, interview with the author (April 7, 2016).
15. Hucker, *The Association for Asian Studies*, 103. Students made up almost one-quarter of AAS membership in 1970.
16. Tom Engelhardt, interview with the author (June 25, 2011).
17. John Berninghausen, interview with the author (April 7, 2016). "The military didn't want conscripts who were over 26, too hard to train, too much trouble, less malleable, more independent, perhaps slightly less physically fit," he explained.
18. "Letter to Secretary/President AAS" (April 21, 1966). Richard Kagan Personal Archive. Among the signatories were Leonard P. Adams, Nina Adams, David Buxbaum, Lawrence Chisolm, Samuel Chu, Edward Farmer, Edward Friedman, Richard Kagan, Lawrence Kessler, Richard Kraus, Arthur Rosenbaum, Richard Williams, and Richard Wilson.
19. "General Report No. 2" (August 12, 1966), Richard Kagan Personal Archive. In the same report, C. Martin Wilbur, then professor of Chinese history at Columbia, replied, citing his experience as a board member of IPR during its five-year struggle to regain tax-exempt status. Charles O. Hucker (1919–1994) was professor at the University of Michigan, specializing in the history of the Ming dynasty. Karl J. Pelzer (1909–1980) was a Southeast Asia specialist and a professor at Yale University.
20. Another professional group, the American Anthropological Association (AAA), continued to declare its apolitical standing through the 1940s and 1950s, even while, as David Price has shown, it was establishing ties with the CIA and the Department of State. Even the AAA, however, voted (by a large majority) in support of a resolution against the Vietnam War in December 1967. David H. Price, *Threatening Anthropology: McCarthyism and the FBI's Surveillance of Activist Anthropologists* (Durham, NC: Duke University Press, 2004), 320.

21. "General Report No. 3" (September 24, 1966), Richard Kagan Personal Archive. Similar papers were presented at the first CCAS conference in 1968.
22. Robert Sakai, quoted in "General Report No. 4" (November 17, 1966), Richard Kagan Personal Archive.
23. "Letter from Robert Sakai to Edward Friedman" (November 9, 1966), CCAS Archives.
24. Mark Selden, interview with the author (April 6, 2014). Among the early members of CCAS, Marilyn Young, Jon Livingstone, James Peck, Tom Engelhardt, and Herbert Bix were all graduate students at Harvard.
25. Marilyn Young, interview with the author (June 27, 2011).
26. Nancy Hodes, "Report," *Harvard Crimson* (April 17, 1968). Fairbank did not feel the need to call on the "ladies," even if several women were present at the meeting.
27. CCAS Archives.
28. Hodes, "Report."
29. "Excerpts from a Statement on U.S. Policy in Asia Made by 14 American Scholars," *New York Times*, December 20, 1967, 14. The fourteen scholars were Edwin O. Reischauer, I. Milton Sacks, Robert A. Scalapino, Lucien Pye, Leo Cherne, Guy J. Parker, Harry D. Gideonse, A. Doak Barnett, Oscar Handlin, William W. Lockwood, Richard L. Park, Paul Seabury, Fred von der Mehden, and Robert E. Ward. "Fourteen U.S. Scholars Sign Statement Backing American Presence in Asia," *Montreal Gazette*, December 20, 1967, 7.
30. Hodes, "Report." I. Milton Sacks was professor of political science at Brandeis University and a specialist in Vietnam and Southeast Asia. He had served in the State Department as director of Vietnamese affairs. He died in 1981. "Obituaries: I. Milton Sacks, 62, Professor and an Authority on Vietnam," *New York Times*, August 18, 1981, www.nytimes.com/1981/08/18/obituaries/i-milton-sacks-62-professor-and-an-authority-on-vietnam.html.
31. "CCAS Meeting" (July 26, 1968), CCAS Archives.
32. "A Position Paper for the CCAS Convention: CCAS Berkeley Chapter" [1968?], CCAS Archives.
33. "Vietnam on Their Minds," *Newsweek*, April 14, 1969. The article also made reference to a meeting of the American Sociological Association where young scholars denounced their senior colleagues as "house servants in the corporate establishment."
34. "A Position Paper for the CCAS Convention."
35. Dick Wilson, "Professors in Conflict," *Far Eastern Economic Review* (May 22, 1969): 457. I explore the relationship with AAS in chapter 2.
36. "CCAS Meeting" (July 26, 1968).
37. Richard Kagan, "Agenda of the Executive Committee Meeting" (March 27, 1969), CCAS Archives.
38. CCAS published three issues of the *Newsletter* between May 1968 and March 1969. The name was then changed to the *Bulletin of Concerned Asian Scholars*

(BCAS) in May 1969 (vol. 1, no. 4), while the *Newsletter* continued to be printed and sent to all the members, as a house organ of sorts. The first three issues of the *Newsletter* are considered to be part of the run of BCAS. All the other issues of the *Newsletter* are available at the CCAS Archives in Madison.

39. "A Position Paper for the CCAS Convention."
40. The statement was approved on March 28–30, 1969. The activities of the Concerned in 1969 did not pass unnoticed, and they spurred reactions from the AAS leadership. William Theodore De Bary, the president of the association, delivered his presidential address in 1970 largely in response to the issues raised by CCAS. "The Association for Asian Studies: Nonpolitical but not Unconcerned," *Journal of Asian Studies* 29 (August 1970): 751–759. De Bary also set up a presidential panel for the 1970 convention specifically on the issues of funding and politics.
41. "CCAS Statement of Purpose," criticalasianstudies.org/about-us/bcas-founding-statement.html. Emphasis mine.
42. "CCAS Statement of Purpose."
43. Among the participants to the seminar were Herbert Bix, Tom Engelhardt, Richard Kagan, Leigh Kagan, Jon Livingston, Victor Nee, Jim Peck, Judith Coburn, Paul Winnacker, plus, obviously, Friedman and Selden. I discuss the seminar in detail in chapter 2.
44. Friedman and Selden, "Introduction," xv.
45. Friedman and Selden, "Introduction," xvi. Emphasis mine.
46. I am simplifying Foucault's much more complex idea of power/knowledge. Michel Foucault, *Power/Knowledge: Selected Interviews and Other Writings* (New York: Pantheon, 1980).
47. A stunning example of that recognition of subjectivity can be found in the report of a meeting between North American women groups and a delegation of Indochinese women in Vancouver, Canada, in April 1971. During the encounter, it was the American women who asked the Indochinese for guidance, with questions such as "What should we do?" "Should we unite with non-revolutionary groups?" and "Do we need a revolution?" Kathleen Aberle, "An Indochinese Conference in Vancouver," *BCAS* 3 (summer–fall 1971): 2–29. Judy Tzu-Chun Wu analyzes the Indochinese Women's Conference in the last three chapters of her book *Radicals on the Road: Internationalism, Orientalism, and Feminism during the Vietnam Era* (Ithaca, NY: Cornell University Press, 2013).
48. Leigh Kagan, "Proposals," *CCAS Newsletter* (May 1968): 7.
49. Mark Selden, "People's War and the Transformation of Peasant Society: China and Vietnam," in Friedman and Selden, *America's Asia*, 360. Selden explored these issues further in his *The Yenan Way in Revolutionary China* (Cambridge, MA: Harvard University Press, 1971). He revised the volume years later in *The Yenan Way Revisited* (Armonk, NY: M. E. Sharpe, 1995).
50. Selden, "People's War," 360.

51. "Ed Friedman to Steve Andors," *CCAS Newsletter* Supplement B (February 1974): 4.
52. Mark Selden, interview with the author (March 8, 2014). Steve Andors and Jonathan Unger both echoed the same point (interviews with the author). China was connected to Vietnam because of the domino theory, and U.S. policymakers were always linking Vietnam with their policy toward China.
53. Committee of Concerned Asian Scholars Friendship Delegation to China, "Interview with Zhou Enlai," *BCAS* 3 (summer–fall 1971): 50.
54. Mark Selden, interview with the author (March 8, 2014).
55. On China-U.S. relationships, see Chen Jian, *Mao's China and the Cold War* (Chapel Hill: University of North Carolina Press, 2001).
56. Victor Lippit, "Economic Development and Welfare in China," *BCAS* 4 (summer 1972): 76.
57. Lippit, "Economic Development," 83.
58. John Gurley, "Capitalist and Maoist Economic Development," in Friedman and Selden, *America's Asia*, 345. Gurley expanded his argument in his book *China's Economy and the Maoist Strategy* (New York: Monthly Review Press, 1976). Gurley was then professor of economics at Stanford University.
59. Noam Chomsky, *American Power and the New Mandarins* (New York: Pantheon, 1969), 332. Chomsky was referencing Walter W. Rostow and Richard W. Hatch, *An American Policy in Asia* (Cambridge, MA: MIT Press, 1955).
60. Stephen Andors, *China's Industrial Revolution: Politics, Planning, and Management, 1949 to the Present* (New York: Pantheon Books, 1977), 23.
61. Andors, *China's Industrial Revolution*, 243.
62. Gurley, "Capitalist and Maoist Economic Development," 348.
63. In 1977, CCAS member Ed Hammond compared the situation at the time with that of ten years earlier (when CCAS was founded) and pondered how the task of advanced scholars was no longer "to explain how Chinese are human too." Ed Hammond, "Some Thoughts for the Convention—1978," *CCAS Newsletter* (October 1977): 3.
64. Selden, "People's War," 360. Emphasis mine.
65. Gurley, "Capitalist and Maoist Economic Development," 348. Emphasis mine.
66. Jim Peck, "The C.C.A.S. Summer Seminar," *CCAS Newsletter* 1 (October 1968).
67. Christian Bay, "The Cheerful Science of Dismal Politics," in *The Dissenting Academy*, ed. Theodore Roszak (New York: Pantheon, 1968), 222. Emphasis mine.
68. In 1972 and 1976, the national CCAS conventions featured panels on Asian Americans. "Confrontation with AAS Brewing," *CCAS Newsletter* (April 1973): 20; "The 1976 National Convention," *CCAS Newsletter* (February 1976): 2.
69. Orville Schell and Jim Peck, "National Coordinators Report," *CCAS Newsletter* (October 1969): 14.
70. In 1967, John K. Fairbank called China "our biggest problem" during a public lecture titled "East Asia and Our Future." Accessed August 2016, vimeo.com

/50776144. I discuss the lecture later in the chapter. See also Fairbank's presidential address for the American Historical Association in 1968: John K. Fairbank, "Assignment for the '70s. Presidential Address, AHA December 1968," *American Historical Review* 74 (February 1969): 861–879.

71. Mark Selden to Orville Schell and Jim Peck (September 6, 1969), CCAS Archives. The *Bulletin* also planned to do a joint issue with *Ampo*. Beheiren (Citizen's League for Peace in Vietnam) was a nonviolent movement that organized major protests against the Vietnam War between 1965 and 1974. See Thomas R. H. Havens, *Fire Across the Sea: The Vietnam War and Japan, 1965–1975* (Princeton, NJ: Princeton University Press, 1987). *Ampo: Japan-Asia Quarterly Review* was founded in 1969 as the organ of Beheiren. It ceased publication in 2000.
72. Selden and Friedman, "Introduction," xiv–xv.
73. Selden and Friedman, "Introduction," xvii.
74. "CCAS Convention Report, Boston, March 30–April 4 1974," *CCAS Newsletter* (May 1974): 11. Gail Omvedt was one of the presenters for the panel "Transforming Societies: The Socialist Alternative."
75. Gail Omvedt, Agrarian Crisis in India: A Review Essay," *BCAS* 6 (November–December 1974): 20.
76. Richard W. Franke, "Solution to the Asian Food Crisis: Green Revolution or Social Revolution?" *BCAS* 6 (November–December 1974): 10. On the Green Revolution and its relationship to the Maoist experiments, see Sigrid Schmalzer, *Red Revolution, Green Revolution: Encounters with Scientific Farming in Socialist China* (Chicago: University of Chicago Press, 2016).
77. CCAS South Asia Committee, "An Open Letter to South Asian Scholars" (undated), CCAS Archives.
78. Gail Omvedt, "Gandhi and the Pacification of the Indian National Revolution," *BCAS* 5 (July 1973): 2–4. It must be noted that, especially in the 1970s, it was the experience of the Chinese revolution that functioned as a model or a point of comparison, not the actual policy of the Chinese state, whose relations to Pakistan were viewed with rightful suspicion by South Asianists. For an example of this distinction, see Kathleen Gough, "The South Asian Revolutionary Potential," *BCAS* 4 (winter 1971): 77–98.
79. I am thinking in particular of Ranajit Guha, *Elementary Aspects of Peasant Insurgency in Colonial India* (Durham, NC: Duke University Press, 1999).
80. Tom Engelhardt, "Ambush at Kamikaze Pass," *BCAS* 3 (winter–spring 1971): 64–84. The book is *The End of Victory Culture: Cold War America and the Disillusioning of a Generation* (New York: Basic Books, 1995). For a different and more somber interpretation of *The Battle of Algiers*, see Wendy Smith, "From Oppressed to Oppressor," *American Scholar* (autumn 2008), accessed December 2015, theamericanscholar.org/from-oppressed-to-oppressors/#.UoMEJ1732zA.
81. In another crucial moment in the film, Colonel Mathieu, the man in charge of the repression of the FLN, when questioned by a journalist about their use

of torture, answers: "I would now like to ask you a question: Should France remain in Algeria? If you answer 'yes,' then you must accept all the necessary consequences." That is the only question that counts, until the very end of the movie (and the success of the revolution). *The Battle of Algiers*, directed by Gillo Pontecorvo (1967). I am thankful to Daniel Vukovich for drawing my attention to this analysis of the final scene of the movie.

82. Christopher Leigh Connery, "Introduction: Worlded Pedagogy in Santa Cruz," in *The Worlding Project: Doing Cultural Studies in the Era of Globalization*, ed. Rob Wilson and Christopher Leigh Connery (Santa Cruz, CA: New Pacific Press, 2007), 78.

83. Connery, "Introduction: Worlded Pedagogy," 92. In 1975, Mark Selden celebrated the end of the Vietnam War in an enthusiastic piece, which remarked the powerful example of Vietnam's actual existence, against all odds: "Human solidarity has triumphed over the awesome and unbridled might of technology. A montagnard arrow slicing a helicopter fuel line, bringing the machine crashing to earth, a diminutive Vietnamese woman leading away a hulking American pilot at gunpoint, these are symbols of the victory of national liberation against overwhelming odds. The defeat of American armed might in Indochina inspires men and women in Asia, throughout the Third World, and in the United States to confront the power of empire and to strive for national independence." "Introduction," BCAS 7 (April–June 1975): 2.

84. Selden, interview with the author (March 8, 2014).

85. Wu, *Radicals on the Road*, 5. A similar criticism of the radical Left was leveled at the time by Jürgen Habermas, who, as Quinn Slobodian has pointed out, not only denied the possibility of any political identification with a global movement of the oppressed, but even proclaimed the need to separate the violent and irrational politics of the non-whites from the "rational engagement and measured protest" that were proper for Western youths. Slobodian, *Foreign Front*, 10.

86. James Peck, "Revolution versus Modernization and Revisionism: A Two-Front Struggle," in *China's Uninterrupted Revolution: From 1840 to the Present*, ed. Victor Nee and James Peck (New York: Pantheon Books, 1975), 185.

87. Judy Perrolle to John Berninghausen (June 19, 1973), CCAS Archives. Perrolle mentioned that she kept a Chinese flag in her office. In his reply, Berninghausen pushed on: "Again it's not crucial but I would encourage you to consider the possible costs of flaunting these symbols. They are not ours to flaunt (display). They belong to someone else. We must belong to ourselves." John Berninghausen to Judy and Paul Perrolle (July 3, 1973), CCAS Archives.

88. Committee of Concerned Asian Scholars Friendship Delegation to China, "Interview with Zhou Enlai," 52.

89. Alain Geismar, *Porquoi nous combattons* [Why we fight] (Paris: Maspero, 1970), 18. Geismar was one of the leaders of the Gauche Prolétarianne, and he was sentenced to eighteen months in prison in October 1970 for re-forming the

organization, which had been declared illegal. See Christophe Bourseiller, *Les Maoïstes: La folle histoire des gardes rouges Français* [The Maoists: The crazy story of the French red guards] (Paris: Points, 2008).

90. Geismar, *Porquoi nous combattons*, 22.
91. "Jean et Colette: An Etabli and His Wife," in Michéle Manceaux, *Les Maos en France* (Paris: Gallimard, 1972), 22.
92. "George, 26 Years Old, Engineering Student Turned Worker," in Manceaux, *Les Maos*, 57.
93. "George, 26 Years Old," in Manceaux, *Les Maos*, 59.
94. "George, 26 Years Old," in Manceaux, *Les Maos* 57.
95. "Two miners from the north," in Manceaux, *Les Maos*, 103.
96. "Il y a bien quelqu'un chez nous avec un nome de chez nous pour faire notre révolution à nous. . . . Le maoïsme, c'est largement ouvert." "A Female Worker," in Manceaux, *Les Maos*, 117.
97. Louis Althusser, in an unsigned 1966 text on the Cultural Revolution, called for Communists all over the world to "borrow" the lesson of the CR. [Louis Althusser], "On the Cultural Revolution," trans. Jason E. Smith, *Décalages* 1, no. 1 (2014), scholar.oxy.edu/decalages/vol1/iss1/9. The text was originally published in the November–December 1966 issue of the *Cahiers Marxistes-Léninistes*.
98. Connery, "Introduction: Worlded Pedagogy," 97.
99. Dipesh Chakrabarty, *Provincializing Europe: Postcolonial Thought and Historical Difference* (Princeton, NJ: Princeton University Press, 2007). Daniel Vukovich illustrates how an orientalist framework is still operating today in Western scholarship on the PRC in his *China and Orientalism: Western Knowledge Production and the PRC* (London: Routledge, 2011).
100. Connery, "Editorial Introduction. The Asian Sixties," 548. I owe this insight into a different significance of the "not yet" to Meera Ashar. Her paper "The 'Not-Yet' in Indian Politics: Language, Epistemology and Coloniality" was presented at the conference "Global Coloniality in the Asian Century," Hong Kong, June 7–8, 2012. See also her "Decolonizing What? Categories, Concepts and the Enduring 'Not Yet,'" *Cultural Dynamics* 27, no. 2 (2015): 253–265.
101. Guha's *Elementary Aspects of Peasant Insurgency in Colonial India*, for example, is heavily informed by a Maoist approach. For a history of sorts of Subaltern studies, see David Ludden, ed., *Reading Subaltern Studies: Critical History, Contested Meaning and the Globalization of South Asia* (London: Anthem Press, 2002).
102. Edwin O. Reischaeur (1910–1990) was professor of Japanese history at Harvard and U.S. Ambassador to Japan (1961–1966). The Institute for Japanese Studies at Harvard University is named after him. See George R. Packard, *Edwin O. Reischauer and the American Discovery of Japan* (New York: Columbia University Press, 2010).
103. Fairbank and Reischauer, "East Asia and Our Future." Fairbank restated the case for the Chinese difference in his presidential address to the American

Historical Association. "China presents a special world problem requiring special treatment," Fairbank argued:

> If China were not the *most distinctive and separate* of the great historical cultures, if the Chinese language were not *so different and difficult*, if our China studies were not so set apart by these circumstances, *our China problem* would not be so great. But the fact is that China is a uniquely large and compact section of mankind, with a specially self-contained and long-continued tradition of centrality and superiority, too big and too different to be assimilated into our automobile–TV, individual–voter, individual–consumer culture. China is too weak to conquer the world but too large to be digested by it.

Later in the address he called the Chinese "the most indigestible and unassimilable of the other peoples" and China "the most pronounced case of 'otherness' on which we need perspective." Fairbank, "Assignment for the '70s," 862–863. Emphasis mine.

104. Recalling her time in graduate school at the University of Chicago, Saundra Sturdevant remarked: "Of course, in those days, you weren't allowed to talk about imperialism. You couldn't use the word." Interview with the author (August 30, 2011).
105. Fairbank and Reischauer, "East Asia and Our Future." Compared to Fairbank's, Edwin Reischauer's talk, while at times indulging in similar generalizations (especially about China), was more somber and pragmatic. He went as far as to state that the strategy of isolating China had failed and that the PRC was not aggressive in a military sense.
106. It is difficult to assess Fairbank's role in and attitude toward the founding of CCAS. Six days after chairing the meeting of the Vietnam Caucus in Philadelphia on March 23, he wrote to the newly established CCAS urging them to "form a *student-faculty committee* of Asia specialists and use it as a vehicle both to study policy problems and to express policy views." He suggested they publish a newsletter to communicate these policies. "John K. Fairbank to CCAS" (March 29, 1968), CCAS Archives. The very name "Committee of Concerned Asian Scholars" seemed to have been proposed by Fairbank, but I found no solid confirmation of this attribution. See also Paul M. Evans, *John Fairbank and the American Understanding of Modern China* (New York: Basil Blackwell, 1988).
107. For an insightful view into Fairbank's undeclared methodological tenets, see Tani E. Barlow, "Colonialism's Career in Postwar China Studies," in *Formations of Colonial Modernity in East Asia*, ed. Tani E. Barlow (Durham, NC: Duke University Press, 1997), 373–411. The essay was originally published in the first issue of *positions: east asia cultures critique* [1 (spring 1993): 224–267].
108. Charles Cell, cited in "CCAS Convention Report, Boston, March 30–April 4, 1974," *CCAS Newsletter* (May 1974): 13.
109. CCAS Berkeley, "Why a New Asian Studies Dept?? An Overdue Challenge to Scholarship on Asia: Learning about China" (undated pamphlet): 1, Joe Moore Personal Archive, hereafter JMPA.

110. Richard M. Pfeffer, "Revolution and Rule: Where Do We Go from Here?" *BCAS* 2 (April–July 1970): 91.
111. Pfeffer, "Revolution and Rule," 89. In recalling this review, Ezra Vogel expressed the view that Pfeffer had been fair. Ezra Vogel, interview with the author (May 15, 2008).
112. Felicia Oldfather, Martha Kendall, and Jack Nicholl, "Why a New Asian Studies Dept?? An Overdue Challenge to Scholarship on Asia" (undated pamphlet): 3, JMPA.
113. Elinor Lerner, "The Chinese Peasantry and Imperialism: A Critique of Chalmers Johnson's *Peasant Nationalism and Communist Power*," *BCAS* 6 (April–August 1974): 44. Chalmers Johnson (1931–2010) was at the time very much a cold warrior. He was a consultant for the CIA from 1967 to 1973 and director of the Center for Chinese Studies at Berkeley from 1967 to 1972. Later in his life, Johnson became a vocal critic of American hegemony, which he saw as a form of global empire.
114. Lerner, *The Chinese Peasantry*, 52.
115. Lerner, *The Chinese Peasantry*, 54.
116. Fairbank and Reischauer, "East Asia and Our Future."
117. Peck, "Revolution versus Modernization and Revisionism," 81.
118. One of the best analyses of the role of Modernization Theory in shaping the social sciences is by Nils Gilman, *Mandarins of the Future: Modernization Theory in Cold War America* (Baltimore: Johns Hopkins University Press, 2003).
119. Andrew G. Walder, "The Transformation of Contemporary China Studies, 1977–2002," in *The Politics of Knowledge: Area Studies and the Disciplines*, ed. David Szanton (Berkeley: University of California Press, 2004), 108–109.
120. Peck, "Revolution versus Modernization and Revisionism," 81.
121. Peck, "Revolution versus Modernization and Revisionism," 86.
122. Cheryl Payer Goodman, "Review: Lucian Pye, *The Spirit of Chinese Politics*," *CCAS Newsletter* 3 (March 1969): 19. Lucien W. Pye (1921–2008) was professor at MIT and served as advisor to the Department of State, the National Security Council, and presidential candidates, including John F. Kennedy. He was one of the early proponents of the Vietnam War.
123. Oldfather, Kendall, and Nicholl, "Why a New Asian Studies Dept??"
124. "Cornell Chapter," *CCAS Newsletter* (May 1969).
125. Orville Schell, "Learning by Doing," *CCAS Newsletter* (January 1970): 8.
126. Schell, "Learning by Doing," 9.
127. James Peck, "Reflections on the Implications of the Vietnam Caucus," *CCAS Newsletter* (May 1968): 3. The criticism was recognized—if largely dismissed—by Wm. Theodore De Bary in his 1970 AAS presidential address. "The Association for Asian Studies: Nonpolitical but Not Unconcerned."
128. *Columbia CCAS Newsletter* 2 (April 27, 1970): 1.
129. Jesse Lemisch, *On Active Service in War and Peace: Politics and Ideology in the American Historical Profession* (Toronto: New Hogtown Press, 1975), 72.

130. Ellen W. Schrecker, *No Ivory Tower: McCarthyism and the Universities* (Oxford, UK: Oxford University Press, 1986); Robert P. Newman, *Owen Lattimore and the "Loss" of China* (Berkeley: University of California Press, 1992). John K. Fairbank defended his friend Lattimore publicly and was called to testify in front of the McCarran Committee in 1952; yet in his memoir, he still argued that there were "enough Communist infiltrations to justify setting up a government loyalty-security apparatus." John K. Fairbank, *Chinabound: A Fifty-Year Memoir* (New York: Harper and Row, 1982), 333.

131. Orville Schell, "Melby: The Mandate of Heaven," BCAS 2 (January 1970): 54.

132. Robert R. Tomes, *Apocalypse Then: American Intellectuals and the Vietnam War, 1954–1975* (New York: NYU Press, 1998).

133. "On the Fallacy of Non-involvement" (unsigned), CCAS Newsletter (September 1970): 4.

134. Judith Coburn, "Asian Scholars and Government: The Chrysanthemum on the Sword," in Friedman and Selden, *America's Asia*, 84.

135. "On the Fallacy of Non-involvement," 4.

136. John W. Lewis is now professor emeritus of Chinese politics at Stanford. He was teaching at Stanford at the time he founded and directed the Center for Asian Studies (1969–1970).

137. Coburn, "Asian Scholars," 85.

138. Ron Robin, *The Making of the Cold War Enemy: Culture and Politics in the Military-Intellectual Complex* (Princeton, NJ: Princeton University Press, 2001), 30.

139. Robin, *The Making of the Cold War Enemy*, 32.

140. Michael E. Latham, *Modernization as Ideology: American Social Science and "Nation Building" in the Kennedy Era* (Chapel Hill: University of North Carolina Press, 2000), 8.

141. Latham, *Modernization as Ideology*, 13.

142. "Draft Statement of Purpose" (May 9, 1968), CCAS Archives.

143. CCAS Berkeley Chapter, "The State of the Profession: A Proposed Examination." (1968?), JMPA.

144. "Draft Statement of Purpose."

145. James Peck, "The Roots of Rhetoric: The Professional Ideology of America's China Watchers," in Friedman and Selden, *America's Asia*, 47. Peck reprised his investigation into U.S. government rhetoric in his later books: *Washington's China: The National Security World, the Cold War and the Origins of Globalism* (Amherst: University of Massachusetts Press, 2006) and *Ideal Illusions: How the U.S. Government Co-opted Human Rights* (New York: Metropolitan Books, 2010).

146. Peck, "The Roots of Rhetoric," 45.

147. Peck, "The Roots of Rhetoric," 50–51.

148. Peck, "The Roots of Rhetoric," 51.

149. "An Exchange" (John K. Fairbank and Jim Peck), BCAS 2 (April–July 1970): 52.

150. "An Exchange," 56.
151. "An Exchange," 57.
152. "An Exchange," 67. The May Fourth Movement of 1919 was the first instance of modern student activism in China. It marked the culmination of a longer process (the New Culture Movement) that combined political and intellectual activism. See Fabio Lanza, *Behind the Gate: Inventing Students in Beijing* (New York: Columbia University Press, 2010).
153. "Orville Schell to Stewart" (September 20, 1969), CCAS Archives.
154. "Letter from Mark Selden to Orville Schell" (February 12, 1970), CCAS Archives.
155. "Orville Schell to Stewart."
156. "Letter from the Berkeley and Stanford Chapters on the Conference Organization" (1969), CCAS Archives.
157. "Mark Selden to Stephen Andors, Nina Adams, and Jon Livingston" (December 18, 1973), *CCAS Newsletter* Supplement B (February 1974): 5.
158. Two volumes appeared under the collective authorship of the Committee: *The Indochina Story: A Fully Documented Account* (New York: Pantheon Books, 1970), and *China! Inside the People's Republic* (New York: Bantam Books, 1972). Other books that are directly associated with CCAS are Nina S. Adams and Alfred W. McCoy, *Laos: War and Revolution* (New York: Harpher Colophon, 1970), Nee and Peck, *China's Uninterrupted Revolution*, and Friedman and Selden, *America's Asia*.
159. Carl Riskin, "Maoism and Motivation: Work Incentives in China," in Nee and Peck, *China's Uninterrupted Revolution*, 416.
160. Carl Riskin, "Maoism and Motivation: Work Incentives in China," *BCAS* 5 (July 1973): 21.
161. Carl Riskin, "China's Economic Growth: Leap or Creep? Comments on Some Recent Pekinological Revisionism," *BCAS* 2 (January 1970): 22.
162. Riskin, "China's Economic Growth," 22.
163. Steve Andors, "Hobbes and Weber vs. Marx and Mao: The Political Economy of Decentralization in China," *BCAS* 6 (September–October 1974): 26.
164. Andors, "Hobbes and Weber vs. Marx and Mao," 27. Emphasis in the original.
165. Andors, *China's Industrial Revolution*, 135.
166. Andors, *China's Industrial Revolution*, 160.
167. Andors, *China's Industrial Revolution*, 246.
168. The need for a political rethinking of "economics" has remained an undercurrent in post-Mao China, where the New Left has deployed this part of the Maoist legacy to challenge the path of the economic reform. And it is a need that is now heavily felt globally, as economists (and mathematicians) have unchained financial speculation from social considerations, with disastrous effects.
169. This tradition was obviously dominant within the PRC, and it represented a significant strand of academic research in Europe. In France, the work of Jean Chesneaux is notable.

170. Joseph Esherick, "Harvard on China: The Apologetics of Imperialism," BCAS 4 (December 1972): 15.
171. See, for example, James L. Hevia, *Cherishing Men from Afar: Qing Guest Ritual and the Macartney Embassy of 1793* (Durham, NC: Duke University Press, 1995).
172. Transcript of the "Wither Chinese Studies" panel (1970), CCAS Archives, 12.
173. "CCAS Eastern Regional Conference Report" (1970), CCAS Archives.
174. "Letter from Bryant Avery on CCAS panels at AAS," *CCAS Newsletter* (October 1975): 5.
175. "CCAS Summer Retreat," *CCAS Newsletter* (October 1972): 2. The same report included another honest and startling admission: "Let's face it . . . CCAS has made some contribution to the intellectual side of the anti-war movement, and a few of our members have become deeply involved in anti-war organizing. But as our own internal critics have pointed out, we've done far too little to integrate ourselves in the on-going movement." In other words, there was an acknowledgment of the failure in both scholarship *and* activism.
176. Harootunian adds, "To be sure, when the historians of this newer generation began to appropriate Norman, they recognized the intimate relationship between historical and social-scientific scholarship and politics." H. D. Harootunian, "Review of *E. H. Norman: His Life and Scholarship* by Roger W. Bowen," *Journal of Asian Studies* 47 (November 1988): 879. For Norman's own writings, see E. H. Norman, *Origins of the Modern Japanese State: Selected Writings of E. H. Norman*, ed. John Dower (New York: Pantheon Books, 1975).
177. Latham, *Modernization as Ideology*.
178. Rancière, *Althusser's Lesson*, 142. Emphasis in the original.
179. Slavoj Žižek, *The Sublime Object of Ideology* (New York: Verso, 1989), 32–33.

2: TO BE, OR NOT TO BE, A SCHOLAR

1. "Intellectuals and Power: A Conversation between Michel Foucault and Gilles Deleuze," in Michel Foucault, *Language, Counter-Memory, Practice: Selected Essays and Interviews*, ed. Donald F. Bouchard (Ithaca, NY: Cornell University Press, 1977), 205–217. Also available at libcom.org/library/intellectuals-power-a-conversation-between-michel-foucault-and-gilles-deleuze.
2. Gayatri Chakravorty Spivak, "Can the Subaltern Speak?" in *Marxism and the Interpretation of Culture*, ed. Cary Nelson and Lawrence Grossberg (Urbana: University of Illinois Press, 1988), 271–313.
3. Spivak, "Can the Subaltern Speak?" 275.
4. Spivak, "Can the Subaltern Speak?" 272. Jacques Derrida's reference was to Chinese writing. See *Of Grammatology*, trans. Gayatri Chakravorty Spivak (Baltimore: Johns Hopkins University Press, 1998), 80.
5. See Gayatri Chakravorty Spivak, "Subaltern Studies: Deconstructing Historiography," in *Selected Subaltern Studies*, ed. Ranajit Guha and Gayatri Chakravorty Spivak (New York: Oxford University Press, 1988), 3–32. See also

her "The New Subaltern: A Silent Interview," in *Mapping Subaltern Studies and the Postcolonial*, ed. Vinayak Chaturvedi (London: Verso, 2000), 324–340.
6. I am thankful to Tani Barlow for pushing me on this point.
7. Jacques Rancière, *Althusser's Lesson*, trans. Emiliano Battista (London: Continuum, 2011), 14.
8. Charles Bingham and Gert J. J. Biesta, with Jacques Rancière, *Jacques Rancière: Education, Truth, Emancipation* (London: Continuum, 2010), 40.
9. Peter Hallward, "Jacques Rancière and the Subversion of Mastery," in *Jacques Rancière: Aesthetics, Politics, Philosophy*, ed. Mark Robson (Edinburgh: Edinburgh University Press, 2005), 26.
10. Rancière, *Althusser's Lesson*, 21. The realization is described vividly by Colette, an *etabli* member of the Gauche Proletarienne, who recalled how the experience of the "Comités Vietnam de Base" (CVB) was fundamental for the encounter between intellectuals and the masses and for the realization that intellectuals did not know everything, that what they knew came solely from books and that they were removed from reality. Michéle Manceaux, *Les Maos en France* (Paris: Gallimard, 1972), chapter 1.
11. Sigrid Schmalzer, *Red Revolution, Green Revolution: Encounters with Scientific Farming in Socialist China* (Chicago: University of Chicago Press, 2016).
12. On the Huxian peasants' paintings, see the documentary film by Hu Jie and Ai Xiaoming, *Painting for the Revolution: Peasant Paintings from Huxian, China* (Wei geming huahua) (Hong Kong: Xianggang Zhongwendaxue Zhongguo yanjiu fuwu zhongxin, 2006).
13. See Mao Zedong, "Talk on Questions of Philosophy" (August 18, 1964), www.marxists.org/reference/archive/mao/selected-works/volume-9/mswv9_27.htm. Virginie Linhart wrote a beautiful account both of the French Maoist trajectory and of its legacy based on the traumatic effect that the 1968 eruption of mass activism had on her father, then the Althusserian leader of the Maoist student association in Paris. He had a nervous breakdown and stopped talking. Virginie Linhart, *Le jour où mon père s'est tu* [The day my father stopped talking] (Paris: Éd. du Seuil, 2008).
14. This is Alain Badiou's view. See his *The Communist Hypothesis* (London: Verso, 2010). On the global fortune of the Little Red Book, see Alexander Cook, ed., *Mao's Little Red Book: A Global History* (Cambridge: Cambridge University Press, 2014).
15. Bingham and Biesta, *Jacques Rancière*, 40.
16. Ding Ling's last story "Du Wanxiang" is a reminder that Chinese women (poor farmers/workers) also thought, and precisely in the terms outlined here. Tani E. Barlow, with Gary J. Bjorge, ed., *I Myself Am a Woman: Selected Writings of Ding Ling* (Boston: Beacon Press, 1989), 329–354.
17. The Confucian philosopher Mencius articulated the division of labor in these terms: "Some labour with their minds, and some labour with their strength. Those who labour with their minds govern others; those who labour with their

strength are governed by others. Those who are governed by others support them; those who govern others are supported by them." James Legge, trans., *The Chinese Classics*, vol. II (London: Trübner, 1875), 50.

18. Rancière, *Althusser's Lesson*, 15, emphasis mine. The same expression "over there" was used by John Fairbank in the talk I analyzed in chapter 1; however, that "over there" conveyed a completely different meaning. With Fairbank, it indicated the geographical, cultural, and political distance of a problem; with Rancière (and the French Maoists in general), it marked the connection of a shared political horizon.
19. Rancière, *Althusser's Lesson*, 54.
20. Alain Badiou, *The Adventures of French Philosophy* (London: Verso, 2012), 3. Once again, there is an important elision here, which must be noted. It was, one should add, the intelligence of Chinese women that should have forced male intellectuals everywhere to reconsider how the political subjectivity of women everywhere gets assimilated and erased in their analyses. It was, eventually, the intervention of feminist critique that would lay bare the gendered character of the male philosopher's universal pretenses, his unfettered use of "he" as a universal pronoun.
21. Alain Geismar, *Porquoi nous combattons* [Why we fight] (Paris: Maspero, 1970), 6–7.
22. Jacques Rancière, *The Philosopher and His Poor* (Durham, NC: Duke University Press, 2004), xxvi.
23. Robert J. C. Young, "White Mythologies Revisited," in *White Mythologies: Writing History and the West* (London: Routledge, 2004, 2nd ed.), 19.
24. "Cambridge Summer Seminar Meeting July 19, 1968," CCAS Archives.
25. "Cambridge Summer Seminar Meeting July 19, 1968."
26. "Cambridge Summer Seminar Meeting July 19, 1968." This statement on the need for a new vocabulary was accompanied by a reference to the Chinese vernacular movement of the 1910s and 1920s.
27. Theodore Roszak, "On Academic Delinquency," in *The Dissenting Academy* (New York: Pantheon, 1968), 34.
28. Orville Schell, "Wither Chinese Studies" panel (1970), CCAS Archives.
29. "Cambridge Summer Seminar August 1, 1968," CCAS Archives.
30. "Cambridge Summer Seminar August 1, 1968."
31. "Cambridge Summer Seminar July 19, 1968." Here the CCAS debate addresses one of the defining characteristics of sixties politics, the declared expansion of the political outside its "proper" locations and into the private realm, most notably epitomized by the feminist slogan "the personal is the political."
32. I am not stating that this was unprecedented. Masses had been vocal and thoughtful before, within and outside China, and each instance of mass assumption of the right to speech and politics has always forced a rethinking of the positions of intellectuals and activists. Mao's own "Report on an Investigation of the Peasant Movement in Hunan" is a vivid example of that process,

www.marxists.org/reference/archive/mao/selected-works/volume-1/mswv1_2.htm.
33. "August 27, 1968, Meeting at Mark Selden's Apartment," CCAS Archives.
34. Minutes of the meetings "July 29, 1968, Monday Afternoon" and "August 1, 1968," CCAS Archives. Chomsky took part in the July 29 meeting.
35. "July 29, 1968, Monday Afternoon."
36. Noam Chomsky, "The Asian Scholar and the American Crisis," BCAS 1 (May 1969): 15.
37. Stephen Andors, interview with the author (June 23, 2011). Chomsky's political views were the object of intense scrutiny just a few years later, during his famous debate with Michel Foucault. The French philosopher criticized Chomsky for his postulation of definitions of "justice" and "human nature" as ultimately detached from social and historical conditions. Using Marxist (and at times Maoist) language, Foucault exposed Chomsky's inability to see the complex functioning of power (and ideology) in shaping the very categories deployed by the intellectual. Noam Chomsky and Michel Foucault, "Human Nature: Justice versus Power. Noam Chomsky Debates with Michel Foucault (1971)," accessed March 2016, www.chomsky.info/debates/1971xxxx.htm.
38. Felicia Oldfather, quoted in "Discussion Group on Asian Studies, First Meeting" (Berkeley, October 7, 1968), 3. CCAS Archives.
39. A few years later, Edward Said would make clear how exposing the lies of an ideological construction is not enough to dismantle it. "One ought never to assume that the structure of Orientalism is nothing more than a structure of lies and myths which, were the truth about them to be told, would simply blow away." Edward Said, *Orientalism* (New York: Vintage, 1979), 6.
40. Richard Pfeffer, "Wither Chinese Studies."
41. Orville Schell, "Wither Chinese Studies." This was in response to David Keightley's criticism, quoted in one of the epigraphs at the beginning of the chapter. Schell added: "We see that it is essential that people who act think and that people who think act."
42. Saundra Sturdevant commented on how this division was partially lifted when she joined CCAS in 1969: "It was the first time in my academic career that my study and my political activity went together." Interview with the author.
43. "Cambridge Summer Seminar Meeting, July 19, 1968."
44. Ed Hammond, "Berkeley Chapter," *CCAS Newsletter* (July–August 1972): 10.
45. Geismar, *Porquoi nous combattons*, 6–7. Here is Geismar's original: "ou on l'apprend aux opprimés que le savoir c'est dans le livres et à l'université, que ce n'est pas pour eux. Dans les universités, on n'apprend rien mais on forme les chiens de garde de la bourgeoisie." [where we teach the oppressed that knowledge is in the books and in the university, and that's not for them. In the universities, nothing is learned but that's where the watchdogs of the bourgeoisie are formed.]
46. "Ramblings of a Berkeley Chapter, CCAS, Member."

47. "Ramblings of a Berkeley Chapter, CCAS, Member."
48. Selden, "August 27, 1968, Meeting at Mark Selden's Apartment."
49. "July 29, 1968, Monday Afternoon," CCAS Archives. Tom Engelhardt eventually acted on that conviction. He told me that the decision was easier for him because he was not really interested in the academic career. Interview with the author (June 25, 2011). Engelhardt went on to a successful career in publishing. He returned to more directly political action after 9/11, when he created Tomdispatch, first as an email publication (November 2001) and then as a website (December 2002), www.tomdispatch.com. It provides commentary and news alternative to the mainstream media.
50. John Berninghausen, "Wither Chinese Studies" panel, 14.
51. "CCAS Meeting July 26, 1968," 5–6.
52. Julien Besançon, ed., *Les murs ont la parole* [The walls have the word] (Paris: Claude Tchou, 1968), 36.
53. "John Berninghausen to David [Marr]" (October 31, 1969), CCAS Archives.
54. "Marilyn Young to Orville Schell" (1970), CCAS Archives.
55. BCAS 3 (summer–fall, 1971). The special supplement, titled "Modern China Studies: How the Foundations Bought a Field," included the exposé by the Columbia Chapter of CCAS, a reply from John K. Fairbank, an essay by Moss Roberts on the structure and direction of contemporary China studies, and a vitriolic text by David Horowitz. Columbia CCAS, "The American Asian Studies Establishment" (92–103); John K. Fairbank, "Comment" (104–111); Moss Roberts, "The Structure and Direction of Contemporary China Studies" (113–141); David Horowitz, "Politics and Knowledge: An Unorthodox History of Modern China Studies" (143–172). For an analysis of how postwar funding dramatically shaped the research priorities of a different discipline, see David H. Price, *Cold War Anthropology: The CIA, the Pentagon, and the Growth of Dual Use Anthropology* (Durham, NC: Duke University Press, 2016), in particular chapter 4.
56. "The JCCC Boycott: A Necessary First Step towards Self-Determination in Asian Studies" [draft, 1972?], CCAS Archives.
57. "Andrea Faste to Coordinators" (January 27, 1974), CCAS Archives.
58. Marilyn Young, interview with the author (June 27, 2011). Young recalls that other leftist female scholars participated in the conference (Norma Diamond, Delia Devlin) and that they managed to have an open session in Berkeley (the conference was otherwise closed to the public).
59. "Carl Riskin to Coordinator and Boycott Committee" (January 4, 1974), CCAS Archives. Riskin was a CCAS member. Initially, JCCC had agreed only to have its first president, George Taylor, write a report, later to be published in the AAS *Professional Review*.
60. "On the Fallacy of Non-involvement" (unsigned), *CCAS Newsletter* (September 1970): 4.

61. Felicia Oldfather, quoted in "Discussion Group on Asian Studies, First Meeting (10/7/1968)," JMPA.
62. "On the Fallacy of Non-involvement."
63. "Discussion Group on Asian Studies, First Meeting" (October 14, 1968), JMPA.
64. "Mark Selden to Al McCoy" (November 14, 1970), CCAS Archives. Emphasis in the original.
65. Mark Selden, "For Circulation among the 'Concerned' in CCAS" (1969), CCAS Archives.
66. "Selden to Schell and the Jims on BCAS" (March 15, 1970), CCAS Archives. "The Jims" addressed were probably James Sanford and Jim Peck.
67. "Letter from Mark Selden to Orville Schell" (February 12, 1970), CCAS Archives.
68. The Harvard CCAS, for example, produced a series of exhaustive "fact sheets" on topics ranging from "Vietnamization" to "Communism in Asia." CCAS Archives.
69. "Excerpts from Jon Livingston's letter to Selden," CCAS Newsletter Supplement B (February 1974): 2.
70. Angela Davis joined the faculty of UCLA in 1969; she was already known as a radical feminist and a political activist, close to the Black Panther Party. Katherine (Kate) Millet, one of the leaders of the feminist movement, taught at Barnard College between 1964 and 1968 and later had other academic positions. Both scholars faced dismissals and massive controversies, including, in the case of Davis, arrest and a trial.
71. "1972 CCAS Summer Retreat," CCAS Newsletter Special Supplement (August 1, 1972): 2.
72. Steve Andors, CCAS Newsletter Supplement B: 1.
73. "Preliminary Statement of Purpose and General Editorial Policy," CCAS Newsletter Supplement B: 6. Emphasis mine.
74. "Letter from Steve Andors to Ed Friedman" (January 8, 1974), CCAS Newsletter Supplement B: 10.
75. "Letter from Steve Andors to Ed Friedman," 10.
76. Edward Friedman admitted that the new journal was meant to provide a venue for "serious scholarship." "Letter from Ed Friedman to Steve Andors," CCAS Newsletter Supplement B: 11.
77. "From Nina Adams to Philip Huang" (November 26, 1973), CCAS Archives.
78. "From Nina Adams" (November 9, 1973), CCAS Archives.
79. "From Nina Adams" (November 9, 1973).
80. "From Nina Adams to Philip Huang" (November 26, 1973), CCAS Archives.
81. "From Nina Adams" (November 9, 1973).
82. Camille Robcis, "'China in Our Heads': Althusser, Maoism, and Structuralism," *Social Text* 110 (spring 2012): 52.
83. Robcis, "'China in Our Heads,'" 64.

84. Rancière, *Althusser's Lesson*, 42.
85. Quinn Slobodian, *Foreign Front: Third World Politics in Sixties West Germany* (Durham, NC: Duke University Press, 2012), 4–5.
86. [Louis Althusser], "On the Cultural Revolution," trans. Jason E. Smith, *Décalages* 1 (February 2010), scholar.oxy.edu/decalages/vol1/iss1/9, 14–15. Emphasis in the original.
87. [Althusser], "On the Cultural Revolution," 15.
88. In his essay on the global impact of Maoism, Andrew Ross makes a similar point when he argues that "culture" in the Cultural Revolution had to do "with the transformation of subjectivity." See Andrew Ross, "Mao Zedong's Impact on Cultural Politics in the West," *Cultural Politics* 1, no. 1 (2005): 17.
89. "CCAS 2nd Annual Conference, San Francisco (April 3–4, 1970)," CCAS Archives. Emphasis mine.
90. See, for example "CCAS Summer Retreat (August 28–September 1)," *CCAS Newsletter* (October 1972): 1–2.
91. Alan Wolfe, "On Strike at Columbia, Kent Hall—May, 1970," *Columbia CCAS Newsletter* 3 (July 8, 1970): 8–9. CCAS Archives.
92. On the impact of Maoism in the black and multinational radical movement in the United States, see Michael C. Dawson, *Blacks In and Out of the Left* (Cambridge, MA: Harvard University Press, 2013), in particular his analysis of the League of Revolutionary Struggle (M-L), which united formerly national Communist groups (black, Chicano, Asian American).
93. Joe Esherick, "China Week in Ann Arbor," *CCAS Newsletter* (March 1971): 4–8.
94. Orville Schell, "Berkeley," *CCAS Newsletter* (May 1969): 5.
95. "CCAS Regional Conference in New Haven" (1970), CCAS Archives.
96. The questions in the West Coast opinion poll were: "Do you consider CCAS to be a political organization? If no, how strongly do you object to others considering it a political organization?" "If yes, how would you suggest resolving the contradiction between your view of CCAS and the views of those who consider it to be a broadly-based organization of people involved in anti-imperialist research?" "West Coast CCAS—Informal Opinion Poll" (July 1, 1973), CCAS Archives. Unfortunately, the results of the polls are not in the archives.
97. "Letter from Steve Andors at USC," *BCAS* 2 (October 1969): 7.
98. Janet Salaff, "Notes Taken at Workshop, The New McCarthyism" (1971 CCAS meeting), CCAS Archives.
99. Orville Schell, "Learning by Doing," *CCAS Newsletter* (January 1970): 9.
100. Schell, "Learning by Doing," 9.
101. Schell, "Learning by Doing," 10.
102. Rebecca E. Karl, "Culture, Revolution and the Times of History: Mao and 20th-Century China," *China Quarterly* 187 (2006): 695.
103. "John Berninghausen's Letter on CCAS and Its Future" (August 1, 1973), 2, CCAS Archives.

104. The China trips are discussed at length in chapter 3.
105. "Letter from Jon [Livingston?] to Judy Perrolle" (August 11, 1973), CCAS Archives.
106. "Nina to Steve, Jon, Felicia, Moss" (January 24, 1974), JMPA.
107. "Judy Perolle to Elaine Emling" (July 29, 1973), CCAS Archives. Emphasis in the original.
108. "Chris [White?] to Judy Perolle" (July 23, 1973), CCAS Archives. Emphasis in the original. In her reply, Perrolle seemed to agree that, in the end, CCAS expressed only a vague intellectual position, a research orientation. "Judy Perolle to Chris [White?]" (August 8, 1973), CCAS Archives.
109. "CCAS Convention Report, Boston, March 30–April 4 1974," *CCAS Newsletter* (May 1974): 3.
110. "Andrea Faste to Coordinators" (January 27, 1974), CCAS Archives.
111. Carl Jacobson, "Letter from the Editor," *CCAS Newsletter* (September 1973): 15–16.
112. "Jon Livingston to Kathleen Gough" (January 14, 1975), JMPA.
113. *CCAS Newsletter* (April 1976): 1; *CCAS Newsletter* (June 1976): 1; "The Co-coordinators' Report," *CCAS Newsletter* (October 1976): 2.
114. *CCAS Newsletter* (February 1977): 1.
115. Marjorie King, "Coordinator's Final Report," *CCAS Newsletter* (March 1978): 4.
116. *CCAS Newsletter* (February 1977): 1.
117. "Letter from Bryant Avery," *CCAS Newsletter* (May 1979): 2.

3: SEEING AND UNDERSTANDING

1. *CCAS Newsletter* (April 1973): 14.
2. "Letter from Vivienne Shue," *CCAS Newsletter* (May–June 1973): 1.
3. Committee of Concerned Asian Scholars, *China! Inside the People's Republic* (New York: Bantam Books, 1972), 1.
4. John Berninghausen, "Tentative Proposal for 2nd CCAS Friendship Delegation to China," CCAS Archives.
5. Richard Bernstein, "A Bridge to the Love of Democracy," *New York Times*, December 29, 2010.
6. The essays were originally published in the blog of the newspaper *Hsin pao* and then collected with other recollections in *My First Trip to China*. Liu Kin-ming, ed., *My First Trip to China: Scholars, Diplomats and Journalists Reflect on Their First Encounter with China* (Hong Kong: East Slope, 2012).
7. Eric Hayot highlights (and takes seriously) the psychological significance of China for the *Tel quel* group in France, with China becoming "the living, vivid manifestation of the West's unconscious." The turn eastward "involved not only seeing the other side of the world, but the other side of themselves." Eric R. Hayot, *Chinese Dreams: Pound, Brecht, Tel Quel* (Ann Arbor: University of Michigan Press, 2003), 122.

8. Committee of Concerned Asian Scholars, *China!*
9. Orville Schell, "Foreword. A China Frontier: Once the Border of Borders," in *My First Trip to China*, ed. Liu Kin-ming, 13, 16–17.
10. Schell, "Foreword. A China Frontier," 16–17.
11. Perry Link, "Dawn in China," in *My First Trip to China*, ed. Liu Kin-ming, 49–55.
12. Jonathan Mirsky, "From Mao Fan to Counter-Revolutionary in 48 Hours," in *My First Trip to China*, ed. Liu Kin-ming, 24–28.
13. Mirsky, "From Mao Fan to Counter-Revolutionary," 27.
14. Mirsky commented on the *Hsin Pao* version of Selden's account: "Well, there it is again, the Selden proposition, again, that I was surprised that poor people should put their best foot forward. I remember him saying that. That wasn't what happened; our CP minders faked it, and if by chance I hadn't stumbled into that Potemkin 'typical worker' when he—the bravest Chinese I ever met—told me the truth I would have swallowed the garbage for a few days more. The worker didn't put his best foot forward; his minders did it for him." Comment on Mark Selden, "Understanding China and Ourselves," accessed December, 2016, http://forum.hkej.com/node/62926.
15. Mark Selden, "Understanding China and Ourselves," in *My First Trip to China*, ed. Liu Kin-ming, 42.
16. Selden, "Understanding China and Ourselves," 43. Emphasis mine.
17. Committee of Concerned Asian Scholars, *China!*, 2.
18. Marianne Bastid, one of the participants in the debate, told me about her experience as a young student at Beijing University in the 1960s, just before the Cultural Revolution. Interview with the author (February 11, 2010). Bastid had been a member of CCAS and a participant in the Harvard Summer Seminar in 1968.
19. "En Chine, on ne glane que des impressions, par nature subjectives et discutables. On n'apprend rien, on n'ajoute rien qui ne fût déjà connu et répertorié: tous voient à peu près les mêmes choses et le répètent à satiété." Claude Aubert et al., *Regards froids sur la Chine* (Paris: Seuil, 1976), 60.
20. ". . . je crois cependant que le séjour en Chine—surtout si l'on parle chinois et si l'on est autorisé à y demeurer un certain temps—permet d'apprécier, de sentir la réalité de ce que les journaux expriment souvent de façon assez arbitraire ou elliptique, tout simplement parce que le Chinois sont au courant et comprennent à demi-mot." Aubert et al., *Regards froids sur la Chine*, 23–24.
21. The editors of the journal *Tel Quel* became declared supporters of Maoism in 1971. In 1974 Philippe Sollers, Marcelin Pleynet, François Wahl, Roland Barthes, and Julia Kristeva visited China. See Hayot, *Chinese Dreams*. The *Tel Quel* group was particularly fascinated by Maria Antonietta Macciocchi's book on her own trip to China, which Sollers considered important "not only for its account of the Chinese Cultural Revolution, but also for its theoretical analysis (of Marxism)." In 1971 the *Tel Quel* group broke with the French Communist

Party, when the book (published in French as *De La Chine*) was banned at the annual PCF festival. See Danielle Marx-Souras, *The Cultural Politics of Tel Quel: Literature and the Left in the Wake of Engagement* (University Park: Penn State University Press, 1996), 165.

22. Paul Hollander, *Political Pilgrims: Western Intellectuals in Search of the Good Society*, 4th ed. (New Brunswick, NJ: Transaction, 1998), 321. Hollander argues that it was the sanctioned critique of the Cultural Revolution in the immediate post-Mao era that made it more acceptable to criticize China.

23. In the English-language historiography of the Cultural Revolution, there has been a progressive shift away from analyses focused on the power struggles internal to the CCP and the mechanisms of authoritarianism (which still largely followed a Cold War paradigm). New studies have proposed a reappraisal of the political meaning of the movement for different actors (including students and workers) and have tried to describe these experiences at the grassroots level. This shift is only marginally due to the availability of new archival sources, as the material on the Cultural Revolution period is still strictly guarded.

24. Aubert et al., *Regards froids sur la Chine*, 48–49.

25. "Dans le cas particulier des sinologues français, je suis surprise de constater qu'ils n'ont pas encore pris la peine d'analyser et de comprendre la fin de leur vieux rôle, qui était, classiquement, d'exercer depuis l'Occident une sorte d'hégémonie culturelle sur la Chine, à l'image de ces formes de néo-colonialisme, vaguement 'idéologisantes,' à travers lesquelles se poursuit objectivement l'œuvre de conquête impérialiste des marchés sous-développés." Quoted in Aubert et al., *Regards froids sur la Chine*, 51–52.

26. "Ce livre . . . est une contribution au mouvement, que l'auteur a pu écrire parce qu'elle est elle-même déjà engagée dans l'action. . . . Son expérience pratique militante étant une pré-condition pour connaître la Chine." Quoted in Aubert et al., *Regards froids sur la Chine*, 53.

27. Selden, "Understanding China and Ourselves," in *My First Trip to China*, ed. Liu Kin-ming, 46.

28. Marcel Proust, *Time Regained*. Volume 6 of *In Search of Lost Time*, trans. Andreas Mayor and Terence Kilmartin; revised by D. J. Enright (New York: Modern Library, 1999), 506.

29. Proust, *Time Regained*, 504.

30. Sigrid Schmalzer, "On the Appropriate Use of Rose-Colored Glasses: Reflections on Science in Socialist China," *Isis* 98 (2007): 582. In the same piece, Schmalzer cautions against searching the truth somewhere in the middle between the pro-Maoist accounts and the post-Mao ones, but rather invites us to engage both at once, so that "we can think critically about the history in question while remembering to be equally critical of our own assumptions" (583).

31. CCAS Hong Kong Chapter, "To the National Coordinators" (June 9, 1971), CCAS

Archives. The trip lasted one day longer because of a typhoon in Hong Kong. They returned on July 24. In light of CCAS's assumption that they had been invited because of their political leanings, it is quite ironic that their sojourn in China overlapped with Henry Kissinger's secret meetings with Zhou Enlai (July 9–11). See the excellent timeline provided by the USC U.S.-China Institute, "Getting to Beijing: Henry Kissinger's Secret 1971 Trip" (July 21, 2011), accessed August 2016, china.usc.edu/getting-beijing-henry-kissingers-secret-1971-trip.

32. The U.S. ping-pong team was invited to visit China in April 1971 while participating in the World Table Tennis Championship in Japan. It was the first visit by an official U.S. delegation to the PRC. See Margaret MacMillan, *Nixon and Mao: The Week That Changed the World* (New York: Random House, 2008).

33. Paul Pickowicz, interview with the author (March 20, 2014).

34. "John Berninghausen to Molly, Al, Bill, Steve and other CCAS/CASS Comrades" (July 25, 1971), CCAS Archives. The trip participants were Anthony and Jean Garavente, Kay Ann Johnston, Ann and Uldis Kruze, Kenneth Levin, Paul Levine, Paul Pickowicz, Susan Shirk, Raymond and Rhea Whitehead, and Judy and Kim Woodard. Berninghausen, who was in Hong Kong at the time of the first trip, remarked that most of the people in the delegation had no connection with CCAS and that "we were jealous as hell." John Berninghausen, interview with the author (March 24, 2011).

35. CCAS Hong Kong Chapter, "To the National Coordinators."

36. CCAS Hong Kong Chapter, "To the National Coordinators." Emphasis mine.

37. Charles Cell, "Letter to the 13" (June 17–18, 1971). Emphasis in the original. It is difficult to underestimate how personally exhilarating the possibility of actually going to China was for people who had spent years studying it. John Berninghausen mentioned that he had studied China for nine years by the time he finally visited it with the second delegation in 1972. His fellow delegation member Jonathan Mirsky had studied and taught China for seventeen years. John Berninghausen, interview with the author.

38. "Kim Woodard to Molly Coye" (August 3, 1971), CCAS Archives.

39. "It seems to us that in the context of the rapidly changing U.S. relations with China, CCAS can play a very constructive role as a united front organization bridging the movement and the establishment media, and trying to influence the content of establishment media commentaries (e.g., in negotiations with networks we've been insisting on providing the *commentary*)." "Christine White to Molly Coye" (July 23, 1971), CCAS Archives.

40. "Karen McCornell to Molly Coye" (July 26, 1971), CCAS Archives.

41. "John Berninghausen to Molly, Al, Bill, Steve and other CCAS/CASS Comrades." Published in English, *Peking Review* (or *Beijing Review*) was the official voice of the PRC government in the rest of the world.

42. "Molly Coye to the Hong Kong Chapter" (July 29, 1971). CCAS Archives. Jonathan Unger was at the time supposed to write the article in question for Pacific

News Service, but the members of the delegation reserved the right to veto anything he wrote, leading to a piece that "looked like agit-prop." Interview with the author (April 1, 2011).
43. Susan Shirk, interview with the author (February 16, 2014).
44. See Helen Kruger, "Acupuncture in America?" *Village Voice*, September 16, 1971.
45. "Molly Coye to the Hong Kong Chapter" (August 11, 1971), CCAS Archives. Emphasis in the original. When we talked, Coye had a very different recollection of her reaction to the interview, saying she thought it was terrific that a CCAS member had appeared on national TV.
46. Susan Shirk, interview with the author.
47. Paul Pickowicz argued that the participants, while not active with CCAS nationally, were active in Hong Kong. "Letter from Paul Pickowicz" (August 5, 1971), CCAS Archives.
48. "CCAS Goes to China: Questions on Future Relationships," CCAS *Newsletter* (July–August 1971): 4. The perception that CCAS had privileged access to Beijing also made the group very attractive for people who were of very different political and intellectual persuasions. John Berninghausen recalled that people "who were enemies of CCAS" started calling to say that they were members and wanted to go to China. "They would have signed a loyalty oath to Mao," he commented. John Berninghausen, interview with the author.
49. "CCAS Goes to China: Questions on Future Relationships," 5.
50. "Retreat in Review," CCAS *Newsletter* (October 1971): 1.
51. "Letter from Mark Selden" (September 15, 1971), CCAS Archives.
52. "Letter from Mark Selden."
53. "Retreat in Review," 1. The guidelines reflected those proposed by John Berninghausen after consultation with the Hong Kong chapter. See his "Tentative Proposal for 2nd CCAS Friendship Delegation to China."
54. "Seattle Chapter Protests Delegation Selection Procedure," CCAS *Newsletter* (February 1972): 1. Cindy Frederick, member of the selection committee, complained in a letter dated December 6, 1971: "god! how did we ever get involved in this thing??? I have already received 34 applications, and know that at least a dozen more are on the way. it's going to be hell." "Cindy Frederick to the Selection Committee," CCAS Archives.
55. "CCAS is not a travel agency and its members and chapters should not spend much time and energy on this one limited activity. The real work of CCAS is in going to the people of America and raising their knowledge and level of consciousness about US involvement in Asia and about Asia itself." Berninghausen, "Tentative Proposal for 2nd CCAS Friendship Delegation to China."
56. "John Berninghausen to Molly, Al, Bill, Steve and other CCAS/CASS Comrades."
57. "Richard Kagan to Peg Roston, Ric Pfeffer, Sandy Sturdevant, Molly Coye, Paul Pickowicz, Dorothy Kehl" (October 30, 1971), CCAS Archives.
58. "Stanford Chapter: Statement on National Priorities," CCAS *Newsletter* (No-

vember 1971): 10. John Berninghausen summarized the whole argument with a pithier comment: "The Vietnam War was more important than sticking our tongue up Beijing's ass." Interview with the author.

59. "John Berninghausen and Janet Swislow to Peg Roston, Ric Pfeffer, Sandy Sturdevant, Molly Coye, Paul Pickowicz, Dorothy Kehl, Richard Kagan, Cindy Frederick" (December 2, 1971), CCAS Archives.
60. "John Berninghausen and Janet Swislow."
61. "Elaine Cell to Peg Roston, Ric Pfeffer, Sandy Sturdevant, Molly Coye, Paul Pickowicz, Dorothy Kehl, Richard Kagan, Cindy Frederick" (December 6, 1971), CCAS Archives.
62. "Molly Coye to Chuck and Elaine Cell" (December 10, 1971), CCAS Archives.
63. "Molly Coye to Chuck and Elaine Cell."
64. "Molly Coye to Chuck and Elaine Cell."
65. "Letter to John Berninghausen" (December 14, 1971), CCAS Archives. The letter was probably signed, but the last page is missing.
66. "Letter to John Berninghausen."
67. Sandy Sturdevant, "Report on Plans for Chinese Visit to the US," CCAS Newsletter (March 1972): 2.
68. For example, the reactions of U.S. Black liberation activists to the U.S.-China rapprochement were varied but generally worried. See Frazier, *The East Is Black*, and Robin D. G. Kelley and Betsy Esch, "Black Like Mao: Red China and Black Revolution," *Souls: A Critical Journal of Black Politics, Culture, and Society* 1, no. 4 (1999): 6–41. Anne-Marie Brady recounts how Zhou Enlai announced the news of the upcoming Nixon visit to a large group of American friends (including members of the Black Panthers) during a reception in the Great Hall of the People, on October 5, 1971. Anne-Marie Brady, *Making the Foreign Serve China: Managing Foreigners in the People's Republic* (Lanham, MD: Rowman and Littlefield, 2003): 180–181.
69. "CCAS Resolution on Return Delegation to US" (March 24, 1972), CCAS Newsletter (April 1972): 12.
70. Hayot, *Chinese Dreams*, 130.
71. The members of the second delegation were Jane Barrett (Ann Arbor), Louise Bennett (Ann Arbor), John Berninghausen (Hong Kong), Richard Bernstein (Taiwan), Leo Cawley (New York), Charles Cell (New York), Gene Cooper (Hong Kong), Ben Cox (McAlister), Molly Coye (Stanford), Alfred Crofts (Denver), Jean Doyle (Boston), Robert Entenmann (Stanford), Christine Frank (New York), Steve Graham (St. Louis), Chad Hansen (Ann Arbor), Nancy Jervis (New York), William Joseph (Stanford), Leigh Kagan (Ann Arbor–Tokyo), Steve MacKinnon (Phoenix), Joanne Mei (Boston), Mitch Meisner (Chicago), Jonathan Mirsky (New Hampshire), Nina Moore (McAlister), Stephen Uhalley (Honolulu), Moss Roberts (New York), Jim Sanford (Boston), Mark Selden (St. Louis), Christine White (Hong Kong), Gordon White (Hong Kong), and Lynda Womack (New York). CCAS Newsletter (February 1972): 1.

72. The retreat took place March 2–6, 1972. "Information Package for the Second Delegation," CCAS Archives. John Berninghausen, who was already in Hong Kong, was in charge of welcoming the rest of the delegation, and he had planned the retreat as a very practical "how to behave in China" session. He recalled that some of the members came with a very "hardcore agenda" and pushed it through the meeting. They had three major requests: the first day the delegation arrived in Canton, they had to ask to be taken to the North Vietnamese consulate; they had to ask the Chinese to be allowed to go to Tibet, so they "could undo the damage of the anti-Chinese propaganda about the mistreatment of the Tibetans"; and, finally, they wanted to visit prisons (the Attica prison riot had just happened, so they thought it was a good idea to compare Chinese and American prisons). Interview with the author.
73. Quoted in Helen Chauncey, "CCAS Summer Retreat," *CCAS Newsletter* (October 1972): 8. MacKinnon cited another piece of evidence of the utility of the China trips within the field. Apparently John K. Fairbank had gone to China later in the spring and "was infuriated that the Chinese accepted CCAS analysis of the organization and purposes of Asian Studies in the U.S."
74. Helen Chauncey, "CCAS Summer Retreat," 8–9. The CEC members were Helen Chauncey (Stanford), Keith Hazelton (Minneapolis), Jean Doyle (Boston), Louise Bennett, and Jane Barrett (both Ann Arbor).
75. While the CEC was tasked with surveying the participants in the two delegations, no member from the first trip responded.
76. "An Evaluation of CCAS Friendship Delegations to China and Recommendations for a Third Trip," *CCAS Newsletter* (January 1973): 9–10. DRV stands for Democratic Republic of Vietnam, that is, North Vietnam.
77. "An Evaluation of CCAS Friendship Delegations," 10.
78. "An Evaluation of CCAS Friendship Delegations," 7.
79. "An Evaluation of CCAS Friendship Delegations," 12. There is a certain degree of embarrassment in this assessment, in part because the trip was the main element behind one of CCAS's book-length publications (*China! Inside the People's Republic*). Also, the members of the group had toured the United States in a speaking tour jointly organized with AFSC, which they proposed on the basis of their unrestricted access to China: "We were permitted total freedom to photograph and ask questions as we pleased. We were encouraged to preserve a complete account of our meetings with Premier Chou En-Lai and Prince Sihanouk. As a result, the group now has available more than 3,000 color slides, a one hour 'super 8' movie, nearly 1,000 black and white photographs, several tape recordings, and volumes of transcripts and notes." "Joint AFSC-CCAS Speaking Tour on China (Proposals and Plans)" (August 3, 1971), CCAS Archives.
80. "An Evaluation of CCAS Friendship Delegations," 7.
81. "An Evaluation of CCAS Friendship Delegations," 13.
82. Molly Coye, interview with the author.

83. "An Evaluation of CCAS Friendship Delegations," 12.
84. "Responses to Initial Report of the China Exchange Committee," *CCAS Newsletter* (March 1973): 9.
85. This was John Berninghausen's formulation. "Responses to Initial Report," 10.
86. "Responses to Initial Report," 10.
87. "Responses to Initial Report," 10–11. Emphasis mine.
88. Special *CCAS Newsletter* Supplement (April 6, 1973). The new CEC was Judy Perrolle and Ric Pfeffer (East), Leigh Kagan and Mitch Meisner (West), and Andrea Faste (West).
89. Special *CCAS Newsletter* Supplement (April 6, 1973). Emphasis in the original.
90. John Berninghausen, "Letter to the CEC Concerning the Third Trip" (April 22, 1973), CCAS Archives.
91. Special *CCAS Newsletter* Supplement (April 6, 1973). Sigrid Schmalzer illustrates how the group Science for the People was torn by a very similar debate when they had to select the members of their China delegation in 1972. Sigrid Schmalzer, "Speaking about China, Learning from China: Amateur China Experts in 1970s America," *Journal of American–East Asian Relations* 16 (winter 2009): 326.
92. Berninghausen, "Letter to the CEC Concerning the Third Trip."
93. Michelle Loi, *L'Intelligence au pouvoir. Un Monde Nouveau: La Chine* (Paris: Maspéro, 1973), 9. Loi was a specialist in Chinese modern literature.
94. François Hourmant, *Au pays de l'avenir radieux: Voyages des intellectuels Français en URSS, à Cuba et en Chine populaire* (Paris: Aubier, 2000).
95. Schmalzer, "Speaking about China," 1.
96. Hourmant, *Au pays de l'avenir radieux*, 87.
97. Maria-Antonietta Macciocchi, *Daily Life in Revolutionary China* (New York: Monthly Review Press, 1972), 15.
98. The literary genre of the travelogue to Maoist China was quite popular, especially in the long sixties. Some examples in English include Janet Goldwasser and Stuart Dowty, *Huan-Ying: Workers' China* (New York: Monthly Review Press, 1975); Victor W. Sidel and Ruth Sidel, *Serve the People: Observations on Medicine in the People's Republic of China* (New York: Beacon Press, 1974); Ruth Sidel, *Women and Child Care in China* (New York: Hill and Wang, 1972); and Arthur Galstone with Jean S. Savage, *Daily Life in People's China* (New York: Crowell, 1973). There were also several reports written by people who had been allowed longer stays in China, such as Jan Myrdal, *Report from a Chinese Village* (New York: Pantheon Books, 1965); Neale Hunter, *Shanghai Journal* (New York: Praeger, 1969); and Nancy Milton and David Milton, *The Wind Will Not Subside: Years in Revolutionary China, 1964–1969* (New York: Pantheon, 1976).
99. The long list of contributors includes the entire first delegation plus Andrew Andreasen, Lorraine Broderick, Halsey Beemer, Cynthia Chennault, Helen Chauncey, Maryruth Coleman, Joel Coye, Robert Delfs, Richard Doner,

Tom Engelhardt, Robert Entenmann, Gardell Feurtado, June Gordon, Harry Harding, Kathleen Hartford, Ted Huters, David Kelly, Michael David Lampton, Daniel Lindheim, Jonathan Lipman, Jon Livingston, Earl Martin, Vera Morrissey, Felicia Oldfather, Sue Ann Ritchie, Stephen Thomas, Christina Turner, Jon Unger, Carter Weiss, and Judith Welch. Committee of Concerned Asian Scholars, *China!*

100. John Berninghausen did not hide his disgust for this book and his relief for not having had any part in it: "I am proud of my association with CCAS, but I am not proud of that book." Interview with the author (March 24, 2011). Susan Shirk shared similarly disparaging comments. Interview with the author (February 16, 2014).
101. Committee of Concerned Asian Scholars, *China!*, 1.
102. Committee of Concerned Asian Scholars, *China!*, 3.
103. Macciocchi, *Daily Life*, 24.
104. Macciocchi, *Daily Life*, 265. Macciocchi had been a (somewhat heretical) member of the Italian Communist Party since its underground days during the German occupation. She traveled to China as a journalist for *L'Unità*, the party newspaper, together with her then husband, Alberto Jacoviello, also a journalist for *L'Unità*. She was expelled from the Party in 1977 for her supports of Maoist groups in Bologna. John Francis Lane, "Obituary: Maria Antonietta Macciocchi," *Guardian*, May 21, 2007, www.theguardian.com/news/2007/may/21/guardianobituaries.italy.
105. Committee of Concerned Asian Scholars, *China!*, 150.
106. Hayot, *Chinese Dreams*, 153.
107. Committee of Concerned Asian Scholars, *China!*, 50.
108. On 1968 as a process of displacement and dislocation of politics, see Kristin Ross, *May '68 and Its Afterlives* (Chicago: University of Chicago Press, 2004), 25.
109. They compared the situation in Maoist China to that in the United States where, they wrote, "the usefulness of a degree from an elite college is as great today as in the past. But in China, while the overall level of education is still not as high as in America, the *need* for education as a means to a better job is far less important and becoming less so because of these new programs." Committee of Concerned Asian Scholars, *China!*, 195. Joel Andreas made a similar point on the successes of rural education in his "Leveling the Little Pagoda: The Impact of College Examinations, and Their Elimination, on Rural Education in China," *Comparative Education Review* 48 (February 2004): 1–47.
110. Committee of Concerned Asian Scholars, *China!*, 101–102. On the May Seventh Schools, see Yinghong Chen, *Creating the New Man: From Enlightenment Ideals to Socialist Realities* (Honolulu: University of Hawai'i Press, 2009).
111. Hollander, *Political Pilgrims*, 334.
112. Committee of Concerned Asian Scholars, *China!*, 276.
113. Both Saundra Sturdevant and John Berninghausen mentioned the impact of a gendered internal criticism in my interviews with them.

114. Committee of Concerned Asian Scholars, *China!*, 279. There is no explanation why only the seven female members of the CCAS delegation went to this meeting.
115. Roland Barthes, *Travels in China*, ed. Anne Herschberg Pierrot (Cambridge: Polity, 2009), 177.
116. Roland Barthes, *Carnets du voyage en Chine* (Paris: Christian Bourgois/IMEC, 2009), 196.
117. During my interviews, both Saundra Sturdevant and John Berninghausen commented on the separation that existed in CCAS since its founding, between people who were simply antiwar and people who were anti-imperialist (or anticapitalist—revolutionaries, Maoists). In Sturdevant's opinion, it was the normalization of the relationships with China, the possibility of going to China, that made that separation explode. In the end, she bleakly commented, "it turns out that there weren't many who were anti-imperialist." Interviews with the author.
118. On the AFSC, see Richard Madsen, *China and the American Dream: A Moral Inquiry* (Berkeley: University of California Press, 1995).
119. On March 26, 1972, CCAS decided to allow a voluntary committee of CCAS members to approach the AFSC "to request that they organize—in conjunction with those CCAS members who express an interest in helping—a small informal visit of Chinese students." "Helen Chauncey to Frank Kehl" (June 1972), CCAS Archives. Part of the funding for the trip came from the various speeches that members of the two delegations gave after their return to China. "AFSC Memorandum" (March 29, 1972), CCAS Archives. The Committee received $4,500 back from AFSC after the failure of the return trip. "Jon Livingston to BCAS Board" (April 2, 1976), CCAS Archives.
120. Stanley Karnow, "Radicals Dislike China's New Foreign Policy," *Washington Post*, May 28, 1972. Peck's role in the article did gain him a fair amount of criticism within CCAS. See "Richard Kagan to Chris" (May 21, 1973); and "Letter from AFSC and Committee to Peck" (September 25, 1972), CCAS Archives.
121. John Gittings, "Mixed up about Mao," *Guardian*, August 30, 1972, 11.
122. "Larry Lifschultz Report" (September 15, 1972), CCAS Archives.
123. Ray Whitehead, "A Time for Unity and Strength" (September 29, 1972), CCAS Archives.
124. "Frank Kehl to Gene Cooper" (May 19, 1973), CCAS Archives.
125. "Jean Doyle to Christina Gilmartin" (November 12, 1972), CCAS Archives.
126. *CCAS Newsletter* (May–June 1973). The final list included Len Adams, Fred Blake, Marc Blecher, John Clancey, Deborah David Freeman, Dick Gaulton, Gary Glick, Carol Lee Hamrin, Richard Heitler, Jeff Hermanson, Helena Hershel, Ahmee Hewitt, Aleen Holly, Carol Jacobson, Richard Kagan, Tony Kane, Betsy Kanwit, Rich Levy, Robert Marks, John McClendon, Angus McDonald, Cheryl Payer, Pierre Perrolle, Mary Ellen Quintana, Les Ross, Pat Stanford,

Sandy Sturdevant, Janet Swislow, Ralph Thaxton, V'Ella Warren, David Wilson, Martha Winnacker, and Katsu Young.
127. "CCAS Summer Retreat," *CCAS Newsletter* (October 1972): 15. John Israel had accepted a JCCC grant for 1973–74, and Marilyn Young "intended to participate in a JCCC conference as a discussant." "China Exchange Committee Explains Removal of John Israel and Marilyn Young from the Delegation," *CCAS Newsletter* (May–June 1973): 5.
128. See *CCAS Newsletter* (July–August 1973).
129. "Jonathan Mirsky to Judy Perrolle" (June 22, 1973), CCAS Archives.
130. "Letter from Angus McDonald to the Members of the Third Delegation" (June 25, 1973), CCAS Archives.
131. Sandy Sturdevant, "Statement on the Removal of Marilyn Young and John Israel" (June 14, 1973), CCAS Archives.
132. *CCAS Newsletter* (May–June 1973): 11.
133. "Martha Kendall Winnacker to the China Exchange Committee" (June 25, 1973), CCAS Archives.
134. Cheryl Payer to the China Exchange Committee" (June 23, 1973), CCAS Archives. Also Leigh Kagan, in *CCAS Newsletter* (July–August 1973): 3.
135. "Judy Perrolle to Jonathan Mirsky" (June 17, 1973), CCAS Archives.
136. "Jon Livingston to Marilyn Young" (September 3, 1973), CCAS Archives.
137. "Report from Jan Emmert on the Conference of National Committee of US-China Relations at Wingspread Conference Center in Wisconsin" (September 27, 1972), CCAS Archives.
138. "Statement on U.S. China Exchanges" (December 20, 1972), CCAS Archives. John K. Fairbank, Ezra Vogel, A. Doak Barnett, Alexander Ekstein, Albert Feuerwerker, Robert Scalapino, Chalmers Johnson, and John W. Lewis were directly named in the statement.
139. Richard Kagan, quoted in "Minutes of the National Convention," *CCAS Newsletter* (April 1975): 8.
140. Angus McDonald, "Coordinator's Notes," *CCAS Newsletter* (October 1975): 2.
141. Lin Biao had risen to become Mao's "closest comrade-in-arms and successor" during the Cultural Revolution. By 1971, his relationship to Mao had soured and his support within the Army had declined. He died in a plane crash in Mongolia after allegedly attempting a coup. See Jin Qiu, *The Culture of Power: The Lin Biao Incident in the Cultural Revolution* (Stanford, CA: Stanford University Press, 1999).
142. For the importance of "friendship" and "friendship delegations" in PRC foreign policy, see Brady, *Making the Foreign Serve China*.
143. Hayot, *Chinese Dreams*, 128.
144. Dora Zhang, "The Sideways Gaze: Roland Barthes's *Travels in China*," *Los Angeles Review of Books*, June 23, 2012, lareviewofbooks.org/essay/the-sideways-gaze-roland-barthess-travels-in-china.

4: FACING THERMIDOR

The second epigraph is translated as "Maoism does not exist. It never existed. Without doubt, that's what explains its success."

1. "Bryant Avery to Editors" (January 10, 1981), SSPA.
2. On the reversal of fortune of the Dazhai model (and its main representative, Chen Yonggui), see Qin Huailu, *Ninth Heaven to Ninth Hell: The History of a Noble Chinese Experiment*, ed. William Hinton (New York: Barricade Books, 1995).
3. Maurice Meisner, *Mao's China and After: A History of the People's Republic*, 3rd ed. (New York: Free Press, 1999), chapters 22–23.
4. Alessandro Russo, "How Did the Cultural Revolution End? The Last Dispute between Mao Zedong and Deng Xiaoping, 1975," *Modern China* 39 (May 2013): 239–279.
5. Alain Badiou, *Metapolitics* (London: Verso, 2005), 136.
6. Sophie Wahnich, *In Defence of the Terror: Liberty or Death in the French Revolution* (London: Verso, 2012), 91. This restriction of political speech and action is perhaps most clearly exemplified in the Chinese case by the substitution of Mao's "four great freedoms" ("speak out freely, air views freely, hold great debates, and write big-character posters") with Deng's "Four Cardinal Principles" ("upholding the socialist road, the dictatorship of the proletariat, the leadership of the Communist Party, and Marxism-Lenism-Mao Zedong thought). Meisner, *Mao's China and After*, 436–437.
7. The issues were both in vol. 13 (April–June 1981 and July–September 1981).
8. On the economic/political shift of the late 1970s, see David Harvey, *A Brief History of Neoliberalism* (Oxford: Oxford University Press, 2007).
9. One of the elements of division among various Red Guards groups was precisely the question of what defined the "class status" of a student. In opposition to an almost "genetic" definition based on family background, some students aligned with one that took into consideration present political attitudes and practice. See Walder, *Fractured Rebellion: The Beijing Red Guard Movement* (Cambridge, MA: Harvard University Press, 2009), and Wu Yiching, *The Cultural Revolution at the Margins: Chinese Socialism in Crisis* (Cambridge, MA: Harvard University Press, 2014); see also William Hinton, *Hundred Day War: The Cultural Revolution at Tsinghua University* (New York: Monthly Review Press, 1972).
10. Robert B. Townsend, "Precedents: The Job Crisis of the 1970s," in *Perspectives on History* (April 1997), www.historians.org/publications-and-directories/perspectives-on-history/april-1997/precedents-the-job-crisis-of-the-1970s; Robert B. Townsend, "History in Those Hard Times: Looking for Jobs in the 1970s," in *Perspectives on History* (September 2009), www.historians.org/publications-and-directories/perspectives-on-history/september-2009/history-in-those-hard-times-looking-for-jobs-in-the-1970s.

11. Production of doctorates in Area and Ethnic studies remained constant (but historically high) through the mid-1970s and early 1980s. See the NSF Survey of Earned Doctorate, ncsesdata.nsf.gov/webcaspar/index.jsp?subHeader= WebCASPARHome.
12. *Etablissement* describes the movement of radical students and intellectuals into factories, where they chose to labor as industrial workers. The experience is described by Robert Linhart, one of the early Maoist leaders, in his *The Assembly Line* (Amherst: University of Massachusetts Press, 1981), and by his daughter, Virginie Linhart, in *Volontaires Pour l'Usine* [Volunteers for the factory] (Paris: Éd. du Seuil, 1994).
13. Richard Wolin, *The Wind from the East: French Intellectuals, the Cultural Revolution, and the Legacy of the 1960s* (Princeton, NJ: Princeton University Press, 2010), 21. See also Camille Robcis, "'China in Our Heads': Althusser, Maoism and Structuralism," *Social Text* 110 (spring 2012): 51–69.
14. "Marjorie King to Joyce Overton" (May 26, 1976), CCAS Archives.
15. "Coordinator's Final Report," *CCAS Newsletter* (March 1978): 4.
16. "Briant Avery to Herbert Bix, Jayne Werner, and Bruce Cumings" (December 23, 1977), SSPA.
17. "Gail Omvedt to Saundra Sturdevant" (November 7, 1978), SSPA. See also chapter 1.
18. "CCAS Convention Report, Boston, March 30–April 4, 1974," *CCAS Newsletter* (May 1974): 11.
19. "Helen Chauncey to Bryant Avery" (June 29, 1980), JMPA.
20. "Bryant Avery to the Board" (January 4, 1978), SSPA.
21. "Bryant Avery to Ben Kerkvliet" (February 11, 1980), SSPA.
22. "Bryant Avery to Saundra Sturdevant, Jon Halliday, Jayne Werner, Bruce Cumings, Jon Livingston, Moss Roberts" (February 11, 1979), 2. BCAS lost about two hundred subscribers in 1979. See "Bryant Avery to Editorial Board Members" (October 15, 1980), SSPA.
23. The *Bulletin* was self-produced and self-managed, which meant that most of the work fell on the shoulders of the editor-in-chief (in this period, Bryant Avery), who was the only paid employee and who was in charge of nearly everything, including layout, proofreading, and fundraising. Avery complained incessantly of the financial situation of the journal, which was kept alive by a sizable donation from one person, Felicia Oldfather. The crisis was intensified by the collapse of the movement around the *Bulletin*. As Avery wrote to Jonathan Mirsky, "No longer is there a large and dependable corps of persons out there in clearly definable spots that support us. We are individually and collectively in a period when hussle [sic] keeps us alive." "Bryant Avery to Jonathan Mirsky" (January 26, 1980), SSPA.
24. "Robert Marks to Ben Kerkvliet, Joe Moore, Bryant Avery" (November 11, 1980), SSPA.
25. "Bryant Avery to Robert Marks and Saundra Sturdevant" (August 4, 1980), SSPA.

26. "Bryant Avery to Editorial Board Members" (October 15, 1980), SSPA. Between 1978 and 1981, *Modern China* published essays by Ed Hammond, Mitch Meisner, Ben Stavis, Victor Lippit, Carl Riskin, Marc Blecher, Joseph Esherick, and Bruce Cumings (who wrote on China, not Korea), all former CCASers, some of them members of the BCAS Editorial Board or even former editors of the *Bulletin*. I am thankful to Saundra Sturdevant for pointing this out. Bruce Cumings, for example, published a long, detailed, and theoretically informed analysis of Chinese foreign policy in *Modern China*. Bruce Cumings, "The Political Economy of Chinese Foreign Policy," *Modern China* 5 (October 1979): 411–461.
27. Saundra Sturdevant, interview with the author.
28. "Helen Chauncey to Bryant Avery" (November 17, 1980). The reference is here, among other things, to China's policy on Vietnam in the post-Mao period. Chauncey had been a very critical voice within CCAS in the previous years, and the demurred tone of her letter is revealing of a much deeper sense of inevitability.
29. "Bryant Avery to Editorial Board Members" (October 15, 1980), SSPA. Mark Selden, one of the China specialists on the editorial board, responded to Avery's "serious charge": "Bryant is certainly correct that it is important for the Bulletin to break through in this area; and his criticism of us is correct." "Mark Selden to Bryant Avery, Robert Marks, Joe Moore" (October 18, 1980), SSPA.
30. "Mark Selden to Bryant Avery" (December 18, 1979), SSPA.
31. "Bruce Cumings to Saundra Sturdevant, Jayne Werner, Bryant Avery" (July 29, 1978), SSPA. Among the non-BCAS scholars, Cumings listed Stuart Schram, Benjamin Schwartz, Frederic Wakeman, Ross Terrill, and Tang Tsou.
32. "Bryant Avery to Jon Halliday, Saundra Sturdevant, Bruce Cumings, and Jayne Werner" (August 8, 1978), 6, SSPA.
33. "Saundra Sturdevant to Bryant Avery, Bruce Cumings, Jayne Werner, Jon Halliday" (May 13, 1978), SSPA.
34. "Saundra Sturdevant's Draft of China Symposium Letter" (July 29, 1978), SSPA.
35. "Saundra Sturdevant's Draft of the China Call for Papers, Reworked by Bryant Avery" (June 8, 1979), SSPA.
36. "Richard Pfeffer's Note" (July 25, 1978), SSPA.
37. John Gittings is a British journalist, lecturer, and China expert. From 1983 to 2003, he worked at the *Guardian* as assistant foreign editor and chief foreign leader writer.
38. "Saundra Sturdevant to John Gittings" (January 21, 1981), SSPA. Sturdevant never actually wrote the introduction. She left for China before the issues were published.
39. "Robert Marks to Victor Lippit" (March 5, 1981), SSPA.
40. Victor Nee's essay in the first China special issue is an example of this excitement. See his "Post-Mao Changes in a South China Production Brigade," *BCAS* 13 (April–June 1981): 32–39.

41. One article in the first China issue addressed the question of class under Maoism in a fairly interesting and theoretical way, but the analysis did not extend in any way to the post-Mao period. Peter Moller Christensen and Jorgen Delman, "A Theory of Transitional Society: Mao Zedong and the Shanghai School," BCAS 13 (April–June, 1981): 2–15.
42. On the issue of class during the Cultural Revolution, see Wu Yiching, "How State Enumeration Spoiled Mao's Last Revolution," *Journal of Modern Chinese History* 7, no. 2 (2013): 200–217. See also his *The Cultural Revolution at the Margins*.
43. Jacques Rancière quoted in Mischa Suter, "A Thorn in the Side of Social History: Jacques Rancière and *Les Révoltes logiques*," *International Review of Social History* 57 (April 2012): 65.
44. Alessandro Russo, "The Probable Defeat: Preliminary Notes on the Chinese Cultural Revolution," *positions: east asia cultures critique* 6, no. 1 (1998): 197.
45. Russo, "How Did the Cultural Revolution End?," 249–250.
46. Alain Badiou, "The Cultural Revolution: The Last Revolution?" *positions: east asia cultures critique* 13 (winter 2005): 481–514.
47. Russo, "How Did the Cultural Revolution End?," 269–270.
48. 不管黑猫白猫，捉到老鼠就是好猫 "Buguan heimao baimao, zhuodao laoshu jiu shi haomao" was apparently a Sichuan proverb.
49. Peter Nolan and Gordon White, "Distribution and Development in China," BCAS 13 (July–September 1981): 17.
50. Victor Lippit, "The People's Communes and China's New Development Strategy," BCAS 13 (July–September 1981): 28.
51. "Saundra Sturdevant to Bryant Avery, Robert Marks, Moss Roberts, Stephen Andors, Joe Moore, Ben Kerkvliet" (January 24, 1981), 3, SSPA. "There's a considerable body of literature . . . written in the late 60s and early 70s and I dare say, some by Victor, which make the argument that given the contradictions of Chinese development at that particular time, the policies of the CR were indeed practical. WE MUST ADDRESS OURSELVES TO THIS CONTRADICTION." Emphasis in the original.
52. "Saundra Sturdevant to Brian Avery" (January 24, 1981), 3.
53. "Saundra Sturdevant to Brian Avery" (January 24, 1981), 6.
54. "Saundra Sturdevant to Bryant Avery, Robert Marks, Joe Moore, Ben Kerkvliet" (February 3, 1981), SSPA.
55. "Saundra Sturdevant to Brian Avery" (February 3, 1981).
56. Mitch Meisner and Marc Blecher, "Rural Development, Agrarian Structure and the County in China," BCAS 13 (April–June 1981): 27.
57. "Saundra Sturdevant to Bryant Avery" (February 3, 1981), SSPA. The use of the term "middle-rich peasants" seems a bit anachronistic here, given the collectivization of the Mao era. But I think Sturdevant here refers to the reemergence of class distinctions in the countryside following the NAP.

58. Blecher and Meisner, "Rural Development," 31.
59. Neil G. Burton and Charles Bettelheim, *China since Mao* (New York: Monthly Review Press, 1978), 11–12.
60. Burton and Bettelheim, *China since Mao*, 43–44.
61. Burton and Bettelheim, *China since Mao*, 75, 93.
62. I am not arguing that Bettelheim here was right, but that he presented a more radical view of the enormity of the shift that was taking place. Wang Hui has argued that the rural reforms between 1978 and 1985 were based on a "small peasant socialist" model and that the increase in productivity of peasants "largely originated from flexibility in production and the decrease in the urban-rural gap." It was not due to the opening of markets. See Wang Hui, *The End of the Revolution: China and the Limits of Modernity* (London: Verso, 2009), 23–24.
63. Phyllis Andors, "'The Four Modernizations' and Chinese Policy on Women," BCAS 13 (April–June 1981): 56.
64. Stephen Andors, *China's Industrial Revolution: Politics, Planning, and Management, 1949 to the Present* (New York: Pantheon Books, 1977), 160.
65. Bruno Bosteels, *Badiou and Politics* (Durham, NC: Duke University Press, 2011), 119.
66. Groupe pour la fondation de l'Union des Communistes de France Marxistes-Léninistes, *Le Maoïsme, Marxisme de Notre Temps* (Marseille: Éditions Potemkine, 1976), 19. English translation by Bruno Bosteels, "Maoism, Marxism of Our Time," *positions: east asia cultures critique* 13 (winter 2005): 530.
67. Groupe pour la fondation de l'Union des Communistes de France Marxistes-Léninistes, *Sur le Maoïsme et la Situation en Chine après la mort de Mao Tsé-Toung* (Marseille: Éditions Potemkine, 1976), 4.
68. Natacha Michel, *Ô Jeunesse ! Ô Vieillesse ! Mai 68, le Mai Mao* [Oh Youth! Oh Old Age! May '68, the Maoist May] (Les Conférences du Rouge-Gorge, 2002), 23. Michel also points to the Maoists' uneasiness in using the term "the working class," which belonged to the language of trade unions and was often deployed to mark a separation between workers and students (19).
69. Bosteels, "Maoism, Marxism of Our Time," 526. The original reads: "C'est qui naît avec 68, c'est une autre distinction, un affrontement décisif, entre deux réalités et deux conceptions des luttes de masses elles-mêmes. D'une côté, la conception réactionnaire, de type purement revendicatif, de type ouvriériste, avec son cadre syndical et parlementaire bourgeois inébranlé. De l'autre côté, attaquant de plein fouet le syndicalisme et sa conception politique, la nouveauté d'une lutte de masse politique et autonome." Groupe pour la fondation de l'Union des Communistes de France Marxistes-Léninistes, *Le Maoïsme, Marxisme de Notre Temps*, 10.
70. Groupe pour la fondation de l'Union des Communistes de France Marxistes-Léninistes, *Sur le Maoïsme et la situation en Chine*, 4.
71. "C'est tout au contraire ce par quoi la classe ouvrière dépasse son être élémen-

taire de classe sociale pour devenir une classe politique, une classe dirigeante. C'est ce par quoi elle substitue, à l'horizon borné de sa propre immédiateté de classe, l'espace, non plus seulement de ses propres intérêts revendicatifs, mais celui des intérêts politiques et sociaux de l'ensemble du peuple. La libération de la classe ouvrière exige celle du peuple, donc celle de la paysannerie travailleuse." Groupe pour la fondation de l'Union des Communistes de France Marxistes-Léninistes, *Le livre des paysans pauvres* (Paris: F. Maspero, 1976), 16.

72. "Introduction," *Le Marxiste-Léniniste* 50–51 (1981): 1. Quoted in Bosteels, *Badiou and Politics*, 153.
73. Jacques Rancière, *Althusser's Lesson*, trans. Emiliano Battista (London: Continuum, 2011), xvii.
74. Rancière, *Althusser's Lesson*, 15.
75. Rancière, *Althusser's Lesson*, 152–153.
76. Rancière, *Althusser's Lesson*, 15.
77. Simon Leys, *Chinese Shadows* (New York: Viking, 1977).
78. Edward Friedman, "Simon Leys Hates China; America Loves Simon Leys," BCAS 10 (July–September 1978): 25.
79. Edward Friedman, "Learning about China after the Revolution . . . for the First Time!" BCAS 13 (April–June 1981): 41.
80. Edward Friedman, "The Original Chinese Revolution Remains in Power," BCAS 13 (July–September 1981): 43.
81. See, for example, Mao's famous assessment on the condition of health care in China: "The Ministry of Public Health is not a Ministry of Public Health for the people, so why not change its name to the Ministry of Urban Health, the Ministry of Gentlemen's Health, or even to Ministry of Urban Gentlemen's Health?" "Directive on Public Health," June 26, 1965, in *Selected Works of Mao Tse-tung*, www.marxists.org/reference/archive/mao/selected-works/volume-9/mswv9_41.htm.
82. Friedman, "Learning about China," 42. In the same essay, Friedman attacked his former CCAS comrade Orville Schell for being supposedly critical of Chinese embrace of Westernization in his recent book on post-Mao China. See Orville Schell, *Watch Out for the Foreign Guests! China Encounters the West* (New York: Pantheon, 1980).
83. Wahnich, *In Defence of the Terror*, 91.
84. Wahnich, *In Defence of the Terror*, 93.
85. Christopher Leigh Connery, "The World Sixties," in *The Worlding Project: Doing Cultural Studies in the Era of Globalization*, ed. Rob Wilson and Christopher Leigh Connery (Santa Cruz, CA: New Pacific Press, 2007), 97.
86. "Jon Livingston to the *Newsletter*" (May 26, 1976), CCAS Archives.
87. "Bryant Avery to Earl Coleman" (October 2, 1979), SSPA.
88. "Bryant Avery to Jon Halliday, Saundra Sturdevant, Bruce Cumings, and Jayne Werner" (August 8, 1978), SSPA; "Bryant Avery to Present and Past Editors" (December 10, 1980), SSPA.

89. "Bryant Avery to Herbert Bix, Jayne Werner, and Bruce Cumings" (December 23, 1977), SSPA.
90. Ed Hammond, "Some Thoughts on the Convention" (1977), CCAS Archives.
91. "Angus McDonald to Mark Selden, Jon Livingtone, Felicia Oldfather, and Others" (January 20, 1975), SSPA. The original statement of purpose stated, in this regard: "The Committee of Concerned Asian Scholars seeks to develop a humane and knowledgeable understanding of Asian societies and their efforts to maintain cultural integrity and to confront such problems as poverty, oppression, and imperialism. We realize that to be students of other peoples, we must first understand our relations to them."
92. "Bryant Avery to Present and Past Editors," 2, SSPA.
93. "Bryant Avery to Present and Past Editors," 5. Emphasis mine. There is a similar quick tip of the hat to "imperialism and its attendant evils" in McDonald's statement.
94. "Bryant Avery's Appeal for Subscription" (February 1978), SSPA.
95. "Bryant Avery to Ben Kerkvliet and Others" (June 12, 1980), SSPA.
96. "Bryant to 'Friends' Advertising the Journal" (May 1978), SSPA.
97. "Joe Moore to Jon Livingston" (December 19, 1980), JMPA.
98. "Joseph Tharamangalam's Comments on Bryant Avery's Draft Statement of Purpose" (1981), JMPA.
99. "Bryant Avery to Ben Kerkvliet and Others."
100. "Bryant Avery to Present and Past Editors," 5.
101. The most notable cases were Richard Pfeffer, Angus McDonald, and Stephen Andors.
102. "Briant Avery to Herbert Bix, Jayne Werner, and Bruce Cumings" (December 23, 1977), SSPA.
103. Saundra Sturdevant, interview with the author (February 2013).
104. "Saundra Sturdevant to Bryant Avery, Joe Moore, Ben Kerkvliet" (February 3, 1981), 1, SSPA. Emphasis in the original.
105. "Bryant Avery to Joe Moore, Saundra Sturdevant, Robert Marks, Ben Kerkvliet" (February 26, 1981), SSPA.
106. "Richard Pfeffer to Bryant Avery" (April 17, 1980), SSPA. On the vicissitudes of Richard Pfeffer's career, see Nathan Karnovsky, "The Other Cultural Revolution: The Academic Uprising of the American China Scholar in the 1960s," senior thesis, Haverford College, 2012.
107. "Stephen Andors to Bryant Avery" (March 20, 1978), JMPA.
108. "Bryant Avery to Several People" (March 9, 1978), SSPA.
109. I can only speculate about the failure to publish any analysis of the purges of radical in academia. In part, the secrecy of the tenure and promotion process made it difficult to establish solid connections (even when the larger pattern seemed obvious) so that these cases could be justified (or challenged) one by one on the basis of their specific circumstances and not as part of a wider reaction. More tactically, who was in the position of writing such an analysis,

basically a moral indictment of the entire field? Avery originally asked Noam Chomsky to write a piece, probably because of his unassailable position and authority, but nothing came of that.
110. Orville Schell, "Learning by Doing," *CCAS Newsletter* (January 1970): 9–10.
111. Rancière, *Althusser's Lesson*, 110.
112. Rancière, *Althusser's Lesson*, 15.
113. Donald Reid, "Introduction," in Jacques Rancière, *Proletarian Nights: The Workers' Dream in Nineteenth-Century France* (London: Verso, 2012), xvi.
114. Reid, "Introduction," in Rancière, *Proletarian Nights*, xviii; see also Suter, "A Thorn in the Side of Social History," 75.
115. Schell, "Learning by Doing," 10.

EPILOGUE

1. "Bryant Avery to Robert Marks and Saundra Sturdevant" (August 4, 1980), SSPA. See chapter 4.
2. As Saundra Sturdevant succinctly put it, "academics are very cautious people . . . you sort of pussyfoot through life. I did not think that the sixties was a time for pussyfooting." Interview with the author.
3. Dipesh Chakrabarty, *Provincializing Europe: Postcolonial Thought and Historical Difference* (Princeton, NJ: Princeton University Press, 2007).
4. The special issue was *BCAS* 4 (December 1972).
5. Jon Livingston, Bryant Avery, Joe Moore, and Bill and Nancy Doub, "*The Bulletin of Concerned Asian Scholars* from the Perspective of Past and Present Managing Editors," *BCAS* 21 (April–December 1989): 189.
6. Elizabeth Lasek, "Imperialism in China: A Methodological Critique," *BCAS* 15 (January–February 1983): 50–64.
7. Tim Wright, "Imperialism and the Chinese Economy: A Methodological Critique of the Debate," *BCAS* 18 (January–March 1986): 36–45. Following a pattern adopted by the CCP at the time, Wright also reenlisted Marx in order to claim a positive role for imperialism: "Moreover, the recent 'modes of production' school in Marxist theory attributes a progressive role to both national and foreign capital in undermining the precapitalist (feudal or petty commodity) modes of production which are the root of underdevelopment; indeed, Mao also pointed to this effect" (38).
8. Tani E. Barlow, ed., "Colonialism's Career in Postwar China Studies," in *Formations of Colonial Modernity in East Asia* (Durham, NC: Duke University Press, 1997), 373–411.
9. Barlow, "Colonialism's Career," 395.
10. Phyllis Andors, "Women and Work in Shenzhen," *BCAS* 20 (July–September 1988): 22–41; Jonathan Unger and Jean Xiong, "Life in the Chinese Hinterlands under the Rural Economic Reforms," *BCAS* 22 (April–June 1990): 4–17.
11. Paul A. Cohen, *Discovering History in China: American Historical Writing on the Recent Chinese Past*, 2nd ed. (New York: Columbia University Press, 2010), 190.

12. Robert Marks, "The State of the China Field: Or, the China Field and the State," *Modern China* 11 (October 1985): 488.
13. Harry Harding, "From China, with Disdain: New Trends in the Study of China," *Asian Survey* 22 (October 1982): 953.
14. Harding, "From China, with Disdain," 953; Simon Leys, *Chinese Shadows* (New York: Viking, 1977).
15. Daniel Vukovich, *China and Orientalism: Western Knowledge Production and the PRC* (London: Routledge, 2011), 1.
16. Wang Hui, "Dandai zhongguo lishi jubian zhong de Taiwan wenti" 当代中国历史巨变中的台湾问题 (The Problem of Taiwan within Contemporary China's Historical Transformation), accessed October 15, 2015, wen.org.cn /modules/article/view.article.php?4172/c8.
17. I don't want to give the impression that everything published in the 1980s on Asia or specifically on modern China was untheorized or banal. Among the several excellent books published, I want to single out Gail Hershatter, *The Workers of Tianjin, 1900–1949* (Stanford, CA: Stanford University Press, 1986); Kay Ann Johnson, *Women, the Family, and Peasant Revolution in China* (Chicago: University of Chicago Press, 1983); Arif Dirlik, *The Origins of Chinese Communism* (New York: Oxford University Press, 1989); Anita Chan, Richard Madsen, and Jonathan Unger, *Chen Village: The Recent History of a Peasant Community in Mao's China* (Berkeley: University of California Press, 1985); and Sulamith Heins Potter and Jack M. Potter, *China's Peasants: The Anthropology of a Revolution* (Cambridge: Cambridge University Press, 1990).
18. "BCAS / CAS Statement of Purpose," accessed August 2016, criticalasianstudies .org/about-us/.
19. "BCAS / CAS Statement of Purpose."
20. "*positions*' Statement of Purpose," *positions: east asia cultures critique*, accessed October 16, 2015, positions.rice.edu/Content.aspx?id=153.
21. In her assessment of the evolution of *positions* after twenty years, Tani Barlow, senior editor and founder of the journal, mentioned how they modeled themselves in relation to the Cold War generation of CCAS. "It never entered my mind that these constituencies would conceive of *positions* as hostile or threatening in any way. This is the blessed idiocy of young people. I always considered the Left intellectuals—BCAS, *Critical Inquiry*, the Jamesonians, the senior generation of Harootunian, *Socialist Review*—to be *positions*' natural allies. It never crossed my mind that *positions* would threaten anyone on the scholarly Left or that our appearance as a project would cause conflict." Rebecca Karl, Tom Lamarre, Claudia Pozzana, and Alessandro Russo, "'A Relentlessly Productive Venue': Interview with Senior Editor, Tani Barlow," *positions: east asia cultures critique* 20 (winter 2012): 352.
22. Naoki Sakai, "Positions and Positionalities: After Two Decades," *positions: east asia cultures critique* 20 (winter 2012): 76–77.

23. Harry D. Harootunian, "Postcoloniality's Unconscious/Area Studies' Desire," in *Learning Places: The Afterlives of Area Studies*, ed. Masao Miyoshi and Harry D. Harootunian (Durham, NC: Duke University Press, 2002), 167.
24. H. D. Harootunian and Masao Miyoshi, "Introduction: The 'Afterlife' of Area Studies," in *Learning Places*, 7.
25. As posed by Tani Barlow, this was the question of "what happens after the *critique* of Orientalism. And what sort of scholarship should ensue," "how does one displace habits following a trenchant and definitive critique of them? Are we condemned to put Orientalism on parade year after year? In light of the widespread conventions of the Orientalist view, how could a better style of scholarship emerge out of the critique?" Karl et al., "'A Relentlessly Productive Venue,'" 347–348.
26. Philip Huang, "The Paradigmatic Crisis in Chinese Studies: Paradoxes in Social and Economic History," *Modern China* 17 (July 1991): 303.
27. Huang, "The Paradigmatic Crisis," 335–336.
28. Huang, "The Paradigmatic Crisis, 316.
29. Eagleton, *Literary Theory: An Introduction*, xvii.
30. Huang, "The Paradigmatic Crisis," 333.
31. Similar connections can be traced in the work of some thinkers of the Chinese New Left, such as Wang Hui, who too are a central reference for *positions*.
32. Here it is difficult to talk about an intergenerational debate, unless we confine ourselves to strictly scholarly terms. Hevia was in military intelligence during the Vietnam War and only subsequently went on to an academic career, which places him in the same generation as Esherick.
33. Joseph W. Esherick, "Cherishing Sources from Afar," *Modern China* 24 (April 1998): 136. Esherick's essay was followed by a response by Hevia and a rejoinder by Esherick, both published in the July 1998 issue of *Modern China*. James L. Hevia, "Postpolemical Historiography: A Response to Joseph W. Esherick," *Modern China* 24 (July 1998): 319–327. Joseph W. Esherick, "Tradutore, Traditore: A Reply to James Hevia," *Modern China* 24 (July 1998): 328–332.
34. "It is true . . . that much of the latest theory has passed me by. But . . . the notion that newer is better is consumerism, not scholarship." Esherick, "Tradutore, Traditore," 331.
35. Here I find Harry Harootunian's assessment unimpeachable: "What was staged was a call to return to the sources and the facts so venerated by Chinese scholars, as if native knowledge itself, not to mention either the 'sources' and facticity, the archive, were untroubled and unproblematic concepts capable of revealing their own reason of theory, with little effort." Harootunian, "Postcoloniality's Unconscious/Area Studies' Desire," 162–163.
36. Arif Dirlik's assessment of *positions* follows exactly this pattern, calling (with absolutely no evidence to back his claim) the newly founded journal "antirevolutionary." Arif Dirlik, "Reversals, Ironies, Hegemonies: Notes on the Con-

temporary Historiography of Modern China," *Modern China* 22 (July 1996): 272–275.
37. François Cusset, *French Theory: How Foucault, Derrida, Deleuze and Co. Transformed the Intellectual Life of the United States* (Minneapolis: University of Minnesota Press, 2008), xx–xxi.
38. Cusset, *French Theory*, xv.

BIBLIOGRAPHY

Adams, Nina S., and Alfred W. McCoy. *Laos: War and Revolution*. New York: Harper Colophon, 1970.
Alexander, Robert J. *International Maoism in the Developing World*. Westport, CT: Prager, 1999.
[Althusser, Louis]. "On the Cultural Revolution," translated by Jason E. Smith. *Décalages* 1, no. 1 (2014), scholar.oxy.edu/decalages/vol1/iss1/9.
Andors, Stephen. *China's Industrial Revolution: Politics, Planning, and Management, 1949 to the Present*. New York: Pantheon Books, 1977.
Andors, Stephen. "Revolution and Modernization: Man and Machine in Industrializing Societies, the Chinese Case," in *America's Asia: Dissenting Essays on Asian-American Relations*, edited by Edward Friedman and Mark Selden, 393–444. New York: Pantheon, 1969.
Andreas, Joel. "Leveling the Little Pagoda: The Impact of College Examinations, and Their Elimination, on Rural Education in China." *Comparative Education Review* 48 (February 2004): 1–47.
Andreas, Joel. *Rise of the Red Engineers: The Cultural Revolution and the Origins of China's New Class*. Stanford, CA: Stanford University Press, 2009.
Ashar, Meera. "Decolonizing What? Categories, Concepts and the Enduring 'Not Yet.'" *Cultural Dynamics* 27, no. 2 (2015): 253–265.
Ashar, Meera. "The 'Not-Yet' in Indian Politics: Language, Epistemology and Coloniality." Presented at the conference "Global Coloniality in the Asian Century," Hong Kong, June 7–8, 2012.
Aubert, Claude, Lucien Bianco, Claude Cadart, and Jean-Luc Domenach. *Regards froids sur la Chine* [Cold-eyed perspectives on China]. Paris: Seuil, 1976.
Badiou, Alain. *The Adventures of French Philosophy*. London: Verso, 2012.
Badiou, Alain. *The Communist Hypothesis*. London: Verso, 2010.
Badiou, Alain. "The Cultural Revolution: The Last Revolution?" *positions: east asia cultures critique* 13 (winter 2005): 481–514.
Badiou, Alain. *Metapolitics*. London: Verso, 2005.

Barlow, Tani E. "Colonialism's Career in Postwar China Studies," in *Formations of Colonial Modernity in East Asia*, 373–411. Durham, NC: Duke University Press, 1997.

Barlow, Tani E., ed. *Formations of Colonial Modernity in East Asia*. Durham, NC: Duke University Press, 1997.

Barlow, Tani E., with Gary J. Bjorge, ed. *I Myself Am a Woman: Selected Writings of Ding Ling*. Boston: Beacon Press, 1989.

Barthes, Roland. *Carnets du voyage en Chine*. Paris: Christian Bourgois/IMEC, 2009.

Barthes, Roland. *Travels in China*, edited, annotated, and with a foreword by Anne Herschberg Pierrot. Cambridge: Polity, 2009.

Bay, Christian. "The Cheerful Science of Dismal Politics," in *The Dissenting Academy*, edited by Theodore Roszak, 208–230. New York: Pantheon, 1968.

Bernstein, Richard. "A Bridge to the Love of Democracy." *New York Times*, December 29, 2010.

Besançon, Julien, ed. *Les murs ont la parole* [The walls have the word]. Paris: Claude Tchou, 1968.

Bingham, Charles, and Gert J. J. Biesta, with Jacques Rancière. *Jacques Rancière: Education, Truth, Emancipation*. London: Continuum, 2010.

Bloom, Joshua, and Waldo Martin. *Black against Empire: The History and Politics of the Black Panther Party*. Berkeley: University of California Press, 2013.

Bosteels, Bruno. *Badiou and Politics*. Durham, NC: Duke University Press, 2011.

Bosteels, Bruno, trans. "Maoism, Marxism of Our Time." *positions: east asia cultures critique* 13 (winter 2005): 523–533.

Bourg, Julian. *From Revolution to Ethics: May 1968 and Contemporary French Thought*. Montreal: McGill-Queen's University Press, 2007.

Bourg, Julian. "The Red Guards of Paris: French Student Maoism of the 1960s." *History of European Ideas* 31, no. 4 (2005): 472–490.

Boursellier, Cristophe. *Les Maoïstes: La folle histoire des gardes rouges Français* [The Maoists: The crazy story of the French red guards]. Paris: Points, 2008.

Brady, Anne-Marie. *Making the Foreign Serve China: Managing Foreigners in the People's Republic*. Lanham, MD: Rowman and Littlefield, 2003.

Brown, Jeremy, and Matthew D. Johnson, eds. *Maoism at the Grassroots: Everyday Life in China's Era of High Socialism*. Cambridge, MA: Harvard University Press, 2015.

Burton, Neil G., and Charles Bettelheim. *China since Mao*. New York: Monthly Review Press, 1978.

Chakrabarty, Dipesh. *Provincializing Europe: Postcolonial Thought and Historical Difference*. Princeton, NJ: Princeton University Press, 2007.

Chan, Anita, Richard Madsen, and Jonathan Unger. *Chen Village: The Recent History of a Peasant Community in Mao's China*. Berkeley: University of California Press, 1985.

Chang, Gordon H. *Fateful Ties: A History of America's Preoccupation with China*. Cambridge, MA: Harvard University Press, 2015.

Chen Jian. *Mao's China and the Cold War*. Chapel Hill: University of North Carolina Press, 2001.

Chen Yinghong. *Creating the New Man: From Enlightenment Ideals to Socialist Realities*. Honolulu: University of Hawai'i Press, 2009.

Cheng Jinkuan. *"Jiaoyu geming" de lishi kaocha, 1966–1976* [An investigation of the history of "the educational revolution," 1966–1976]. Fuzhou: Fujian jiaoyu chubanshe, 2001.

Chomsky, Noam. *American Power and the New Mandarins*. New York: Pantheon, 1969.

Chomsky, Noam, and Michel Foucault. "Human Nature: Justice versus Power. Noam Chomsky Debates with Michel Foucault (1971)," accessed October 2015, www.chomsky.info/debates/1971xxxx.htm.

Chow, Rey. *Writing Diaspora: Tactics of Intervention in Contemporary Cultural Studies*. Bloomington: Indiana University Press, 1993.

Clark, Paul. *The Chinese Cultural Revolution: A History*. Cambridge: Cambridge University Press, 2008.

Coburn, Judith. "Asian Scholars and Government: The Chrysanthemum on the Sword," in *America's Asia: Dissenting Essays on Asian-American Relations*, edited by Edward Friedman and Mark Selden, 67–107. New York: Pantheon, 1969.

Cohen, Paul A. *Discovering History in China: American Historical Writing on the Recent Chinese Past*, 2nd ed. New York: Columbia University Press, 2010.

Committee of Concerned Asian Scholars. *China! Inside the People's Republic*. New York: Bantam Books, 1972.

Committee of Concerned Asian Scholars. *The Indochina Story: A Fully Documented Account*. New York: Pantheon Books, 1970.

Connery, Christopher Leigh. "Editorial Introduction. The Asian Sixties: An Unfinished Project." *Inter-Asia Cultural Studies* 7, no. 4 (2006): 545–553.

Connery, Christopher Leigh. "Introduction: Worlded Pedagogy in Santa Cruz," in *The Worlding Project: Doing Cultural Studies in the Era of Globalization*, edited by Rob Wilson and Christopher Leigh Connery, 1–12. Santa Cruz, CA: New Pacific Press, 2007.

Connery, Christopher Leigh. "The World Sixties," in *The Worlding Project: Doing Cultural Studies in the Era of Globalization*, edited by Rob Wilson and Christopher Leigh Connery, 77–108. Santa Cruz, CA: New Pacific Press, 2007.

Cook Alexander C., ed. *Mao's Little Red Book: A Global History*. Cambridge: Cambridge University Press, 2014.

Cook, Alexander C. "Third World Maoism," in *A Critical Introduction to Mao*, edited by Timothy Cheek, 288–312. Cambridge: Cambridge University Press, 2010.

Cumings, Bruce. "The Political Economy of Chinese Foreign Policy." *Modern China* 5 (October 1979): 411–461.

Cusset, François. *French Theory: How Foucault, Derrida, Deleuze and Co. Transformed the Intellectual Life of the United States*. Minneapolis: University of Minnesota Press, 2008.

Dawson, Michael C. *Blacks In and Out of the Left*. Cambridge, MA: Harvard University Press, 2013.

De Bary, Wm. Theodore. "The Association for Asian Studies: Nonpolitical but Not Unconcerned." *Journal of Asian Studies* 29 (August 1970): 751–759.

De Bary, Wm. Theodore, Richard D. Lambert, and Gerald D. Berreman. "The Funding of Asian Studies." *Journal of Asian Studies* 30 (February 1971): 389–412.

Derrida, Jacques. *Of Grammatology*, translated by Gayatri Chakravorty Spivak. Baltimore: Johns Hopkins University Press, 1998.

Dirlik, Arif. "Chinese History and the Question of Orientalism." *History and Theory* 35 (December 1996): 96–118.

Dirlik, Arif. *Marxism in the Chinese Revolution*. Lanham, MD: Rowman and Littlefield, 2005.

Dirlik, Arif. *The Origins of Chinese Communism*. New York: Oxford University Press, 1989.

Dirlik, Arif. "Reversals, Ironies, Hegemonies: Notes on the Contemporary Historiography of Modern China." *Modern China* 22 (July 1996): 243–284.

Eagleton, Terry. *Literary Theory: An Introduction*. Minneapolis: University of Minnesota Press, 2008.

Eley, Geoff. *A Crooked Line: From Cultural History to the History of Society*. Ann Arbor: University of Michigan Press, 2005.

Engelhardt, Tom. *The End of Victory Culture: Cold War America and the Disillusioning of a Generation*. New York: Basic Books, 1995.

Esherick, Joseph W. "Cherishing Sources from Afar." *Modern China* 24 (April 1998): 135–161.

Esherick, Joseph W. "Tradutore, Traditore: A Reply to James Hevia." *Modern China* 24 (July 1998): 328–332.

Evans, Paul M. *John Fairbank and the American Understanding of Modern China*. New York: Basil Blackwell, 1988.

"Excerpts from a Statement on U.S. Policy in Asia Made by 14 American Scholars." *New York Times*, December 20, 1967, 14.

Fairbank, John K. "Assignment for the '70s. Presidential address, AHA December 1968." *American Historical Review* 74 (February 1969): 861–879.

Fairbank, John K. *Chinabound: A Fifty-Year Memoir*. New York: Harper and Row, 1982.

Fairbank, John K., and Edwin Reischauer. "East Asia and Our Future" (lecture), accessed August 2016, vimeo.com/50776144.

Fields, Belden. "French Maoism," in "The 60s without Apology," edited by Sohnya Sayres. Special issue, *Social Text* 9/10 (spring–summer 1984): 148–177.

Fortini, Franco. "Ancora in Cina" [In China once again]. *Quaderni Piacentini* 48 (1973): 119–140.

Foucault, Michel. *Power/Knowledge: Selected Interviews and Other Writings*. New York: Pantheon, 1980.

Foucault, Michel, and Gilles Deleuze. "Intellectuals and Power: A Conversation between Michel Foucault and Gilles Deleuze," in Michel Foucault, *Language, Counter-Memory, Practice: Selected Essays and Interviews*, edited by Donald F.

Bouchard, 205–217. Ithaca, NY: Cornell University Press. Also available at libcom.org/library/intellectuals-power-a-conversation-between-michel-foucault-and-gilles-deleuze.

"Fourteen U.S. Scholars Sign Statement Backing American Presence in Asia." *Montreal Gazette*, December 20, 1967.

Frazier, Robeson Taj. *The East Is Black: Cold War China in the Black Radical Imagination*. Durham, NC: Duke University Press, 2015.

Frey, Marc, and Nicola Spakowski, eds. *Asianisms: Regionalist Interactions and Asian Integration*. Singapore: NUS Press, 2015.

Friedman, Edward, and Mark Selden, eds. *America's Asia: Dissenting Essays on Asian-American Relations*. New York: Pantheon, 1969.

Galstone, Arthur, with Jean S. Savage. *Daily Life in People's China*. New York: Crowell, 1973.

Geismar, Alain. *Porquoi nous combattons* [Why we fight]. Paris: Maspero, 1970.

Gilman, Nils. *Mandarins of the Future: Modernization Theory in Cold War America*. Baltimore: Johns Hopkins University Press, 2003.

Gittings, John. "Mixed up about Mao." *Guardian*, August 30, 1972.

Goldwasser, Janet, and Stuart Dowty. *Huan-Ying: Workers' China*. New York: Monthly Review Press, 1975.

Groupe pour la fondation de l'Union des Communistes de France Marxistes-Léninistes. *Le livre des paysans pauvres*. Paris: F. Maspero, 1976.

Groupe pour la fondation de l'Union des Communistes de France Marxistes-Léninistes. *Le Maoïsme, Marxisme de Notre Temps*. Marseille: Éditions Potemkine, 1976.

Groupe pour la fondation de l'Union des Communistes de France Marxistes-Léninistes. *Sur Le Maoïsme et la Situation en Chine après la mort de Mao Tsé-Toung*. Marseille: Éditions Potemkine, 1976.

Guha, Ranajit. *Elementary Aspects of Peasant Insurgency in Colonial India*. Durham, NC: Duke University Press, 1999.

Gurley, John. "Capitalist and Maoist Economic Development," in *America's Asia: Dissenting Essays on Asian-American Relations*, edited by Edward Friedman and Mark Selden, 324–356. New York: Pantheon, 1969.

Gurley, John. *China's Economy and the Maoist Strategy*. New York: Monthly Review Press, 1976.

Hai Tian and Xiao Wei. *Wo de daxue, 1970–1976: Gong nong bing daxuesheng* [My university, 1970–1976: Students at the worker-peasant-soldier universities]. Beijing: Zhongguo youyi chuban gongsi, 2009.

Hallward, Peter. "Jacques Rancière and the Subversion of Mastery," in *Jacques Rancière: Aesthetics, Politics, Philosophy*, edited by Mark Robson, 26–45. Edinburgh: Edinburgh University Press, 2005.

Harding, Harry. "From China, with Disdain: New Trends in the Study of China." *Asian Survey* 22 (October 1982): 934–958.

Harootunian, Harry D. "Postcoloniality's Unconscious/Area Studies' Desire," in

Learning Places: The Afterlives of Area Studies, edited by Masao Miyoshi and Harry D. Harootunian, 150–174. Durham, NC: Duke University Press, 2002.

Harootunian, Harry D. "Review of *E. H. Norman: His Life and Scholarship* by Roger W. Bowen." *Journal of Asian Studies* 47 (November 1988): 878–880.

Harootunian, Harry D., and Masao Miyoshi, eds. "Introduction: The 'Afterlife' of Area Studies," in *Learning Places: The Afterlives of Area Studies*, 1–18. Durham, NC: Duke University Press, 2002.

Harvey, David. *A Brief History of Neoliberalism*. Oxford: Oxford University Press, 2007.

Havens, Thomas R. H. *Fire across the Sea: The Vietnam War and Japan 1965–1975*. Princeton, NJ: Princeton University Press, 1987.

Hayot, Eric R. *Chinese Dreams: Pound, Brecht, Tel Quel*. Ann Arbor: University of Michigan Press, 2003.

Hershatter, Gail. *The Workers of Tianjin, 1900–1949*. Stanford, CA: Stanford University Press, 1986.

Hevia, James L. *Cherishing Men from Afar: Qing Guest Ritual and the Macartney Embassy of 1793*. Durham, NC: Duke University Press, 1995.

Hevia, James L. "Postpolemical Historiography: A Response to Joseph W. Esherick." *Modern China* 24 (July 1998): 319–327.

Hinton, William. *Hundred Day War: The Cultural Revolution at Tsinghua University*. New York: Monthly Review Press, 1972.

Hodes, Nancy. "Report." *Harvard Crimson*, April 17, 1968.

Hollander, Paul. *Political Pilgrims: Western Intellectuals in Search of the Good Society*, 4th ed. New Brunswick, NJ: Transaction, 1998.

Hourmant, François. *Au pays de l'avenir radieux: Voyages des intellectuels Français en URSS, à Cuba et en Chine populaire* [To the countries of the bright future: Travels of French intellectuals to the USSR, Cuba, and the PRC). Paris: Aubier, 2000.

Hourmant, François. *Le désenchentement des clercs: Figures de l'intellectuel dans l'après-Mai 68* [The disenchantments of the clerks: Features of the intellectual after May '68]. Rennes: Presses Universitaires de Rennes, 1997.

Huang, Philip. "The Paradigmatic Crisis in Chinese Studies: Paradoxes in Social and Economic History." *Modern China* 17 (July 1991): 299–341.

Hucker, Charles O. *The Association for Asian Studies: An Interpretive History*. Seattle: University of Washington Press, 1973.

Hunter, Neale. *Shanghai Journal*. New York: Praeger, 1969.

"Introduction." *Le Marxiste-Léniniste* 50–51 (1981): 1.

Jameson, Fredric. "Periodizing the 60s," in "The 60s without Apology," edited by Sohnya Sayres. Special issue, *Social Text* 9/10 (spring–summer 1984): 178–209.

Jobs, Richard Ivan. *Riding the New Wave: Youth and the Rejuvenation of France after the Second World War*. Stanford, CA: Stanford University Press, 2007.

Johnson, Kay Ann. *Women, the Family, and Peasant Revolution in China*. Chicago: University of Chicago Press, 1983.

Johnson, Matthew D. "From Peace to the Panthers: PRC Engagement with African-

American Transnational Networks, 1949–1979." *Past and Present* 218, supplement 8 (2013): 233–257.

Joseph, Peniel E. *Stokely: A Life*. New York: Basic Civitas Books, 2015.

Karl, Rebecca E. "Culture, Revolution and the Times of History: Mao and 20th-Century China." *China Quarterly* 187 (2006): 693–699.

Karl, Rebecca, Tom Lamarre, Claudia Pozzana, and Alessandro Russo. "'A Relentlessly Productive Venue': Interview with Senior Editor, Tani Barlow." *positions: east asia cultures critique* 20 (winter 2012): 345–372.

Karnovsky, Nathan. "The Other Cultural Revolution: The Academic Uprising of the American China Scholar in the 1960s," senior thesis, Haverford College, 2012.

Karnow, Stanley. "Radicals Dislike China's New Foreign Policy." *Washington Post*, May 28, 1972.

Kelley, Robin D. G., and Betsy Esch. "Black Like Mao: Red China and Black Revolution." *Souls: A Critical Journal of Black Politics, Culture, and Society* 1, no. 4 (1999): 6–41.

Kruger, Helen. "Acupuncture in America?" *Village Voice*, September 16, 1971.

Landsberg, Alison. *Prosthetic Memory: The Transformation of American Remembrance in the Age of Mass Culture*. New York: Columbia University Press, 2004.

Lane, John Francis. "Obituary: Maria Antonietta Macciocchi." *Guardian*, May 21, 2007, www.theguardian.com/news/2007/may/21/guardianobituaries.italy.

Lanza, Fabio. "America's Asia? Revolution, Scholarship and Asian Studies," in *Asianisms: Regionalist Interactions and Asian Integration*, edited by Marc Frey and Nicola Spakoswki, 134–155. Singapore: NUS Press, 2016.

Lanza, Fabio. *Behind the Gate: Inventing Students in Beijing*. New York: Columbia University Press, 2010.

Lanza, Fabio. "Deng's Children: Chinese 'Youth' in the Beijing Spring, 1989," in *Transnational Histories of Youth in the Twentieth Century*, edited by David Pomfret and Richard Jobs, 260–282. Houndmills: Palgrave Macmillan, 2015.

Lanza, Fabio. "Making Sense of 'China' during the Cold War: Global Maoism and Asian Studies," in *De-Centering Cold War History: Local and Global Change*, edited by Jadwiga Pieper Mooney and Fabio Lanza, 147–166. London: Routledge, 2012.

Lanza, Fabio. "Springtime and Morning Suns: 'Youth' as a Political Category in Twentieth-Century China." *Journal of the History of Childhood and Youth* 5, no. 1 (2012): 31–51.

Latham, Michael E. *Modernization as Ideology: American Social Science and 'Nation Building' in the Kennedy Era*. Chapel Hill: University of North Carolina Press, 2000.

Lattimore, Owen. *Ordeal by Slander: The First Great Book of the McCarthy Era*. New York: Carroll and Graf, 2002.

Legge, James, trans. *The Chinese Classics*, vol. II. London: Trübner, 1875.

Lemisch, Jesse. *On Active Service in War and Peace: Politics and Ideology in the American Historical Profession*. Toronto: New Hogtown Press, 1975.

Leys, Simon. *Chinese Shadows*. New York: Viking, 1977.

Linhart, Robert. *The Assembly Line*. Amherst: University of Massachusetts Press, 1981.
Linhart, Virginie. *Le jour où mon père s'est tu* [The day my father stopped talking]. Paris: Éd. du Seuil, 2008.
Linhart, Virginie. *Volontaires pour l'usine* [Volunteers for the factory]. Paris: Éd. du Seuil, 1994.
Link, Perry. "Dawn in China," in *My First Trip to China: Scholars, Diplomats and Journalists Reflect on their First Encounter with China*, edited by Liu Kin-ming, 49–55. Hong Kong: East Slope, 2012.
Liu Kin-ming, ed. *My First Trip to China: Scholars, Diplomats and Journalists Reflect on Their First Encounter with China*. Hong Kong: East Slope, 2012.
Loi, Michelle. *L'Intelligence au pouvoir. Un monde nouveau: La Chine* [Intelligence in power. A new world: China]. Paris: Maspéro, 1973.
Ludden, David, ed. *Reading Subaltern Studies: Critical History, Contested Meaning and the Globalization of South Asia*. London: Anthem Press, 2002.
Macciocchi, Maria Antonietta. *Daily Life in Revolutionary China*. New York: Monthly Review Press, 1972.
MacMillan, Margaret. *Nixon and Mao: The Week That Changed the World*. New York: Random House, 2008.
Madsen, Richard. *China and the American Dream: A Moral Inquiry*. Berkeley: University of California Press, 1995.
Manceaux, Michéle. *Les Maos en France* [The Maoists in France]. Paris: Gallimard, 1972.
Mao, Joyce. *Asia First: China and the Making of Modern American Conservatism*. Chicago: Chicago University Press, 2015.
Mao Zedong. "Directive on Public Health," June 26, 1965, in *Selected Works of Mao Tse-tung*, www.marxists.org/reference/archive/mao/selected-works/volume-9/mswv9_41.htm.
Mao Zedong. "Report on an Investigation of the Peasant Movement in Hunan," March 1927, in *Selected Works of Mao Tse-tung*, www.marxists.org/reference/archive/mao/selected-works/volume-1/mswv1_2.htm.
Mao Zedong. "Talk on Questions of Philosophy," August 18, 1964, in *Selected Works of Mao Tse-tung*, www.marxists.org/reference/archive/mao/selected-works/volume-9/mswv9_27.htm.
Marks, Robert. "The State of the China Field: Or, the China Field and the State." *Modern China* 11 (October 1985): 461–509.
Marx-Souras, Danielle. *The Cultural Politics of Tel Quel: Literature and the Left in the Wake of Engagement*. University Park: Pennsylvania State University Press, 1996.
Meisner, Maurice. *Mao's China and After: A History of the People's Republic*. 3rd ed. New York: Free Press, 1999.
Michel, Natacha. *La Chine Européenne* [The European China]. Paris: Gallimard, 1975.
Michel, Natacha. *Ô Jeunesse! Ô Vieillesse! Mai 68, le Mai Mao* [Oh Youth! Oh Old Age! May '68, the Maoist May]. Les Conférences du Rouge-Gorge, 2002.

Milton, Nancy, and David Milton. *The Wind Will Not Subside: Years in Revolutionary China, 1964–1969*. New York: Pantheon, 1976.

Mirsky, Jonathan. "From Mao Fan to Counter-Revolutionary in 48 Hours," in *My First Trip to China: Scholars, Diplomats and Journalists Reflect on their First Encounter with China*, edited by Liu Kin-ming, 24–28. Hong Kong: East Slope, 2012.

Miyoshi, Masao, and Harry D. Harootunian, eds. *Learning Places: The Afterlives of Area Studies*. Durham, NC: Duke University Press, 2002.

Myrdal, Jan. *Report from a Chinese Village*. New York: Pantheon Books, 1965.

Nee, Victor, and James Peck, eds. *China's Uninterrupted Revolution: From 1840 to the Present*. New York: Pantheon, 1975.

Newman, Robert P. *Owen Lattimore and the "Loss" of China*. Berkeley: University of California Press, 1992.

Norman, E. H. *Origins of the Modern Japanese State: Selected Writings of E. H. Norman*, edited by John Dower. New York: Pantheon Books, 1975.

"Obituaries: I. Milton Sacks, 62, Professor and an Authority on Vietnam," *New York Times*, August 18, 1981, www.nytimes.com/1981/08/18/obituaries/i-milton-sacks-62-professor-and-an-authority-on-vietnam.html.

Packard, George R. *Edwin O. Reischauer and the American Discovery of Japan*. New York: Columbia University Press, 2010.

Passerini, Luisa. *Autobiography of a Generation: Italy, 1968*. Hanover, NH: Wesleyan University Press, 1996.

Peck, James. *Ideal Illusions: How the U.S. Government Co-opted Human Rights*. New York: Metropolitan Books, 2010.

Peck, James. "Revolution versus Modernization and Revisionism: A Two-Front Struggle," in *China's Uninterrupted Revolution: From 1840 to the Present*, edited by Victor Nee and James Peck, 57–217. New York: Pantheon, 1975.

Peck, James. "The Roots of Rhetoric: The Professional Ideology of America's China Watchers," in *America's Asia: Dissenting Essays on Asian-American Relations*, edited by Edward Friedman and Mark Selden, 40–66. New York: Pantheon, 1969.

Peck, James. *Washington's China: The National Security World, the Cold War and the Origins of Globalism*. Amherst: University of Massachusetts Press, 2006.

Piccini, Jon. "'Light from the East': Travel to China and Australian Activism in the 'Long Sixties.'" *The Sixties: A Journal of History, Politics and Culture* 6, no. 1 (2013): 25–44.

Pontecorvo, Gillo, dir. *The Battle of Algiers*. Igor Film; Casbah Film. 1967.

"*positions*' Statement of Purpose." *positions: east asia cultures critique*, accessed October 16, 2015, positions.rice.edu/Content.aspx?id=153.

Potter, Sulamith Heins, and Jack M. Potter. *China's Peasants: The Anthropology of a Revolution*. Cambridge: Cambridge University Press, 1990.

Price, David H. *Cold War Anthropology: The CIA, the Pentagon, and the Growth of Dual Use Anthropology*. Durham, NC: Duke University Press, 2016.

Price, David H. *Threatening Anthropology: McCarthyism and the FBI's Surveillance of Activist Anthropologists*. Durham, NC: Duke University Press, 2004.

Proust, Marcel. *Time Regained*, vol. 6 of *In Search of Lost Time*, translated by Andreas Mayor and Terence Kilmartin, revised by D. J. Enright. New York: Modern Library, 1999.

Qin Huailu. *Ninth Heaven to Ninth Hell: The History of a Noble Chinese Experiment*, edited by William Hinton. New York: Barricade Books, 1995.

Qiu, Jin. *The Culture of Power: The Lin Biao Incident in the Cultural Revolution*. Stanford, CA: Stanford University Press, 1999.

Rancière, Jacques. *Althusser's Lesson*, translated by Emiliano Battista. London: Continuum, 2011.

Rancière, Jacques. *The Philosopher and His Poor*, edited by Andrew Parker; translated by John Drury, Corinne Oster, and Andrew Parker. Durham, NC: Duke University Press, 2004.

Reid, Donald. "Introduction," in Jacques Rancière, *Proletarian Nights: The Workers' Dream in Nineteenth-Century France*. London: Verso, 2012.

Riskin, Carl. "Maoism and Motivation: Work Incentives in China," in *China's Uninterrupted Revolution*, edited by Victor Nee and James Peck, 415–461. New York: Pantheon, 1975.

Robcis, Camille. "'China in Our Heads': Althusser, Maoism, and Structuralism." *Social Text* 110 (spring 2012): 51–69.

Robin, Ron. *The Making of the Cold War Enemy: Culture and Politics in the Military-Intellectual Complex*. Princeton, NJ: Princeton University Press, 2001.

Ross, Andrew. "Mao Zedong's Impact on Cultural Politics in the West." *Cultural Politics* 1, no. 1 (2005): 5–22.

Ross, Kristin. *May '68 and Its Afterlives*. Chicago: University of Chicago Press, 2004.

Rostow, Walter W., and Richard W. Hatch. *An American Policy in Asia*. Cambridge, MA: MIT Press, 1955.

Roszak, Theodore. "On Academic Delinquency," in *The Dissenting Academy*, 3–42. New York: Pantheon, 1968.

Roszak, Theodore, ed. *The Dissenting Academy*. New York: Pantheon, 1968.

Russo, Alessandro. "How Did the Cultural Revolution End? The Last Dispute between Mao Zedong and Deng Xiaoping, 1975." *Modern China* 39 (May 2013): 239–279.

Russo, Alessandro. "How to Translate 'Cultural Revolution.'" *Inter-Asia Cultural Studies* 7, no. 4 (2006): 673–682.

Russo, Alessandro. *Le rovine del mandato: La modernizzazione politica dell'educazione e della cultura cinesi* [The ruins of the mandate: The political modernization of Chinese education and culture]. Milan: Franco Angeli, 1985.

Russo, Alessandro. "The Probable Defeat: Preliminary Notes on the Chinese Cultural Revolution." *positions: east asia cultures critique* 6, no. 1 (1998): 179–202.

Said, Edward. *Orientalism*. New York: Vintage, 1979.

Sakai, Naoki. "Positions and Positionalities: After Two Decades." *positions: east asia cultures critique* 20 (winter 2012): 67–94.

Schell, Orville. "Foreword. A China Frontier: Once the Border of Borders," in *My

First Trip to China: Scholars, Diplomats and Journalists Reflect on their First Encounter with China, edited by Liu Kin-ming, 10–18. Hong Kong: East Slope, 2012.

Schell, Orville. *Watch Out for the Foreign Guests! China Encounters the West*. New York: Pantheon, 1980.

Schmalzer, Sigrid. "On the Appropriate Use of Rose-Colored Glasses: Reflections on Science in Socialist China." *Isis* 98 (2007): 571–583.

Schmalzer, Sigrid. *Red Revolution, Green Revolution: Encounters with Scientific Farming in Socialist China*. Chicago: University of Chicago Press, 2016.

Schmalzer, Sigrid. "Speaking about China, Learning from China: Amateur China Experts in 1970s America." *Journal of American–East Asian Relations* 16 (winter 2009): 313–352.

Schrecker, Ellen W. *No Ivory Tower: McCarthyism and the Universities*. Oxford: Oxford University Press, 1986.

Selden, Mark. "People's War and the Transformation of Peasant Society: China and Vietnam," in *America's Asia: Dissenting Essays on Asian-American Relations*, edited by Edward Friedman and Mark Selden, 357–392. New York: Pantheon, 1969.

Selden, Mark. "Understanding China and Ourselves," in *My First Trip to China: Scholars, Diplomats and Journalists Reflect on their First Encounter with China*, edited by Liu Kin-ming, 41–48. Hong Kong: East Slope, 2012.

Selden, Mark. *The Yenan Way in Revolutionary China*. Cambridge, MA: Harvard University Press, 1971.

Selden, Mark. *The Yenan Way Revisited*. Armonk, NY: M. E. Sharpe, 1995.

Seth, Sanjay. "Indian Maoism: The Significance of Naxalbari," in *Critical Perspectives on Mao Zedong's Thought*, edited by Arif Dirlik, Paul Healy, and Nick Knight, 289–312. Atlantic Highlands, NJ: Humanities Press, 1997.

Shue, Vivienne. "Epilogue: Mao's China—Putting Politics in Perspective," in *Maoism at the Grassroots: Everyday Life in China's Era of High Socialism*, edited by Jeremy Brown and Matthew D. Johnson, 365–379. Cambridge, MA: Harvard University Press, 2015.

Sidel, Ruth. *Women and Child Care in China*. New York: Hill and Wang, 1972.

Sidel, Victor W., and Ruth Sidel. *Serve the People: Observations on Medicine in the People's Republic of China*. New York: Beacon Press, 1974.

Slobodian, Quinn. *Foreign Front: Third World Politics in Sixties West Germany*. Durham, NC: Duke University Press, 2012.

Slobodian, Quinn. "Guerrilla Mothers and Distant Doubles." *Zeithistorische Forschungen/ Studies in Contemporary History* 12 (2015): 39–65.

Slobodian, Quinn. "Maoism in the Global 1960s." Presentation at NYU Shanghai, March 13, 2016. www.academia.edu/26839510/Maoism_in_the_Global_1960s.

Smith, Wendy. "From Oppressed to Oppressor." *American Scholar* (autumn 2008), theamericanscholar.org/from-oppressed-to-oppressors/#.UoMEJ1732zA.

Spivak, Gayatri Chakravorty. "Can the Subaltern Speak?," in *Marxism and the Interpretation of Culture*, edited by Cary Nelson and Lawrence Grossberg, 271–313. Urbana: University of Illinois Press, 1988.

Spivak, Gayatri Chakravorty. "The New Subaltern: A Silent Interview," in *Mapping Subaltern Studies and the Postcolonial*, edited by Vinayak Chaturvedi, 324–340. London: Verso, 2000.

Spivak, Gayatri Chakravorty. "Subaltern Studies: Deconstructing Historiography," in *Selected Subaltern Studies*, edited by Ranajit Guha and Gayatri Chakravorty Spivak, 3–32. New York: Oxford University Press, 1988.

Starn, Orin. "Maoism in the Andes: The Communist Party in Peru—Shining Path and the Refusal of History," in *Critical Perspectives on Mao Zedong's Thought*, edited by Arif Dirlik, Paul Healy, and Nick Knight, 267–288. Atlantic Highlands, NJ: Humanities Press, 1997.

Suter, Mischa. "A Thorn in the Side of Social History: Jacques Rancière and *Les Révoltes logiques*." *International Review of Social History* 57 (April 2012): 61–85.

Szanton, David, ed. *The Politics of Knowledge: Area Studies and the Disciplines*. Berkeley: University of California Press, 2004.

Tomes, Robert R. *Apocalypse Then: American Intellectuals and the Vietnam War, 1954–1975*. New York: NYU Press, 1998.

Townsend, Robert B. "History in Those Hard Times: Looking for Jobs in the 1970s." *Perspectives on History* (September 2009), www.historians.org/publications-and-directories/perspectives-on-history/september-2009/history-in-those-hard-times-looking-for-jobs-in-the-1970s.

Townsend, Robert B. "Precedents: The Job Crisis of the 1970s." *Perspectives on History* (April 1997), www.historians.org/publications-and-directories/perspectives-on-history/april-1997/precedents-the-job-crisis-of-the-1970s.

USC US-China Institute. "Getting to Beijing: Henry Kissinger's Secret 1971 Trip," July 21, 2011, accessed August 2016, china.usc.edu/getting-beijing-henry-kissingers-secret-1971-trip.

"Vietnam on Their Minds." *Newsweek*, April 14, 1969.

Vukovich, Daniel. *China and Orientalism: Western Knowledge Production and the PRC*. London: Routledge, 2011.

Wahnich, Sophie. *In Defence of the Terror: Liberty or Death in the French Revolution*. London: Verso, 2012.

Walder, Andrew G. *Fractured Rebellion: The Beijing Red Guard Movement*. Cambridge, MA: Harvard University Press, 2009.

Walder, Andrew G. "The Transformation of Contemporary China Studies, 1977–2002," in *The Politics of Knowledge: Area Studies and the Disciplines*, edited by David Szanton, 314–340. Berkeley: University of California Press, 2004.

Wang Hui. "Dandai zhongguo lishi jubian zhong de Taiwan wenti" 当代中国历史巨变中的台湾问题 [The problem of Taiwan within contemporary China's historical transformation]. wen.org.cn/modules/article/view.article.php?4172/c8.

Wang Hui. *The End of the Revolution: China and the Limits of Modernity*. London: Verso, 2009.

Wilson, Dick. "Professors in Conflict." *Far Eastern Economic Review* (May 22, 1969): 455–456.

Wilson, Rob, and Christopher Leigh Connery, eds. *The Worlding Project: Doing Cultural Studies in the Era of Globalization.* Santa Cruz, CA: New Pacific Press, 2007.

Wolin, Richard. *The Wind from the East: French Intellectuals, the Cultural Revolution, and the Legacy of the 1960s.* Princeton, NJ: Princeton University Press, 2010.

Wu, Judy Tzu-Chun. *Radicals on the Road: Internationalism, Orientalism, and Feminism during the Vietnam Era.* Ithaca, NY: Cornell University Press, 2013.

Wu Yiching. *The Cultural Revolution at the Margins: Chinese Socialism in Crisis.* Cambridge, MA: Harvard University Press, 2014.

Wu Yiching. "How State Enumeration Spoiled Mao's Last Revolution." *Journal of Modern Chinese History* 7, no. 2 (2013): 200–217.

Young, Robert J. C. "*White Mythologies* Revisited," in *White Mythologies: Writing History and the West*, 2nd ed., 1–31. London: Routledge, 2004.

Zhang, Dora. "The Sideways Gaze: Roland Barthes's *Travels in China.*" *Los Angeles Review of Books*, June 23, 2012, lareviewofbooks.org/essay/the-sideways-gaze-roland-barthess-travels-in-china.

Žižek, Slavoj. *The Sublime Object of Ideology.* New York: Verso, 1989.

ARTICLES PUBLISHED IN THE *BULLETIN OF CONCERNED ASIAN SCHOLARS*

Aberle, Kathleen. "An Indochinese Conference in Vancouver." *BCAS* 3 (summer–fall 1971): 2–29.

Andors, Phyllis. "'The Four Modernizations' and Chinese Policy on Women." *BCAS* 13 (April–June 1981): 44–56.

Andors, Phyllis. "Women and Work in Shenzhen." *BCAS* 20 (July–September 1988): 22–41.

Andors, Steve. "Hobbes and Weber vs. Marx and Mao: The Political Economy of Decentralization in China." *BCAS* 6 (September–October 1974): 19–34.

Andors, Steve. "Letter to the Editors." *BCAS* 2 (October 1969): 6–7.

"BCAS/CAS Statement of Purpose." criticalasianstudies.org/about-us/.

Chomsky, Noam. "The Asian Scholar and the American Crisis." *BCAS* 1 (May 1969): 14–22.

Christensen, Peter Moller, and Jorgen Delman. "A Theory of Transitional Society: Mao Zedong and the Shanghai School." *BCAS* 13 (April–June 1981): 2–15.

Clubb, O. Edmund. "McCarthyism and Our Asia Policy." *BCAS* 1 (May 1969): 23–26.

Columbia CCAS. "The American Asian Studies Establishment." *BCAS* 3 (summer–fall 1971): 92–103.

Committee of Concerned Asian Scholars Friendship Delegation to China. "Interview with Zhou Enlai." *BCAS* 3 (summer–fall 1971): 31–60.

Engelhardt, Tom. "Ambush at Kamikaze Pass." *BCAS* 3 (winter–spring 1971): 64–84.

Esherick, Joseph. "Harvard on China: The Apologetics of Imperialism." *BCAS* 4 (December 1972): 9–16.

Fairbank, John K. "Comment." *BCAS* 3 (summer–fall 1971): 104–111.

Fairbank, John K., and Jim Peck, "An Exchange." *BCAS* 2 (April–July 1970): 51–70.

Franke, Richard W. "Solution to the Asian Food Crisis: Green Revolution or Social Revolution?" *BCAS* 6 (November–December 1974): 2–13.

Friedman, Edward. "Learning about China after the Revolution . . . for the First Time!" *BCAS* 13 (April–June 1981): 41–43.

Friedman, Edward. "The Original Chinese Revolution Remains in Power." *BCAS* 13 (July–September 1981): 42–49.

Friedman, Edward. "Simon Leys Hates China; America Loves Simon Leys." *BCAS* 10 (July–September 1978): 19–27.

Gough, Kathleen. "The South Asian Revolutionary Potential." *BCAS* 4 (winter 1971): 77–98.

Horowitz, David. "Politics and Knowledge: An Unorthodox History of Modern China Studies." *BCAS* 3 (summer-fall 1971): 143–172.

Kagan, Leigh. "Proposals." *CCAS Newsletter* 1 (May 1968): 1.

Kagan, Leigh. "A Statement of Directions." *CCAS Newsletter* 1 (May 1968): 1.

Kagan, Richard. "McCarran's Legacy: The Association for Asian Studies." *BCAS* 1 (May 1969): 18–22.

Lasek, Elizabeth. "Imperialism in China: A Methodological Critique." *BCAS* 15 (January–February 1983): 50–64.

Lerner, Elinor. "The Chinese Peasantry and Imperialism: A Critique of Chalmers Johnson's *Peasant Nationalism and Communist Power*." *BCAS* 6 (April–August 1974): 43–56.

Lippit, Victor. "Economic Development and Welfare in China." *BCAS* 4 (summer 1972): 76–86.

Lippit, Victor. "The People's Communes and China's New Development Strategy." *BCAS* 13 (July–September, 1981): 19–30.

Livingston, Jon, Bryant Avery, Joe Moore, and Bill and Nancy Doub. "*The Bulletin of Concerned Asian Scholars* from the Perspective of Past and Present Managing Editors." *BCAS* 21 (April–December 1989): 180–192.

Meisner, Mitch, and Marc Blecher. "Rural Development, Agrarian Structure and the County in China." *BCAS* 13 (April–June 1981): 16–31.

"Modern China Studies: How the Foundations Bought a Field," special supplement, *BCAS* 3 (summer–fall 1971).

Nee, Victor. "Post-Mao Changes in a South China Production Brigade." *BCAS* 13 (April–June 1981): 32–39.

Nolan, Peter, and Gordon White. "Distribution and Development in China." *BCAS* 13 (July–September 1981): 2–18.

Omvedt, Gail. "Agrarian Crisis in India: A Review Essay." *BCAS* 6 (November–December 1974): 17–23.

Omvedt, Gail. "Gandhi and the Pacification of the Indian National Revolution." *BCAS* 5 (July 1973): 2–4.

Payer Goodman, Cheryl. "Review: Lucian Pye, *The Spirit of Chinese Politics*." *CCAS Newsletter* 1 (March 1969): 18–21.

Peck, Jim. "The C.C.A.S. Summer Seminar." *CCAS Newsletter* 1 (October 1968): 6.

Pfeffer, Richard M. "Revolution and Rule: Where Do We Go from Here?" BCAS 2 (April–July 1970): 88–95.

Riskin, Carl. "China's Economic Growth: Leap or Creep? Comments on Some Recent Pekinological Revisionism." BCAS 2 (January 1970): 19–24.

Riskin, Carl. "Maoism and Motivation: Work Incentives in China." BCAS 5 (July 1973): 10–24.

Roberts, Moss. "The Structure and Direction of Contemporary China Studies." BCAS 3 (summer–fall 1971): 113–41.

Schell, Orville. "Melby: The Mandate of Heaven." BCAS 2 (January 1970): 54–58.

Selden, Mark. "Introduction." BCAS 7 (April–June 1975): 2.

Unger, Jonathan, and Jean Xiong. "Life in the Chinese Hinterlands under the Rural Economic Reforms." BCAS 22 (April–June 1990): 4–17.

Wright, Tim. "Imperialism and the Chinese Economy: A Methodological Critique of the Debate." BCAS 18 (January–March 1986): 36–45.

INDEX

AAA. *See* American Anthropological Association
AAS. *See* Association for Asian Studies
Abernathy, Ralph, 117
ACLS. *See* American Council of Learned Societies
Adams, Nina, 88–89, 95, 201n18
Adorno, Theodore W., 74
AFSC. *See* American Friends Service Committee
Algerian National Liberation Front (FLN), 42
Alinsky, Saul, 117
Althusser, Louis, 10, 65, 70–71, 90–91, 143, 172; and circle at Rue de l'Ulm, 90, 172
American Anthropological Association (AAA), 201n20
American Council of Learned Societies (ACLS), 137
American Friends Service Committee (AFSC), 122, 135, 225n79, 228n119
America's Asia, 24–27, 34–40, 56–59, 75
Ampo: Japan-Asia Quarterly Review, 40, 205n71
Andors, Phyllis, 159, 179, 196n6
Andors, Stephen "Steve," 25, 34, 37–38, 61–62, 78, 87–88, 92, 170, 196n6, 236n101
Association for Asian Studies (AAS), 28–32, 82–85, 97, 146, 151, 201n15, 203n40

Avery, Bryant, 64, 98, 143, 148–50, 166–70, 176, 196n6, 237n109

Badiou, Alain, 10, 12, 73, 155, 160
Bantam Books, 131
Barlow, Tani, 178, 182, 238n21, 239n25
Barnett, A. Doak, 229n138
Barthes, Roland, 18, 101, 135, 141, 220n21
Bastid, Marianne, 107, 220n18
Battle of Algiers, The, 42, 205n80, 206n81
Bay, Christian, 39
BCAS. *See Bulletin of Concerned Asian Scholars*
Beheiren, 40, 205n71
Bernighausen, John, 19, 28, 44, 81–82, 95, 113–14, 117, 129–30, 195n3, 206n87, 222n34, 223n48, 224n58, 224n71, 225n72, 227n100, 228n117
Bernstein, Richard, 103, 105
Bettelheim, Charles, 131, 158, 234n62
Bianco, Lucien, 106–9
Bix, Herbert, 4, 19, 170, 202n24, 203n43
Black Panthers, 7, 92, 217n70
Blecher, Marc, 157, 232n26
Bourseiller, Cristophe, 143
Bulletin of Concerned Asian Scholars, 2, 4, 21, 33, 37, 42, 50, 58, 60–61, 64, 78, 83–85, 87, 88, 96, 124, 161, 162, 165–69, 171, 173, 184–85, 189, 205n71, 231n23; changes name to *Critical Asian Studies*, 184–85, 195n1; in the 1980s,

Bulletin of Concerned Asian Scholars (continued)
177–82; special issue on imperialism, 62–63; special issue on post-Mao China, 143–59, 232n26
Burton, Neil, 158

Carter, Jimmy, 168
Carter, John Vincent, 139
Cavett, Dick, 115
CCAS. *See* Committee of Concerned Asian Scholars
Cell, Charles, 49, 114
Cell, Elaine, 120
Chakrabarty, Dipesh, 45
Chauncey, Helen, 127, 148, 150, 232n28
Chavez, Cesar, 117
Chesneaux, Jean, 109, 211n169
China International Travel Services (CITS), 136, 138
China! Inside the People's Republic, 131–34, 225n79
China Quarterly, 1, 149
Chinese People's Association for Friendship with Foreign Countries. *See* Zhonghuo renmin duiwai youhao xiehui
Chomsky, Noam, 37, 78–80, 85–86, 98, 237n109; debate with Foucault, 215n37
Chu, Samuel, 83, 201n18
CITS. *See* China International Travel Services
Coburn, Judith, 56, 203n43
Cohen, Paul: and China-centered history, 180–82
Columbia University, 12, 19, 91–92, 201n19; CCAS chapter at, 54
Comités Vietnam de Base, 213n10
Committee of Concerned Asian Scholars: Cambridge seminar in 1968, 34, 75–82; and Chinese return trip, 113, 116–22; critique of imperialism, 62–65; dissolution of, 145, 165–66; first China trip, 102, 111–15, 131–35; founding of, 29–31 48, 54, 208n106; and funding of the field, 83, 200n2; and *Modern China*, 87–89; JCCC/SSRC/ACLS boycott by, 83–84, 95, 137; second China trip, 102, 105, 122–26
Committee of Scholarly Communications with the PRC, 138
Connery, Christopher, 42, 164
Cooper, Gene, 126, 224n71
Coye, Molly, 115, 120, 126, 223n45
Critical Asian Studies, 33, 184–85, 195n1
Cultural Revolution, 3–6, 11, 14, 20–21, 35–36, 38–39, 42–43, 45, 48, 62, 66, 70–73, 76, 89–91, 94–95, 99, 108, 122, 131–33, 141, 144–48, 150–51, 154–65, 172; historiography of, 221n23
Cumings, Bruce, 4, 19, 151
Cusset, François, 193

Davies, John, 139
Davis, Angela, 86, 217n70
Dazhai, 70, 144, 157, 230n2
De Bary, William Theodore, 203n40, 209n127
Deleuze, Gilles, 186, 193; dialogue with Foucault, 27, 67–71
Dellinger, David, 117
Democratic Republic of Vietnam (DRV), 118, 125, 135, 225n76
Deng Xiaoping, 4, 143–44, 163, 167; reform era, 21, 145, 150, 154–56, 179
Derrida, Jacques, 68, 186, 193, 212n4
Devlin, Delia, 216n58
Diamond, Norma, 216n58
Doctors Without Borders, 8
Doub, Bill, 178
Doub, Nancy, 178
Dower, John, 4, 65
Doyle, Jean, 137, 224n71, 225n74
DRV. *See* Democratic Republic of Vietnam

Eagleton, Terry, 175, 189
Eastern Horizon, 112
Ekstein, Alexander, 229n138
Engelhardt, Tom, 28, 30, 42, 80, 195n3, 196n6, 202n24, 203n43, 216n49
Esherick, Joseph, 19, 62–63, 92, 177,

232n26, 239n32; critique of James
Hevia, 190–92
Esprit, 106, 108
Etablissment, 147, 172, 231n12

Fairbank, John King, 18, 20, 30, 46–48, 51, 56, 58, 181, 188, 201n14, 202n26, 204n70, 207n103, 210n130, 214n18, 225n73, 229n138
Faste, Andrea, 96, 226n88
Feuerwerker, Albert, 229n138
FLN. *See* Algerian National Liberation Front
Ford Foundation, 12, 83
Fortini, Franco, 1, 8, 197n14
Foucault, Michel, 15, 64, 172, 186, 193, 203n46; debate with Chomsky, 215n37; dialogue with Deleuze, 27, 67–71
Franke, Richard, 41
Friedman, Edward "Ed," 23, 26, 30, 36, 40, 82, 87–89, 151, 153, 162–64, 167, 170, 201n18, 203n43

Gandhi, Mohandas Karamchand, 41
Gang of Four, 20, 152, 169
Gauche Prolétarienne, 44, 90, 147, 172, 206n89, 213n10
Geismar, Alain, 44, 73, 80, 81, 206n89
Gittings, John, 136–37, 152, 232n37
gong nong bing daxue. *See* worker-peasant-soldier universities
Goodman, Cheryl, 52
Gramsci, Antonio, 80, 186, 193
Great Leap Forward, 35, 49, 62, 154, 159
Green Revolution, 41, 205n76
Gurley, John, 34, 37, 38, 61, 204n58

Habermas, Jürgen, 206n85
Hammond, Ed, 79–80, 204n63, 232n26
Harding, Harry, 182
Harootunian, Harry, 65, 187, 212n76, 238n21
Harvard Crimson, 30
Harvard University, 12, 18–19, 30, 34, 46, 75, 171, 202n24, 207n102, 217n68;
and interpretation of Chinese history (Harvard school), 62, 63, 178–79, 192
Hayden, Tom, 117
Hayot, Eric, 123, 219n7
Hevia, James, 190–92, 239n32
Ho Chi-min, 47
Hollander, Paul, 108, 133, 221n22
Hourmant, Francois, 130–31
House Un-American Activities Committee (HUAC), 13
Household Responsibility System, 144
Hua Guofeng, 152
HUAC. *See* House Un-American Activities Committee
Huang, Philip: and *Modern China*, 87–88; and the paradigmatic crisis in Chinese studies, 188–89
Hucker, Charles O., 29, 201n19
Huxian paintings, 71

In Search of Lost Time, 104, 110–11
Indochina War, 24, 37, 118, 124, 136
Institute of Pacific Relations (IPR), 13, 29, 55, 201n19
IPR. *See* Institute of Pacific Relations
Israel, John, 137–38, 229n127

Jacobson, Carl, 97
Jacoviello, Alberto, 227n104
Jameson, Fredric, 6, 186, 238n21
JCCC. *See* Joint Committee on Contemporary China
Johnson, Chalmers, 50, 209n113, 229n138
Johnson, Lyndon B., 37, 47, 51
Joint Committee on Contemporary China (JCCC), 229n127; CCAS boycott of, 83–84, 95
Journal of Asian Studies, 2, 96

Kagan, Leigh, 24, 203n43, 226n88
Kagan, Richard, 117, 201n18, 203n43
Karl, Rebecca, 94
Karnow, Stanley, 136–37
Kehl, Frank, 136
Kennedy, John F., 209n122
King, Marjorie, 148

Kissinger, Henry, 136, 222n31
Korean War, 36
Kristeva, Julia, 220n21

Langer, William, 201n14
Laos, 120
Lasek, Elizabeth, 178
Latham, Michael, 57
Lattimore, Owen, 13, 55, 139, 210n130
Lazarus, Sylvain, 160
League of Revolutionary Struggle, 218n92
League of Revolutionary Workers, 92
Lee Tsung-ying, 112
Lemisch, Jesse, 55
Lerner, Elinor, 50
Lewis, John W., 56, 210n136, 229n138
Leys, Simon (pseud. for Pierre Ryckmans), 162–63, 167, 182
Lifschultz, Larry, 136
Lin Biao, 140, 229n141
Link, Perry, 9, 105, 197n21
Lippit, Victor, 37, 153, 156, 157, 232n26
Livingston, Jon, 86, 95, 138, 165, 196n6, 202n24, 203n43
Loi, Michelle, 130, 226n93
loss of China, 13
Lynd, Staughton, 79, 85–86

Macciocchi, Maria-Antonietta, 107–9, 131–32, 220n21, 227n104
MacKinnon, Stephen, 124–25, 224n71, 225n73
Marks, Robert, 149, 153, 181
Massachusetts Institute of Technology (MIT), 19, 209n122
May Fourth Movement, 59, 211n152
May Seventh schools, 133
May '68, 71, 73, 145, 159–61, 172
McCarthy, Joseph: political persecutions by, 13, 24, 29, 55, 56, 59, 132, 139
McCoy, Al, 84
McDonald, Angus, 137, 139, 166–67, 170, 196n6, 236n101
McGovern, George, 117
Meisner, Mitch, 157, 224n71
Michel, Natacha, 1, 160, 234n68

Middlebury College, 19
Millet, Katherine "Kate," 86, 217n70
Mirsky, Jonathan, 105–6, 110, 137, 220n14, 222n37
MIT. *See* Massachusetts Institute of Technology
MLA. *See* Modern Language Association
Modern China, 1, 70, 87–89, 149, 188–89
Modern Language Association (MLA), 30
modernization theory, 56–59, 181, 187
Monthly Review, 96, 158
Moore, Joe, 17, 168
My First Trip to China, 103–6, 108

Nathan, Andrew, 177
National Committee on U.S.-China Relations, 138
National Defense Education Act (NDEA), 28
National Emergency Committee of Clergy and Laymen Concerned about Vietnam, 195n2
Naxalite movement, 7
NDEA. *See* National Defense Education Act
Nee, Victor, 43, 203n43
New York University (NYU), 18, 19
Newton, Huey, 117
1989 Tiananmen movement, 177, 182
1986 protests, 177, 182
Nixon, Richard, 51, 117; trip to and rapprochement with China, 4, 20, 37, 103, 118–19, 123–24, 129, 136, 151, 224n68
Nolan, Peter, 156
Norman, E. H., 65, 212n176
NYU. *See* New York University

Oldfather, Felicia, 84, 231n23
Omvedt, Gail, 41, 148, 205n74

Pacific News Service, 19, 115, 222n42
Pantheon Books, 19, 23
Parade, 115
Parti Communiste Marxiste Leniniste (PCML), 7
PCML. *See* Parti Communiste Marxiste Leniniste

260 / Index

Peck, James "Jim," 19, 30, 43, 51–52, 54, 57–59, 136, 196n6, 202n24, 203n43, 228n120
Peking Review, 114, 222n41
Pelzer, Karl, 29, 201n19
Perrolle, Judy, 44, 138, 206n87, 226n88
Pfeffer, Richard "Ric," 49, 64, 79, 152, 170, 196n6, 209n111, 226n88, 236n101
Pickowicz, Paul, 19, 112, 223n47
Pimpaneau, Jacques, 195
Plato, 93
Pleynet, Marcelin, 220n21
Pol Pot, 167
Pontecorvo, Gillo, 42, 206n81
positions: asia critique (formerly *positions: east asia cultures critique*), 175, 177, 185–87, 190
Prashad, Vijay, 184
Price, David, 13
Proust, Marcel, 104, 110–11. See also *In Search of Lost Time*
Pye, Lucien, 52, 202n29, 209n122

Ramparts, 96
Rancière, Jacques, 10, 21, 71–73, 93, 143, 147, 154, 161–62, 164–65, 171–72; criticism of Althusser by, 65, 70, 90, 172–73
Red Guards, 3, 5, 8, 32, 90, 132, 198n29, 230n9
Reischauer, Edwin O., 46, 202n29, 207n102, 208n105
Riskin, Carl, 61, 83, 136, 232n26
Robcis, Camille, 90
Roberts, Moss, 19, 195n3, 216n55, 224n71
Robin, Ron, 56
Rostow, Walt, 37
Roy, Arundhati, 184
Russo, Alessandro, 144, 154

Sacks, I. Milton, 31, 202n29, 202n30
Said, Edward, 8, 14, 26, 64, 108, 186–87, 190, 215n39; *Orientalism*, 14, 26, 64, 190
Sakai, Robert, 30
Scalapino, Robert, 229n138

Schell, Orville, 19, 54–55, 76, 92–95, 104, 109–10, 115, 171, 235n82
Schlesinger, Arthur, 55
Schmalzer, Sigrid, 11, 111, 130, 221n30
Schrecker, Ellen, 13
Schurmann, Franz, 19, 115
Science for the People, 226n91
Selden, Mark, 19, 23, 25–26, 34–36, 38, 40, 43, 59, 61, 77, 84–85, 101, 105–6, 109, 116, 151, 153, 195, 203n43, 232n29
Sendero Luminoso, 7
Service, John Stuart, 139
Shining Path. *See* Sendero Luminoso
Shirk, Susan, 112, 115, 222n34, 227n100
Shue, Vivienne, 102, 199n38
Slobodian, Quinn, 9, 206n85
Smith, Adam, 188
Social Science Research Council (SSRC), 83, 137
Sollers, Philippe, 220n21
Spivak, Gayatri Chakravorty, 67–69, 72, 186
SSRC. *See* Social Science Research Council
Stanford University, 204n58, 210n136; CCAS chapter at, 60, 113, 117–21
Sturdevant, Saundra "Sandy," 17, 121, 150, 152, 157–58, 169–70, 195n3, 196n6, 208n104, 215n42, 227n113, 228n117
Su Shaozhi, 182
subaltern studies, 41, 46, 69, 186, 189–90, 193
SUNY Binghamton, 19
SUNY Oswego, 170

Taiwan sunflower movement, 183
Taylor, George, 216n59
Tel Quel, 107, 123, 219n7, 220n21
Tharamangalam, Joseph, 168
Tsinghua University, 70
tuxedo statement, 31

UCF-ML. *See* Union des Communistes de France Marxistes-Léninistes
Unger, Jonathan, 23, 179, 222n42

Union des Communistes de France Marxistes-Léninistes (UCF-ML), 147, 159–61
Union of Concerned Scientists, 195n2
Universities Service Center, 112
University of California Berkeley, 11, 12, 19, 83, 92, 169, 171, 209n113; CCAS chapter at, 49, 52, 60, 79, 80
University of California San Diego, 19
University of Chicago, 19, 196n6, 208n104
University of Michigan, 18, 201n19; CCAS chapter at, 114
University of Washington, 13

Vietnam War, 3, 12, 18, 24, 28, 30, 35, 36, 40, 43, 46, 47, 48, 50, 60, 64, 69, 85, 87, 96, 111, 116, 120, 123, 138, 140, 148, 151, 166, 179, 206n83, 224n58. *See also* Indochina War
Vogel, Ezra, 49, 83, 209n111, 229n138
Vukovich, Daniel, 183, 207n99

Wahl, François, 220n21
Wahnich, Sophie, 144, 164
Wang Hui, 183, 234n62, 239n31
Wherry, Kenneth, 57
White, Gordon, 113, 156, 224n71

White Panthers, 92
Whitehead, Ray, 112, 136, 222n34
Wilbur, C. Martin, 201n19
Wilson, Richard "Dick," 32, 201n18
Wittfogel, Karl, 13
Wolin, Richard, 147
worker-peasant-soldier universities (*gong nong bing daxue*), 133, 198n29
Wright, Tim, 178

xiafang movement, 49, 152
Xidan democracy wall, 182
Xiong, Jean, 179

Yan'an, 19, 133
Young, Marilyn, 3, 18, 30, 82–83, 137, 201n14, 229n127

Zhang, Dora, 141
Zhonghuo renmin duiwai youhao xiehui (Chinese People's Association for Friendship with Foreign Countries), 112
Zhou Enlai, 20, 36, 44, 113–14, 117, 135, 222n31, 224n68
Zinn, Howard, 79, 85–86
Žižek, Slavoj, 66